Facebook

Digital Media and Society Series

Facebook

TAINA BUCHER

polity

First published in 2021 by Polity Press

Polity Press
65 Bridge Street
Cambridge CB2 1UR, UK

Polity Press
101 Station Landing
Suite 300
Medford, MA 02155, USA

ISBN-13: 978-1-5095-3516-3
ISBN-13: 978-1-5095-3517-0 (pb)

A catalogue record for this book is available from the British Library.

Library of Congress Cataloging-in-Publication Data

Names: Bucher, Taina, author.
Title: Facebook / Taina Bucher.
Description: Medford : Polity Press, 2021. | Series: Digital media and
    society | Includes bibliographical references and index. | Summary: "How
    Facebook came to be, how it works, and why it is more powerful than
    ever"-- Provided by publisher.
Identifiers: LCCN 2020047168 (print) | LCCN 2020047169 (ebook) | ISBN
    9781509535163 (hardback) | ISBN 9781509535170 (paperback) | ISBN
    9781509535187 (epub)
Subjects: LCSH: Facebook (Electronic resource) | Online social networks. |
    Social networks--Computer network resources.
Classification: LCC HM743.F33 B83 2021 (print) | LCC HM743.F33 (ebook) |
    DDC 302.30285--dc23
LC record available at https://lccn.loc.gov/2020047168
LC ebook record available at https://lccn.loc.gov/2020047169

Typeset in 10.25 on 13pt Scala
by Fakenham Prepress Solutions, Fakenham, Norfolk NR21 8NL
Printed and bound in Great Britain by TJ Books Limited

For further information on Polity, visit our website:
politybooks.com

Contents

Acknowledgements

The writing of this book is hugely indebted to senior editor at Polity Press, Mary Savigar. If Mary hadn't approached me at the Association of Internet Researchers (AoIR) conference in late 2017 to pitch this project to me, I would never have embarked on it in the first place. I never envisioned myself writing an entire book about Facebook. Like so many of my peers, I was already quite fed up with Facebook. What more was there to say, I thought? As it turned out, quite a lot. Once I distanced myself from thinking of Facebook as a social media platform or social network site only, entire swathes of infrastructural activities became apparent. Sometimes chance encounters that plant the right seeds can be quite life-changing, as my brief meeting with Mary demonstrates. Mary, thanks for thinking of me for this project and for allowing me to prove myself wrong: Facebook is an immensely fascinating phenomenon. It has been an absolute pleasure to write this book, keeping me company amid some happy and challenging life events as Facebook calls them: childbirth, change of jobs, moving countries, pandemic. Thank you to Ellen MacDonald-Kramer and the rest of the Polity Press team for guiding me through the editorial and production process.

Status update: Thank you to everyone who has either explicitly or implicitly contributed to developing the ideas in this book. Thank you: Anne Helmond, David Nieborg, my colleagues in the 'Don't take it personal' project team, and the participants from the Media Aesthetics seminars at the Department of Media and Communication, University of Oslo, for reading drafts at various stages of completion and providing critical feedback. Your comments have greatly improved the final product. Thank you also to the anonymous reviewers for their time and efforts in making this a better book. I am grateful to the many people I have met at conferences, workshops, and seminars, who have provided crucial insights into different aspects of Facebook. I am especially grateful to the informants from various NGOs and human rights organizations whose input and generosity helped to shape my understanding of Facebook. Thank you also to research assistant Louise Bechmann Ødegaard Jensen for her research in the early stages of book writing. This book benefited from financial support by the 'Digitization and Diversity' project funded by the Research Council of Norway. Thank you to project leader Anne-Britt Gran for granting the time and resources to work on this book as part of the project.

Finally, my immense gratitude goes to friends and family. You deserve so much more than a status update. Georg, your patience and support means everything. I dedicate this book to Alvar.

Introduction: Facebook is Facebook

Everybody has a Facebook story. Whether it is the story of how a relationship started, or ended, how people found long-lost loved ones, how they learned about the weddings, births and divorces of old friends and acquaintances, Facebook has played – and still does – an important part in people's personal and professional lives. Facebook entered my own life during the autumn of 2006 when I was a graduate student in London. Online social networking sites were a relatively new phenomenon; my lecturers talked about this new phenomenon called Web 2.0, and MySpace was very much a thing. So, when someone in my university network sent me a Facebook invitation, I did not think twice about it and filled out the blank blueish template with some personal details and started to add friends. My school friends in London all became members around the same time that autumn, approximately two years after Facebook first launched its site for a select few American Ivy League networks. Having gone to secondary school in Oslo, Norway, my Norwegian friends had yet to discover Facebook, so I sent off a couple of email invitations. One of the first messages on my Facebook wall came from one of my best friends, saying: 'Hi Taina! Now I'm here! I'll test this one too … usually sites like these only last a week or two for me, but now I've added a few pics so let's see how it goes.' I guess the rest is history. Not only did the site prove its staying power for my friends and me, but it also turned out to do so for a staggering 2.7 billion people worldwide.

Fifteen years after Facebook first launched, an approximate one-third of the world's population uses one of its apps on a monthly basis (including Facebook, Messenger, WhatsApp and Instagram), nearly half of Americans get their news from the Facebook feed, and four petabytes of data are generated through the site each day. Facebook has become one of the most important advertising venues ever to exist, which essentially makes it an advertising business at its core. With nearly every marketer using Facebook advertising, the company made $75 billion in revenue for the twelve months ending 30 June 2020, along with a market capitalization of $805 billion as of September 2020.[1] These are not just impressive numbers but numbers with profound consequences. The fact that Facebook (and Google) essentially own the market for digital advertising means that other businesses whose business models depend on advertising, such as journalism, face huge problems. As every news executive I have talked to (in the Nordic region) seems to agree, the biggest competition to their respective brands and newspapers is not another newspaper, but Facebook and its powerful grip on the ad market. This is not just a commercial problem but something that has far-reaching consequences for journalism as a whole. Fewer revenues support fewer journalists, and fewer journalists and less time to do quality reporting ultimately means a loss of public-service journalism. Facebook's power as a data-driven and programmatic advertisement platform has also become key to the ways in which politics plays out. While just a few years ago, scholars were mainly concerned with the creation of pages and profiles by election candidates, now we are beginning to see the complex ways in which Facebook's advertising platform is used in political campaigning and what that might mean for election results, public discourse and the spread of misinformation and disinformation.

It may seem strange to begin a book on Facebook with two paragraphs describing the mundaneness of Facebook on the one hand, and the specific nature of Facebook as a data-driven ad company on the other. Yet, this is exactly what Facebook is all about: tensions and transitions. A Facebook ad released shortly after the infamous Cambridge Analytica scandal in 2018 usefully brings some of these tensions and transitions into view. Barely two weeks after Mark Zuckerberg testified in front of the US congressional lawmakers in April 2018, Facebook released its biggest ever brand marketing campaign under the tagline 'Here Together' (see also Chapter 1). Designed as a nostalgic field trip through Facebook's connective potentials, the ad set out to remind people why they had signed up to Facebook in the first place, promising its users to do 'more to keep you safe and protect your privacy so that we can all get back to what made Facebook good in the first place – Friends'. The ad tells a tale familiar to many Facebook users. A story that begins with friendship, develops into an expanded network of 'friends and acquaintances', reaches a point of conflict where *too many* 'Friends' make you participate *less*, or at the very least differently, and ends with a hope for a better future – whether this future includes Facebook or not. Beyond articulating a certain structure of feeling around the ways in which Facebook has changed from a simple friendship site to something much bigger, the ad reiterates another familiar story about Facebook. This is the idea of Facebook as a social medium. In calling for change, Facebook remains firm in positioning itself as a place for friends. Yet, as I will argue in this book, this tale no longer holds true, if it ever did.

Facebook is Facebook

The core argument of the book is that Facebook cannot adequately be understood as a social medium, nor is it another name for the internet, as some would claim. Facebook *is* Facebook. While this may seem like a tautological statement at first, I want to suggest that, far from being useless, claiming that Facebook is irreducible to something else might be more generative than many of the metaphors currently in use to make sense of Facebook. The fact that Facebook is

Facebook speaks not just to its global corporate power but, more profoundly, to Facebook becoming a concept of sorts. Much scholarly, public and corporate discourse tends to talk about Facebook in metaphorical and (sub)categorical terms. In the company's early days, it seemed relatively uncontroversial simply to frame Facebook as belonging to the category of social media or social network site. More recently it has become more common to frame Facebook as a platform or infrastructure. Multiple metaphors abound to help us grasp this thing called Facebook, some of which we will explore in this book. As the company grew bigger, its definitional boundaries exploded. What the many definitions and conceptions of Facebook in newspaper articles, lawsuits, congressional hearings, scholarly papers and company press reports suggest is that there seems to be a growing need for clarification as to what Facebook really is. The ontological question is not just interesting for philosophical and theoretical reasons, but serves a very practical and political purpose. In a world where Facebook and its founder and CEO, Mark Zuckerberg, exercise unprecedented power and the conversation on regulation has gained a new urgency, we might have to come to terms with the notion that Facebook cannot readily be compared to something else but must be taken for what it is – Facebook.

What does suggesting that Facebook is Facebook and entertaining the idea of Facebook as a concept involve? The answer to this question begins from another, a question that I am sure many readers have already asked themselves: 'Why do we need a book on Facebook at this point, fifteen or more years after it first launched?' Or, as one well-meaning colleague put it, 'aren't you afraid that a book on Facebook is going to be a bit dated at this point?' If we think of Facebook as primarily a social network site, there might indeed be something to my colleague's question. But, as I want to suggest, this would be a very specific and frankly outdated way of understanding Facebook. If you think Facebook is not for you, that it has lost its cool, or doesn't affect how you live your life, think again.

Facebook is no longer, if it ever was, just a social network site. It's a global operating system and a serious political, economic and cultural power broker. The Facebook that certain people, especially in the West, got accustomed to and signed up for more than a decade ago is far from the Facebook of today. There are many dimensions to this. One obvious point would be to say that Facebook is a work in progress. From its mission statements to its user base, technology, underlying code and design, Facebook is always changing. Along with the changing interfaces, functions and underlying system, our conceptions of what Facebook is have changed as well. If we were to go back in time, say to the beginning of the 2010s, much scholarly research on Facebook centred around questions of self-presentation, effects on self-esteem and well-being, personality traits of users, motivations for use, social capital and networking practices. In articles published at that time, Facebook was commonly considered a specific instance or subset of the broader category of social network site (SNS). Then, the label 'social network site' somehow lost its resonance along the way, only to be replaced by other broad categories and classification systems such as social media and platform.[2]

Many of the people who claim that Facebook has become insignificant or uninteresting say so because they still think of Facebook as primarily a social network site or social medium, whatever that means. Let us think of it as one of the particularly prevailing myths about Facebook. There are many more. Some myths, such as the myth of Facebook in decline and the myth of Facebook as primarily a social medium, overlap. This is not to say that Facebook isn't declining, or that it hasn't lost its cool. To some users, Facebook has certainly lost its appeal. A Pew study on teens' use of social media and technology, for example, showed that while 71% of US teens reported using Facebook in 2014–15, the numbers had declined to 51% in 2018 (Anderson and Jiang, 2018). Reports from the Scandinavian countries show a similar tendency among the younger generations. In Norway, for example, 81% of people aged 15 to 25 reported using Facebook on a daily basis in 2019, a decline of 12 percentage points from two years prior (Kantar, Forbruker and Media). Reports of shrinking user numbers notwithstanding, revenue and profit continue to rise. The earnings report of the first quarter 2020 showed a 17% revenue growth, which is considerable taken the onset of a global pandemic into account (Facebook, 2020a). In other words, despite numerous campaigns that have urged people to leave and quit Facebook, business has never been better.

Insignificance, then, is a highly relative term. While the main service, Facebook.com, might have become less important as a communication channel among Western elites and younger generations, Facebook is important in many other ways – even among the very people who feature in the headlines on Facebook's apparent demise. As Sujon et al. found in a longitudinal study on Facebook use, it is not so much that Facebook has become meaningless to young people, but rather that its meaning has changed. While in 2013, users reported using Facebook mostly to connect with others, five years later the same respondents reported using Facebook mainly as a 'personal service platform' for coordinating events, archiving photos and for relationship maintenance (Sujon et al., 2018). In other words, teenagers still use Facebook, just not necessarily in the same ways that they used to, or in the way that their parents use Facebook for that matter. In a *WIRED* magazine story commemorating Facebook's fifteenth anniversary, teenagers reported mostly using Facebook for controlling what their parents post. Under the headline 'Teens Don't Use Facebook, But They Can't Escape It Either', one of the teenagers explained that Facebook had just always been there, both in terms of playing an essential part in family life, and also in a more abstract sense as a felt presence: 'Even before Jace could understand the concept of Facebook, he felt its influence every time his dad had him stop what he was doing and pose for photos that were destined to be shared online' (Dreyfuss, 2019a). This notion of concept and felt presence is important and one of the reasons why Facebook cannot be easily dismissed.

Feeling Facebook

Invoking the feeling of Facebook, of its felt presence, confronts its alleged status as a social network site, social medium or platform. The memory of having to pose for your parents' Facebook-friendly photos, or, as one of the speakers at an arts festival told the audience, the experience of 'not being able to visit a new city without searching for the perfect new vertical cover photo for Facebook', suggests that the question of what Facebook is and why it matters cannot be answered adequately by referring back to other high-order labels. The way in which Facebook touches the lives of so many, whether this touching is barely noticed or significantly sensed, attests to its atmospheric force. This book suggests that one of the ways in which we might understand Facebook is through notions of atmosphere, affect and imaginaries. More collo-quially, atmosphere is used to describe the ambiance or feel of a place.

Scholars in human geography have taken up the term from Gernot Böhme's writings on aesthetics (1993) as a way of theorizing the unique backdrop of everyday life (Anderson, 2009). According to Bille et al., atmospheres refer to the 'spatial experience of being attuned in and through the material world' (2015: 35). It's a feeling of in-betweenness that cannot readily be attributed to either an object or subject, but needs to be thought of as something that emerges in an encounter between people and things and seems to fill a space with a certain tone or mood. What Jace is describing when he recounts growing up and posing for Facebook photos is essentially the experience of being attuned in certain ways rather than others. If, for Böhme (1993), atmospheres are about the perceived presence of something and their reality in space, we might think of Jace's experience of growing up as a way of feeling the atmospheric force of Facebook. Stopping what he was doing in order to pose for his dad's Facebook photo also became a way of being attuned to the meaning of family and a certain way of staging what a happy family life looks like.

Jace's story is not unique. Most of us have felt the presence of Facebook in one way or another. There are the ways in which we dance and have fun in front of the camera in case it gets posted on Facebook as evidence of a good time, the strategic status updating to boost the sense of personal success, or the way in which we make sure others know that we voted. If we include Instagram, the Facebook-owned image-sharing app, many more examples come to mind. The felt presence of Facebook as a 'family of apps', consisting of Messenger, Instagram, WhatsApp and Facebook, can be seen in the ways that restaurants make dishes appear 'Instagram-worthy' or the ways in families coordinate their daily routines and communicate in smaller groups using WhatsApp or Messenger. Bille et al. (2015) describe how architects and designers work to stage atmospheres, by intentionally shaping spaces for certain emotional responses. While the authors mainly have physical buildings in mind, Facebook, too, should be seen as a designed space that seeks to affect people's moods and guide their behaviour for utilitarian and commercial purposes.

Beyond the pre-individual scales of measure, or intensities, that are often taken to be at the heart of how *affect* is theorized (Clough, 2008), the notion of feeling Facebook is very much part of the articulable realm. When people feel the presence of Facebook in their lives, it is not necessarily beyond discourse and conscious representation, as certain strands of affect theory would have it (Massumi, 1995). While the force of Facebook may be difficult to articulate, in terms of pointing to what exactly it is about Facebook that spurs a specific sensation or emotion, there is no denying the fact that Facebook means a lot to individuals, organizations and institutions alike. The presence of Facebook is felt everywhere, whether it is in the very real sense of threatening the livelihood and condition of an entire institution, such as journalism and the news industry, or more subtly as in the ways in which the health sector has to grapple with Facebook as an alternative information-seeking forum for patients. From the perspective of other businesses and organizations, Facebook means affected revenue streams, changing workflows, new job titles, opportunities for organizing protests, breaking and redefining news, a new political platform and regulatory challenges.

Far from being insignificant, then, Facebook matters. It matters because Facebook orients people. Following cultural theorist Sara Ahmed, we might say that Facebook's power has to do with such orientations. 'Orientations matter,' Ahmed writes, because they 'shape how the world coheres' (Ahmed, 2010: 235). While Ahmed specifically speaks about being oriented in the world from the perspective of 'queer phenomenology' and the ways in which the world coheres around certain bodies rather than others, we might think about Facebook in similar ways. We are oriented towards Facebook, whether we like it or not, and Facebook is oriented towards us. Take Jace, from the *WIRED* feature: he might not use Facebook personally, but it still orients his family's life and the way in which family life is performed. Moreover, my well-meaning colleague might think Facebook has lost its cool, but that does not take away the fact that to many people and organizations, coolness is not even an issue. Talk to the editor-in-chief of a major newspaper that has lost its advertising money to Facebook, and they will not care whether Facebook shows a slight decline in active monthly users among the younger generations. All they will probably care about is their newspaper, the journalists and what it means for the future of journalism. Or talk to a Rohingya refugee whose life has been threatened by the atrocities in Myanmar following the spread of propaganda on Facebook by Buddhist ultranationalists. I am sure their Facebook story will provide an answer to why Facebook matters.

An orientation approach asks us to attend to the ways in which the object of analysis affects 'what is proximate' and 'what can be reached' (Ahmed, 2006: 3). What matters in how 'we come to find our way in the world' (Ahmed, 2006: 1), however, is not always a given. As Ahmed writes, 'depending on which way we turn', the world may take on new shapes and meanings. The question is what makes us turn one way or the other in the first place? In this book, I suggest that Facebook constitutes one particularly powerful orientation device, in that it shapes '"who" or "what" we direct our energy and attention toward' (Ahmed, 2006: 3). This holds true whether we think of Facebook's algorithms and platform design directing people's attention, its *de facto* role as a dominant news source, or its persistent position as a centre of attention in policy circles, electoral politics and surveillance capitalism. True, even the slightest sound, strange smell, or unexpected touch can make us turn, but nothing seems quite as disorienting and commanding of our attention in the algorithmic media environment as Facebook. When things orient, they take up space, they make an impression, render other things more or less probable, provide a path for further direction, suggest what is important, put in place. As we will see throughout this book, this is exactly what Facebook does. Importantly, as a global orientation device of massive scale, Facebook does not merely take up space. It also shapes it in fundamental ways.

Origin story

Facebook has become so deeply engrained into culture and society that the company's origin story as a college network for the few and privileged, programmed by former Harvard student and dropout Mark Zuckerberg and a couple of his friends, is well known. The founding myth tells the story of a 2003 date night gone bad. Bitter and frustrated, young Zuckerberg decides to create a juvenile 'hot-or-not' site called FaceMash, which asked fellow Harvard students to compare their female classmates and judge their relative attractiveness. Zuckerberg hacked into the websites of nine Harvard houses to gather the photos of the women. He then wrote the code to compute rankings for every vote received. Thirteen weeks after the creation of FaceMash, and after almost having been expelled from Harvard University as a result, Facebook launched as a Harvard-only social network in February 2004.

In an early interview with the American news channel CNBC, Zuckerberg described Facebook as:

> An online directory that connects people through universities and colleges through their social networks there. You sign on. You make a profile about yourself by answering some questions, entering some information such as your [...] contact information [...] and, most importantly, who your friends are. And then you can browse around and see who people's friends are and just check out people's online identities and see how people portray themselves and just find some interesting information about people. (CNBC, 2004)

In subsequent interviews, Zuckerberg has reiterated these humble beginnings, stressing the fact that all he wanted was simply to connect his school. 'We were just building this thing because we thought it was awesome', Zuckerberg said in a 2011 interview to aspiring entrepreneurs at the Startup School. In a grandiose gesture of 'bringing the world closer together', Zuckerberg spoke at the first Facebook Community Summit in 2017: 'I always thought one day someone would connect the whole world, but I never thought it would be us. I would have settled for connecting my whole dorm' (Zuckerberg, 2017a). Zuckerberg's origin story frames Facebook almost as an accident. He never even intended for Facebook to be a company, he claimed, it just happened (Zuckerberg,

2011a). The first attempts at setting up the company were 'a disaster'. As the inexperienced college freshmen they were, Facebook was initially set up in Florida because one of the co-founders 'happened to live' there at the time. Even moving to Silicon Valley didn't seem like much of a thought-out plan. Zuckerberg and his friends didn't want to stay in Boston over the summer, so they went to Silicon Valley because it seemed like a 'magical place' for start-ups. After a year of working from their five-bed Palo Alto home, Zuckerberg and his friends finally moved to a real office in 2005. Zuckerberg seals the start-up narrative by casting himself in the role of the dedicated and nerdy software programmer. All he ever looked forward to when growing up, Zuckerberg said in a 2010 interview, was to write software after school.

Mark Zuckerberg and his company have come a long way from the nerdy college beginnings. These early stories are not just fraught with myths about the passionate hacker, free from commercial motivations. Narratives like these have helped to strategically build the story of Facebook and Mark Zuckerberg as a hero of geek power. As Alice Marwick shows in her ethnography of the Silicon Valley start-up scene at the end of the 2000s, Mark Zuckerberg quickly became the epitome of the next-generation tech entrepreneur, founder and millionaire. His genius status was further cemented by extensive media coverage, conference appearances, and endless references in blogs and magazines, essentially creating a sense of celebrity that propelled people's interest in the Zuck as a meritocratic myth (Marwick, 2013). Roughly fifteen years later, countless personal portraits have been written about the Zuck: he's been named *TIME* 'Person of the Year' 2010, and the biographical drama *The Social Network* is probably the only film about a nerdy CEO of an internet start-up that has been nominated for eight Academy Awards. Yet, Zuckerberg's journey as the CEO of one of the world's biggest software companies is not just a happy tale. At least since the 2016 US election, with all its emphasis on fake news and Russian interference,

Zuckerberg has evolved from a cultural hero for the start-up generation to something of a global privacy villain. Although Facebook had been involved in many scandals prior to that – in fact, the company is famous for its many privacy scandals – it wasn't until around 2016 that Facebook started to look bigger, more powerful and more dangerous.

Originally, Facebook was merely a website that displayed individual profiles. In 2006, its most prevalent feature, the News Feed, was introduced. That same year, Facebook launched the first version of the Facebook API, 'enabling users to share their information with the third-party websites and applications they choose' (Morin, 2008). In 2007, Facebook released Facebook Platform, a set of tools and products for developers to make and adapt applications for the Facebook ecosystem. Launched at f8, Facebook's annual developer conference, Zuckerberg called on developers 'to build the next generation of applications with deep integration into Facebook' (Facebook, 2007a). Facebook Platform was presented as a win-win situation and a new business opportunity for developers (and Facebook). Zuckerberg explained how developers would be able to build their businesses by getting distribution of their apps through 'the social graph', a term he has consistently used to describe people's real-life connections, including friendships, business connections and acquaintances. Users, for their part, would benefit from new choices available to them through Facebook.

Also, in 2007, Facebook launched Facebook Ads. According to the company's statement, the new ad system would allow 'businesses to connect with users and target advertising to the exact audiences they want' (Facebook, 2007b). For advertisers, Facebook Ads enabled them to create branded pages, run targeted ads and have access to the data pertaining to Facebook's millions of users. Alongside Facebook Ads, two products were launched: Beacon, which caused the company's first major privacy outcry, and Marketplace, which is still in use to this day. While critics doubted that users would be adding Cola as their friend, Zuckerberg's vision for social advertising proved bigger, and more cynical. 'People influence people', he said, so by combining the social actions of friends with an advertiser's message, 'advertisers could deliver more tailored and relevant ads' (the ad system will be discussed in much greater detail in Chapter 5).

In 2008, Facebook Connect was launched; an updated version of the Platform product, which allowed 'users to "connect" their Facebook identity, friends and privacy to any site' (Morin, 2008). Instead of having to register anew when signing in on a new Web service or app, Facebook Connect allowed users to log in using their Facebook identity. The Facebook-enabled one-click login system not only removed barriers for users to access new sites, but importantly, for those websites to access users' Facebook profile information (Facebook, 2008). Moreover, as the company put it, Facebook Connect would allow developers to add 'social context' to their sites by showing users which friends had already made accounts and to 'share content and actions taken on a third-party site with friends back on Facebook' (ibid.).

Facebook's perhaps most iconic feature, the 'Like' button, was introduced in 2009 and became an important game-changer in the business. In a thread on the question-and-answer platform Quora, one of Facebook's most prolific engineers, Andrew 'Boz' Bosworth, recounts how the Like button first started off as 'the awesome button' (2014). Bosworth writes how he and others conceived of the button at a hackathon in July 2007, and how the project immediately gathered interest among different product teams at Facebook. While everyone at Facebook seemed to love the idea, to Bosworth's great surprise, the Like button did not get the positive feedback from Mark Zuckerberg that he had hoped for, and so it remained a 'cursed' project until February 2009 when it was finally launched to the public. As with all publicly available accounts told by company insiders, statements like these need to be treated with a pinch of salt.

This is important to keep in mind, as I will refer to such PR speak from time to time throughout the book, but will not always reiterate this analytical caveat. In the case of the Like button and the meticulous timeline that Bosworth (2014) provides in the Quora thread, we also need to bear in mind how it conveniently places the invention of the button before FriendFeed's Like button, which Facebook was accused of copying at the time.

If everybody has a Facebook story, so do Facebook's own employees and spokespersons. The stories told by so-called insiders – employees, former employees, collaborators, partners, tech journalists etc. – raise questions about their validity and reliability. It might be tempting to treat insider accounts as being of higher order and somehow more truthful. Yet, we must be reminded that insider accounts are stories too, accounts that are fraught with their own methodological and interpretative challenges (Cunliffe, 2010; Herod, 1999). Public claims made by Facebook employees and other insiders are often characterized by the discourse of public relations, which usually aims to portray the company in a favourable manner (Bhatia, 2010). That said, I will not critically scrutinize the truth value of every public Facebook statement or other insider account referenced in this book. This does not mean, however, that we can take their claims at face value. Corporate speech is a discursive construction; it both 'reflects and shapes a social order' (Hoffmann et al., 2018: 201). As with any other form of narrative and storytelling, Facebook's press releases, blog posts, corporate presentations, public speeches, revenue reports and anecdotes, are performative. Consider, for example, how Leah Pearlman, then product manager at Facebook, and part of the team that developed the awesome button, announced the launch of the button in a blog post:

> This is similar to how you might rate a restaurant on a reviews site. If you go to the restaurant and have a great

> time, you may want to rate it 5 stars. But if you had a particularly delicious dish there and want to rave about it, you can write a review detailing what you liked about the restaurant. We think of the new 'Like' feature to be the stars, and the comments to be the review. (Pearlman, 2009)

In an attempt to frame the new Like button as a service to Facebook's users, Pearlman strategically describes it as an overly positive metric. Of course, as has been raised time and again since, there was never an option to dislike, which would be the equivalent of being able to give a restaurant a one-star rating. While the concept of rating and numbering is hugely controversial (Espeland and Sauder, 2007; Esposito and Stark, 2019), it would be safe to say that the ability to hand out a five-star rating is worth nothing without the ability to also hand out a one-star rating. Yet, as Esposito and Stark remind us, ratings never mirror reality but need to be seen as second-order observations. Ratings function not to 'inform us about how things are but because they provide an orientation about what others observe' (2019: 3). Herein also lies the value for Facebook. Providing a Like button was not about mirroring reality but about orientation, creating a positive feedback mechanism that essentially circulates value to advertisers. The discursive construction and the use of metaphor in Perlman's official announcement of the Like button is ultimately about corporate storytelling. Not only is Pearlman's analogy wrong, but the ex-Facebook employee later professed regret for having played a role in creating one of the most addictive feedback loops in the advertising economy (Lewis, 2017; Karppi and Nieborg, 2020). Comparable to a five-star rating, the Like button isn't like the restaurant rating on a reviews site. What Pearlman, Bosworth and the others conceived of back then is more akin to the reviews one would find in a travel guidebook. The whole idea behind guidebooks is to provide a selection of the best tips – or have you ever travelled to a new city with a guidebook full of mediocre suggestions?

A guidebook to Facebook?

Let's stay with the guidebook metaphor a while longer. If the Like button laid the foundation for a carefully engineered attention economy centred on advertising, where is the guidebook for? Put differently, if we were to imagine Facebook as a geographical destination, where, in the travel book section, would we find its guidebook? Would it be like a city, or a state? Would Facebook even warrant a whole continent? And if we were to imagine a guidebook to the internet, where would Facebook be located? Would it be a website with a dedicated URL, under the apps section, a protocol or something else entirely? Media scholar Siva Vaidhyanathan (2018) calls Facebook the greatest contender for becoming the operating system of our lives. The repercussions of this are much greater than competing for people's laptops or mobile devices. Acting as the operating system of people's lives means having the power to 'measure our activities and states of being and constantly guide our decisions' (p. 99). As Vaidhyanathan contends, Facebook is:

> [t]he most influential media company in the world. It shapes the messages that politicians, dictators, companies, religions and more than two billion people wish to send in the world. It increasingly serves us news content, or content that purports to be news. It is the most powerful and successful advertising system in the history of the world. It's increasingly the medium of choice for political propaganda. (2018: 101)

Government officials, the news media and scholars alike, have used all kinds of spatial metaphors to reckon with Facebook's global power. Perhaps the most prevalent spatial metaphor has been to think of Facebook as a town square (Tussey, 2014). Whereas media and communication scholars have debated the public/private nature of Facebook since the very beginning, pointing to its porous and malleable boundaries, Zuckerberg has consistently framed Facebook as a public space. In an open letter describing a more privacy-focused vision of social networking, Zuckerberg (2019a) claims that Facebook and Instagram for the past fifteen years have served as the 'digital equivalent of a town square' (see also next chapter). The idea of Facebook as a digital town square is far from just empty company rhetoric. In Packingham vs North Carolina, the Supreme Court spoke forcefully about social media like Facebook as being vital for 'speaking and listening in the modern public square, and otherwise exploring the vast realms of human thought and knowledge' (Livni, 2017). In June 2017, the court unanimously overturned a North Carolina law that prohibited registered sex offenders from accessing social media for being unconstitutional. While the town square metaphor helps to illuminate Facebook's role in accessing information and communicating with one another, the metaphor may give the wrong impression as to the nature of speech on privately owned platforms. As Ethan Zuckerman writes, 'speech on these platforms is less like holding a rally in a public park – it's more like giving a speech in a shopping mall [...] where private actors have a great deal of control over speech that takes place on their property' (2014: 152). The town square metaphor may also not be very suitable for making sense of the global reach and scale of Facebook. Besides, town squares generally don't warrant guidebooks.

Nations, however, are great candidates for guidebooks. Indeed, Facebook is routinely described as a country. It is not too uncommon to read things like 'if Facebook were a country, it would be the largest in the world', or to hear Mark Zuckerberg being referred to as the head of the Facebook nation. While careful to not frame itself explicitly as a nation (with all that this entails), the metaphor has been used in several of Facebook's public-facing ad campaigns as a way of describing how nations are like Facebook. In a cinematic ad entitled 'The Things That Connect Us' from 2012, the voice-over lists all the things that are just like Facebook, including 'great nations', because it 'is something people build, so that they can have a place where they belong' (more on this ad in Chapter 2).

In fact, Mark Zuckerberg has gone to great lengths to frame himself and Facebook as a global do-gooder and democratic force. In a longer piece about Facebook's mission to build a global community, Zuckerberg (2017a) puts Facebook firmly in the democratic driving seat. Zuckerberg notes how Facebook's mission is to develop social infrastructure for a community – 'for supporting us, for keeping us safe, for informing us, for civic engagement, and for inclusion of all'. Whether it is about developing new drone, satellite or laser technologies to build the next-generation broadband infrastructure, or disaster relief funds and safety check functionalities, Facebook's social services and infrastructure projects are often framed in terms of a humanitarian and democratic effort. For example, in 2013 when launching Internet.org, a consortium between Facebook, mobile handset makers, a browser company (Opera) and network infrastructure manufacturers, Zuckerberg basically outlined a techno-political vision for addressing economic disparities by means of internet connectivity.

Zuckerberg does not merely invoke global politics in public discourse about Facebook. He is also more directly involved in domestic and foreign politics. He is, for example, the co-founder of the political lobby organization fwd.us, a bipartisan immigration reform advocacy group who are pressing for immigrant rights. If Zuckerberg's framing of immigrants as 'dreamers' and Silicon Valley as 'an idealistic place' is not exemplary of political rhetoric, then what is?

Despite Facebook's attempts to define itself as a social infrastructure and community builder, 'Zuckerberg is careful to avoid indicating that the site is anything more than a simple tool' (Rider and Murakami, 2019: 646). Against the allegation of filter bubbles or fake news, for example, Zuckerberg has consistently framed Facebook as a facilitator and conduit of information rather than a gatekeeper or publisher. When Zuckerberg had to testify in front of congress after the Cambridge Analytica scandal in spring 2018, he explicitly told them that Facebook is not a media company. 'I consider us to be a technology company', Zuckerberg said, 'because the primary thing that we do is have engineers who write code and build product and services for other people' (Castillo, 2018). So, in Zuckerberg's terms, having a workforce made up primarily of coders, makes Facebook a tech company. In addition, Rider and Murakami (2019) note how Zuckerberg draws consistently on the idea of Facebook as a facilitator by hosting networks. Accordingly, when pressed for answers on the spreading of mis- and disinformation, for example, Zuckerberg is quick to point out that it is people's networks, not Facebook, that show us content. When drawing on the network metaphor for an explanation, Zuckerberg is clearly leaning on the myth of the internet as a stateless, democratic force that knows and shows no boundaries. The idea of the internet as a stateless cyberspace is not well founded. We know from the body of literature on internet governance and internet infrastructure (Mueller, 2010; DeNardis, 2014) that the internet knows and obeys state boundaries. The locality of the internet matters. Although largely regulated through multi-stakeholder groups and global organizations, the internet is both a very physical and political entity that is not just controlled by state actors but looks and feels different in different geographical locations.

Where does this selective and strategic differential framing of Facebook as either a town or nation leave us in terms of locating Facebook? If Facebook's locality depends on who and when you ask, what, then, is the guidebook for? Put differently, what territory is being mapped out? Rather than thinking of Facebook in terms of fixed spatial metaphors such as squares, cities or states, the notion of topology offers a language for articulating the instabilities and fluctuations characteristic of malleable and changing entities such as

Facebook. In its mathematical origin, topology is concerned with the theorem of the continuum, of how the properties of objects are preserved under continuous deformations (Lury et al., 2012). In contrast to '"Euclidean" space with its familiar geometry of stable, singular entities positioned against the external backdrop of a static space and linear time', a topological approach accentuates how the infinite and differential character of relations has the capacity to generate its own 'space-time, with its particular scales, extension and rhythms' (Marres, 2012: 292). Whereas Cartesian coordinates enable us to measure a certain space, topology is not concerned with size and measurement as such but with the ways in which 'relationships between various points/ agents enact a space themselves' (Decuypere and Simons, 2016: 374). A topological approach, especially as it has been adopted within the social sciences and the humanities, sees space and time not as a priori but as something produced by 'entities-in-relation' (Marres, 2012: 289). The primary analytic category is relationality, where change is not an exception but fundamental to how spaces are configured.

Bringing a topological approach to bear on Facebook means paying close attention to unfolding configurations and reconfigurations (Suchman, 2007), and grappling with the variations and multiplicities that Facebook produces. Such a view has multiple implications. First, it means we have to get rid of thinking of Facebook as one thing, with a stable and invariant core. In this sense, Facebook is multiple, coming together in various ways as a result of different configurations. This means that what we take Facebook to be is a result of different elements being gathered in a specific way at a specific time. For example, patents, earning reports, profit margins, code stacks and features may come together in a board meeting temporality stabilizing and producing one single object that we conventionally call Facebook. In a different instance, for the human rights activist in Tunisia, what is called Facebook comes together through government censorship, content policies, the lack of information about political ad spending, the inexplicable removal of an activist's video and content moderation. This brings us to a second point that we need to get rid of when adopting a topological approach to Facebook, which is the idea that these stories and configurations hang easily together or cohere. Although the world, especially the scientific world, generally demands some form of consistency, we need to recognize that Facebook and the telling of stories about Facebook are much messier than that. As John Law argues (2004), coherence can only be achieved in theory and not in practice. The fact that there are different stories and gatherings of elements should not be confused with perspectivalism, the idea that there are different perspectives on a stable object (Mol, 2002). When we talk about non-coherence with regard to Facebook it is to acknowledge its elusiveness and ambivalence. While it might be challenging to work with multiplicity, relationality, non-coherence or gatherings as analytical categories, this is only the case if we expect the story to follow a 'smooth and singular narrative of the kind offered by a textbook' (Law, 2004: 98). Alas, this is not the goal of this book.

It's complicated

Facebook is no easy target. Just as telling the story of Facebook, as if there was one coherent and neat story to tell, is not really possible; neither is delineating the target in the first place. What Facebook is depends not just on whom you ask but when you ask. Ontologically, we might say that Facebook is not just variable in the technical sense as it is constantly evolving, changing and developing as a programmed entity with certain features and functionalities that only exist in a given instantiation, at a specific point in time. What matters to different people, stakeholders and other actors is highly variable too. In the same way that the internet is not one thing but 'has always been multiple' with different histories (Driscoll and Paloque-Berges, 2017: 48), there are not just multiple stories to tell about Facebook, but Facebook itself needs to be seen as multiple.

Drawing on a relational ontology reminiscent of science and technology studies (see Mol, 2002; Law, 2002), this book works from the assumption that there is not just one Facebook but many. This statement is true on many levels. As anthropologist Daniel Miller suggests, there are different Facebooks depending on where in the world you are and whom you ask. As a scholar who has specialized in doing fieldwork in Trinidad, Miller's Facebook, if you will, differs from the Facebook you would find in Denmark or Norway. This does not mean that one version is more authentic or real than the other. Reporting from a large ethnographic study of how social media is used in five different geographical locales around the world, Miller et al. stress how there is no core to what Facebook is, because 'Facebook only ever exists with respect to specific populations' (2016: 15). A similar point can be made with regard to the many different versions of Facebook depending on its stakeholders: Facebook for Business, Facebook for Advertisers, Facebook for Developers and so forth. Facebook is not just a company, a partner or adversary. Facebook may be all, some or none of these things, or something else entirely, depending on how it is practised in specific situations. This is not to say that there isn't a corporation, a technical stack and infrastructure, an organization and a board of directors behind this thing that we call Facebook. Indeed, there is only one board of directors that has the steering power and one company called Facebook, but how these things come together and matter in specific circumstances varies.

The idea, then, that Facebook needs to be understood as multiple is not about adding different perspectives to illuminate the meaning of a singular thing or to say that there are indefinite versions of Facebook that exist in parallel. As

Annemarie Mol (2002) has argued in her anthropological study of how a medical diagnosis is practised, different practices do not just produce different perspectives on the disease, they enact different realities as well. This is not to say that everything is relative and that it all depends or that every reality made is equal in terms and effects. The trouble is not that the world is multiple and ambiguous but the fact that it seems singular because much work and politics have gone into making it appear this way. If we begin from the assumption that the world is already vague and indefinite, what should be of concern is explaining why many versions seem to hang together and overlap to begin with – not least to 'make sure that they overlap in productive ways' (Law, 2004: 55). For analytical reasons, Facebook may look like a singular object and be referred to as a social network site, a platform or infrastructure, respectively. There is nothing wrong in adopting these singular labels per se, it might even be the most pragmatic option to take. After all, how can you write sensibly about a topic while having to make amendments and caveats every time you use a certain label? Yet, pragmatism should not be an excuse for not explicating or operational-izing one's terms of use. Throughout the book, I will try to be as concrete and transparent as possible with regard to the different labels used, bearing in mind that they will only ever serve as a shorthand and placeholder for the much more abstract concept lingering underneath – a concept called Facebook.

So, we have arrived at the notion of the concept, at last. At the beginning of this chapter, I suggested that Facebook is Facebook, hinting at the ways in which Facebook has become something of a concept. This is to say that, as time has passed, what we take Facebook to be has acquired a life of its own. It is no longer just a word, or a label for a technological platform or a social network site (if it ever was). As the example of Jace mentioned earlier attests to, we are living in a society where people are routinely socialized into acquiring a concept of Facebook, sometimes even without being an active user themselves. Facebook routinely figures in policy discussions, academic discourse, news reports and public controversies. It plays a habitual role in people's everyday lives and exists more broadly as a global sociotechnical imaginary. As such, we might think of Facebook as a 'basic concept' (Koselleck, 2011) of sorts. For Koselleck, 'a concept is basic if it plays a central role in our sociopolitical language'; something we cannot do without when accounting for 'the most urgent issues of a given time' (Berenskoetter, 2017: 157).

To situate Facebook as a basic concept, then, means thinking of its power as something that can guide thought and action beyond specialized academic domains as it becomes part of a wider public imaginary. At the same time, for media and communication studies, thinking of Facebook as a concept and not simply as an instance of social media, means grappling with the fact that this company has gained the same kind of currency in our common vocabularies as more overarching media forms such as broadcast or the internet.[3] While I will not make any totalizing claims about the unprecedentedness of Facebook's conceptual status in the longer history of media and communication, it is safe to say that Facebook has fostered both new concepts (e.g. 'Liking', News Feed, filter bubble) and helped to reconfigure existing ones (e.g. friendship, publicness, privacy).

The point here is not to provide a definition of Facebook; quite the opposite. In *What is Philosophy?* Deleuze and Guattari suggest that concepts have no identity, only a becoming. 'There are no simple concepts', they write. 'Every concept has components and is defined by them' (Deleuze and Guattari, 1994: 15). This means that concepts are neither fixed nor unambiguous. Instead, concepts are multiplicities that converge around the accumulation of their different conceptions and components.[4] A concept includes all the conceptions people have about it, but those particular understandings are never completely stable or shared. So all our different ideas about Facebook come to form the concept of Facebook but these different ideas may not necessarily overlap.[5] Because of their curious status as 'similar enough' but 'not necessarily overlapping', Mieke Bal proposes the notion of the 'travelling concept' – the capacity of concepts to travel between disciplines, historical periods and dispersed communities (Bal, 2002: 24). Because concepts are dynamic, Bal suggests we might be better off studying the work that concepts do instead of chasing their particular meanings. This means that we have to pay attention to how the application of the concept of Facebook is 'situated in a particular context and shapes (our understanding of) the latter' (Berenskoetter, 2017: 160). Facebook can be understood as many things, only a fraction of which may be called social media. How Facebook is variously situated in journalism or electoral politics, for example, has performative effects on how we understand these domains today (see also Chapters 4 and 6). While Bal's travels take her primarily between different scholarly disciplines, this book provides a different sort of travelling. It contains time travels (back and forth in time) as well as space travels (both geographical and topological). We will travel to specific domains, such as politics and news, and we will consider those who might not conventionally be able to travel (for political, socio-economic or bodily reasons). But before briefly outlining the book's chapters, let us travel to a concrete geographical place with its specific conception of Facebook that may help to illuminate how Facebook is Facebook.

Facebook is everything

Facebook fully entered Myanmar around 2014. People had been using Facebook well before that, but they were only a tiny fraction of the population, early adopters and those who could afford a SIM card. Up until then, the military junta had imposed artificial caps on access to smartphones and SIM cards. In 2014, the cost of a SIM card suddenly dropped from a staggering 1500 GBP to 0.7 GBP. Mobile shops were swamped and the telecom industry expanded from one state-controlled operator to several new competitors, including the Norwegian Telenor. The thing you need to understand about Facebook, Nyan, a former employee of an international NGO that collaborated closely with the government and now funder of a local NGO, tells me, is that for most people in Myanmar, Facebook was introduced to them as a pre-installed app on their new mobile phones. Once the cost of SIM cards dropped, people went into one of the many mobile phone shops that had started to pop up all over the country to purchase a phone with a data plan. Most shop owners not only pre-installed Facebook and Viber, a messaging app, but also made sure they opened up a new Facebook account on the customer's behalf. Because of the country's restrictive communications policies and access to the internet, it wasn't as if people knew how to use the internet, or even had a clear understanding of what the internet, or social network sites, were for. So it only made sense that shop owners had a stack of email addresses and pre-made Facebook accounts at the ready. Nyan says that there are many stories of people who got their new Facebook accounts already equipped with pre-installed friends, and in many cases celebrities and a collection of hot girls, so as to get their Facebook experience going from the very start. In Myanmar, for the millions of people who were able to buy a SIM card, Facebook was not a social network site, or even the internet, but something called Facebook, Nyan says. When talking about the role Facebook has played in Myanmar, about its role in the recent genocide and Facebook's response or lack of response, Nyan says that there is one fundamental thing that Facebook needs to get right and understand. They act as if they are a social media company, but in Myanmar, Facebook is everything, Nyan says. Facebook is Facebook.

Book outline

Writing a book about Facebook feels like writing a book about the internet. Too much to cover, too many developments, too many twists and turns, too much that is already history by tomorrow. Consider this book an incomplete and unfolding travel guide – a book that cannot be filed under any conventional category found in the travel book section. As a topological mapping of sorts, this book will necessarily provide a partial picture of Facebook. That is OK, even to be expected of a book of this nature. Just like the internet itself, the fact that Facebook is difficult to grasp doesn't mean there isn't a concrete origin, prevailing myths, dominant discourses, social histories, cultural contexts, politics, technical developments and imaginary futures. It's all there and part of what makes Facebook Facebook.

In Chapter 1, I look at the framing of Facebook, both by the company itself, as well the discourses that surround it, especially as it pertains to Facebook's early days. This chapter gives readers a sense of where Facebook came from, providing more grounds to the origin story started in this chapter. By analysing Mark Zuckerberg's public statements, this chapter considers the discursive and rhetorical framing of Facebook and the prevailing metaphors used to define what Facebook is and should be. By situating an analysis of metaphors in the cultures and histories of the internet more broadly, this chapter shows how Facebook is very much built on techno-libertarian ideologies of communalism and hacking that have helped to spur Facebook's culture of moving fast and breaking things.

Chapter 2 explores Facebook as an infrastructure. Using two analytical figures – electric light and chairs – this chapter grapples with Facebook's scale and relational qualities by way of an infrastructural reading. Using Zuckerberg's own analogy between Facebook and the electric light as a starting point, I draw on science and technology studies and histories of electrical light to account for Facebook as a large technical system. Using the Like button and Open Graph as cases in point, this chapter makes the argument that even the most technical features contain a rich texture of economic principles, political forces and social concerns. Moreover, analysing one of Facebook's most grandiose television ads, which compares chairs to Facebook, the metaphor of the chair is used to question what and whom Facebook is for.

Chapter 3 considers Facebook sociality by situating questions of identity and friendships in a discussion of Facebook's real name policy. Beginning from Facebook's (early) identity as a social network site, this chapter looks at how networks became social and first had to be deanonymised. By way of a discussion of authenticity, the bulk of the chapter is concerned with the ways in which friendships have been strategically mobilized in the creation of Facebook's business model. Ultimately this chapter shows how a foundational element of what makes Facebook, Facebook, is that it is 'grounded in reality'.

In Chapter 4, I cover some historical and evolutionary grounds again. This chapter is dedicated to the mapping of Facebook's techno-economic development in terms of its most significant business decisions and technical features. If Chapter 1 provided an account of Facebook's history in terms of its discursive and metaphorical work, and Chapter 2 scaled up the discussion to the level of large technical systems and infrastructure, this chapter is concerned with the specific business decisions Facebook has made along the way and how those strategies have been implemented in specific features. The main objective of this chapter is to provide readers with a discussion of Facebook's two main features, the News Feed and its algorithms. By examining how these features are modelled on notions of journalism and news, this chapter reveals the importance of not just understanding what the features are or do, but how they are made to signify to begin with.

Chapter 5 examines Facebook as an advertising company. In this chapter, I argue that Facebook must be considered as a capitalist machine constituting and constituted by an ad-tech-surveillance complex. It provides readers with an overview of digital advertising and how the Web became a commercial space through the implementation of tracking technologies such as cookies, and how Facebook has built on these logics to create an enormous digital tracking and advertising infrastructure. Knowing more about the specifics of Facebook as an advertising company also serves to ground some of the discussions in the next chapter, as knowing what the economic rationales are and how they are technically implemented helps to ground the higher level ethical questions surrounding democracy and politics.

Chapter 6 addresses the complicated and convoluted terrain of politics. While focusing on the intersections of Facebook and electoral politics and campaigning, the chapter makes a case for understanding Facebook politics in the widest possible way. Facebook politics is just as much about electoral politics, as it is also about protests, activism, regulation, technical artifacts, institutional structures, laws and the values in design. By combining a discussion of Facebook's role in the growing landscape of digital behavioural advertising, with cases studies of the Cambridge Analytica scandal and the atrocities in Myanmar, this chapter investigates how Facebook's design and business model help to shape a polluted information landscape. It ultimately shows how the politics of Facebook is concerned with its world-making power, of that which is allowed to take root, to evolve, and to take shape because of Facebook's central position.

In the concluding chapter, I synthesize the book's case studies by considering the different ways in which the assertion that Facebook is Facebook can be understood and why it matters. The argument is made that Facebook became new only recently, when existing words, categories and concepts ceased to be able to describe and explain it adequately.

Furthermore, this chapter makes the case that Facebook has become a hyperobject of sorts, a thing too distributed in time and space, for us to get our heads around it. This unclarity, however, invites renewed attention and reflection, not just about what Facebook is but what we would like it to be.

CHAPTER ONE

Metaphors at work: Framing Facebook

> As I think about the future of the internet, I believe a privacy-focused communications platform will become even more important than today's open platforms.
>
> Mark Zuckerberg (2019a)

On 16 March 2019, Mark Zuckerberg published an open letter titled 'A Privacy-Focused Vision for Social Networking'. The letter detailed a radical new vision for the company that intends to move Facebook away from a public social media platform towards a private messaging platform. Unlike previous announcements, this seemed consequential. After all, most people have come to think of Facebook as a more or less public or semi-public space. When public and private institutions and companies say things like 'we have to be where the people are' as a way of defending their Facebook presence, it attests to the widespread notion of Facebook as a public space. The announcement that Facebook is planning to venture into more private communication channels, possibly at the expense of its most prominent feature, the News Feed, should not be taken lightly. While time will tell whether this move is going to be effectuated, to what extent and with what consequences, just trying to *think* of Facebook as a private messaging platform first, and a 'public' feed-based channel second, is not just strange but almost unimaginable.

In order to understand why this change in company vision seems more radical than any of its previous announcements, we need to revisit some of the developments that led to the normalization of public sharing in the first place. Like the many Facebook stories, this is not a story of a unified linear historical development, but of overlapping and converging social, cultural, political, technical and economic forces. The goal of this chapter is to provide the reader with an understanding of *where* Facebook came from and *how* it evolved, in order to give them a first sense of why Facebook looks as it does at the brink of a new decade. We have already touched briefly upon Facebook's origin history in the previous chapter. In this chapter we will look more closely at the underlying cultural values and ideologies guiding Facebook, from the very cultural and technical roots of the internet itself through to the ideas and discourses shaping the origins of Web 2.0. Grounded in Mark Zuckerberg's public appearances, interviews and statements, this chapter considers the discursive and rhetorical framing of Facebook.

Mark Zuckerberg's letters and notes are part and parcel of a unified communication strategy and an attempt to speak with one coherent voice. As Anna Lauren Hoffmann et al. (2018) point out, Zuckerberg's public utterances offer important evidence as to the discursive strategies used by Facebook in stabilizing the meaning and potential uses of the platform. Discourse, in the Foucauldian sense of the term, refers to a set of statements about the world that have organizing effects.[1] Using language in certain ways (and not others) works in reflecting and shaping social order. As Charles Bazerman has argued in his book *The Languages of Edison's Light* (2002), technology is business, and dealing with the media, the public, financiers and government agencies can be as important to an invention's success as effective product development. Nothing about a technology or invention is inevitable, and it is as much about the symbols and communication as it is about the product itself. Analysing Zuckerberg's letters and notes as a set of statements about social media entails acknowledging their constructive role in shaping how we come to think of the current media environment and the ways in which talk and text can sustain particular practices.

Just like Edison and his corporation, then, Mark Zuckerberg and Facebook should be seen as self-conscious and strategic actors whose rhetorical work plays a crucial role in making Facebook Facebook.

The reading of these statements is guided by a critical awareness of the rhetorical power embedded in language use. Yet, discourse is not limited to language. The affordances and material possibilities and constraints of Facebook, hold discursive powers too. The chapter makes a case for an understanding of Facebook's success through a material-discursive reading that considers a diverse set of secondary sources, including public statements made by Zuckerberg and Facebook employees found in blog posts, insider accounts, press releases and public speeches. By analysing company discourse against the backdrop of Facebook's cultural context and placement in Silicon Valley, this chapter addresses the techno-libertarian ideologies characteristic of contemporary tech companies and internet platforms, the cult of entrepreneurship and the hacker ethic, as well as the symbolism entailed in office and interface designs, metaphors, cultural tropes and company visions.

This chapter is organized into four parts, each of which deals with the discursive framing of Facebook. The first part outlines the new Facebook vision by giving an account of the most recent developments that have led to a 'privacy-focused communications platform' becoming the proposed solution (Zuckerberg, 2019a). The second part revisits the social history of the internet as it relates to the cultures and visions guiding Facebook, particularly with regard to the prevailing normative ideas of openness, sharing and community. The third part of the chapter goes into more detail on the ways that the culture of openness and entrepreneurship manifests itself in Facebook's company culture and work ethic. The fourth part of the chapter takes a broader perspective again by considering the work that metaphor and discourse performs.

From town square to living room

Ask anyone what Facebook is and most people would probably answer something quite similar. A social network(ing) site, a social media platform, a public forum, a semi-public news feed, a place to connect with friends and family, a mini version of the internet where you can find information on businesses and organizations of interest, a place to share news and discuss topics of interest, ask for recommendations and find interesting events. A 'privacy-focused messaging platform'? Not so much. We have become so accustomed to thinking of social media platforms as a form of public broadcasting that Facebook's new vision of turning the company into a platform for private and encrypted communication is not just radical but points to a complete redefinition of what social media is and should be. In the letter announcing the change, Zuckerberg talks about it as a transformation that would entail Facebook feeling less like a 'town square' and more like the intimate spaces of a 'living room'. If a town square leaves people wondering with whom they are communicating and who might be listening in, a living room arguably feels more secure and safe. Public broadcasting, according to Zuckerberg, serves many important functions on Facebook, from 'telling all your friends about something, using your voice on important topics or organizing fundraisers'. Yet, as Zuckerberg says, 'many people prefer the intimacy of communicating one-on-one or with just a few friends'. In order to cater to what is seen as a growing demand for more private communication, Zuckerberg's vision for 'privacy-focused social networking' focused on integrating Facebook's main messaging apps and platforms, Instagram, WhatsApp and Messenger. As Zuckerberg (2019a) boldly proclaimed, 'in a few years, I expect future versions of Messenger and WhatsApp to become the main ways people communicate on the Facebook network'.

How did Mark Zuckerberg arrive at this drastic conclusion, and seemingly change direction completely? While paradoxical in terms of how Facebook has always presented itself as an open platform that helps the whole world to connect, the sudden focus on private communication and moving away from a publicly oriented news feed should not come as a big surprise. After years of privacy scandals, a changing political climate that spurred the proliferation of terms such as 'fake news' and 'disinformation', and an increasingly harsher climate for public discourse that rewards extreme opinions and viral content, Facebook had to come up with more than an apology. More than simply answering to years of privacy mishaps, the new emphasis on private communication is also a strategic business decision that sees Facebook taking big steps in confronting its main competitor and only large hurdle towards consolidating globally – China's WeChat.

If Facebook has spent the majority of its seventeen years of existence on 'making the world more open and connected', the new 'pivot to privacy' came amid a more rampant move towards redefining the company's mission in the aftermath of the 2016 US presidential election. With an increasingly hate-plagued platform that saw Facebook triple its security and moderation staff in the years following the election, Zuckerberg had come to the realization that product change was in order. The first signs of redefining Facebook's service came in 2017 when Facebook changed its mantra for the first time in over a decade. Zuckerberg's lengthiest attempt at a redefinition came in the form of an open letter to the Facebook 'community' in February 2017. The letter, titled 'Building Global Community', explained how Zuckerberg had come to rethink Facebook's role in society (Zuckerberg, 2017a). Over the course of a staggering 2,000 words, the letter, which became more colloquially known as the Facebook manifesto, made a case for seeing Facebook – and himself – as global community builders. In contrast to Facebook's earlier conceptualizations of community that had foregrounded global expansion, the post-2016 election period seemed to bring about a more inward-looking mode, whereby Zuckerberg had taken it upon himself to strengthen people's bonds. In a rather monumental tone that had many commentators speculating about Zuckerberg's political ambitions, Zuckerberg asked rhetorically whether 'we are building the world we all want'. Zuckerberg suggested that Facebook had spent more energy trying to connect people than maintaining those connections after the fact. The company was thus changing direction going forward, developing communities for support, safety and an informed public. 'In times like these', Zuckerberg wrote, 'the most important thing we at Facebook can do is develop the social infrastructure to give people the power to build a global community that works for all of us' (Zuckerberg, 2017a).

A few months later, in June 2017, Zuckerberg finally unveiled Facebook's new mission statement. Speaking at the first ever Facebook Community Summit, Zuckerberg suggested that the time had come to change the company's long-time mantra of 'making the world more open and connected'. 'To set our course as a company for the next decade', Zuckerberg declared, Facebook's new mission would be 'to give people the power to build community and bring the world closer together' (Zuckerberg, 2017b). At the core of the new mission was an emphasis on the somewhat nebulous term 'meaningful communities'. In the Facebook manifesto, Zuckerberg had already described how they had found that 'more than 100 million people on Facebook are members of what *we* call "very meaningful" *groups*' [emphasis added]. These are essentially the Facebook groups that turn out to be particularly important and relevant to those joining them, for example parenting groups for new parents. At the Community Summit, the 'we' and 'groups' of the previous message had been subtly replaced by 'they' [Facebook users] and 'communities', respectively, making it appear as if the term 'meaningful communities' had originated with Facebook users themselves (see Zuckerberg, 2017b).

The change from 'very meaningful groups' to 'meaningful communities' was far from coincidental. The marriage of the terms 'meaningful' and 'communities' was essentially part and parcel of a branding operation that gained particular urgency after trouble spiralled in 2016. While the history of Facebook includes a series of privacy scandals and political controversies, there was something about the scale and gravity of a new kind of reality that seemed to demand a more serious redefinition of what Facebook is and should be. Caught up in multiple data breaches, free-speech controversies, accusations of Russian interference in the 2016 US presidential election and a proliferation of fake accounts, it is safe to say that Facebook found itself miles away from its original image as a network of friends. As a result, the focus on private communication via groups and 'meaningful communities' became a central force in fostering a more positive image of a community-geared 'social infrastructure'.

While the recasting of Facebook from public broadcasting to private communication might be difficult to grasp at first, there is nothing inevitable or natural about the idea of Facebook as a town square to begin with. Just consider how Zuckerberg described the ways in which the meaning of public sharing and openness first had to be established:

> When I built the first version of Facebook, almost nobody I knew wanted a public page on the internet. That seemed scary. But as long as they could make their page private, they felt safe sharing with their friends online. Control was key. With Facebook, for the first time, people had the tools they needed to do this. That's how Facebook became the world's biggest community online. We made it easy for people to feel comfortable sharing things about their real lives. (Zuckerberg, 2011b)

Contrary to the prevailing discourse around social media, this description suggests that public sharing is not something people do naturally, it has to be invented and repeated until it seems like a natural thing to do. Here we are reminded of

Paul Edwards' study of politics and technology during the Cold War, in which he showed how technologies and the terms under which they are understood are 'quite literally fought inside a quintessentially semiotic space' (1997: 120). Some discourses stick more than others and help to frame not just how people think of a technology or a company, but perhaps more importantly how those discursive dimensions sift into and become integrated into cultural life and subjective experience in general.

Techno-utopianism and the open internet

Facebook is both shaped by and shapes the history of the internet. To understand the cultural values at play in Facebook, and how these values are starting to turn on themselves, we need to revisit the social history and cultures out of which the company grew. First, there is the longer history of the internet itself, which originated as a non-commercial network created by government researchers and computer scientists for the purpose of connecting anyone on the network to anyone else (Zittrain, 2008: 27). Secondly, the discourse of Facebook must be understood against a certain way of thinking and talking about the intersection of technology, economy and society reminiscent of the techno-scientific communities of the Californian Bay Area that helped to shape the contemporary landscape of digital networking technologies. For all its discourse of openness, connectivity and sharing, Facebook didn't invent it.

The internet was originally cast as a liberatory and open space, where networking and sharing were the dominant ideals. The 'standard folklore' of the internet, as Tom Streeter (2011) calls it, has always emphasized its imagined openness and freedom as a defining characteristic. This folklore usually starts with the internet's ARPANET origins as a computer network in the US military complex and its quest for technological superiority over the Soviet Union in the 1960s to

1970s, continues with the hobbyist's personal computers and networks in the 1970s to 1980s, and a mention of the open-source movement commencing in the 1980s, before arriving at the emergence of the World Wide Web in the 1990s.[2] In contrast to the scientific image of the early internet and computing, the 1970s and 1980s were also a time when computers were portrayed as educational and communal (Rankin, 2018). As Kevin Driscoll writes, 'many of the technical structures and cultural practices that we now recognize as social media were first developed by amateurs tinkering in their free time to build systems for computer-mediated collaboration and communication' (2016: 56). Decades before the advent of Facebook, then, computer users were communicating and sharing important information about everything from the then emerging AIDS epidemic to the most recent news on popular TV shows using bulletin-board systems (BBSs).

The New Communalists, as Fred Turner (2006) called the generation of techno-utopianists who helped to shape the early Web and the platforms that were built as a result, strongly believed in the power of the internet to build alternative, creative and decentralized communities. Institutions and governments were to be mistrusted, while upholding a belief in the power of the internet to engender social change. By the mid-1980s, the computer industry in California was rapidly growing and many of its future leaders, including Steve Jobs, were inspired by the techno-utopianist rhetoric surrounding the Communalists. An important aspect of the Communalist rhetoric emphasized the idea of sharing for the good of the community, which became one of the core tenets of the open-source movement as well.[3] While numerous books have been written on the ideology behind open-source software development, including its internal differences and multiple constituencies, suffice it here to emphasize how the model of frequent borrowing and code sharing has not only influenced Facebook's company rhetoric but also been widely adopted in many of the software products that the company has created.[4] As recent reports suggest, Facebook is among the top five companies in the world contributing to major open-source repositories. As Adrian Mackenzie points out, 'from its earliest implementations, Facebook has relied on a relatively generic but iconic set of open-source software technical elements such as the Linux operating system, Apache Web server, MySQL relational database and PHP programming scripts, the so-called LAMP stack' (2019: 2001). If, for some, Facebook's open-source initiatives provide a 'reason not to hate Facebook' (Hecht, 2019), others see it as just another recruitment and PR tool. However one looks at it, open-source software plays an important role in the company's ideological and technological mission to 'create community and bring the world closer together' (Flory, 2018).

As the personal computer industry grew throughout the 1980s and the first version of the Web was invented, thanks to the hypertext standards developed by Tim Berners-Lee in the early 1990s, the information-sharing and communal rhetoric that had characterized the pre-Web decades were merged with a new kind of techno-libertarianism and commercial hype. Richard Barbrook and Andy Cameron (1996) coined the term 'the Californian ideology' in the mid-1990s to describe how two seemingly opposing ideological camps, Californian hippies and market fundamentalists, came to be united by shared ideals of technological determinism and anti-statism. As Karina Rider and David Murakami Wood explain, the rise of the Web was not just fuelled by a profound faith in its emancipatory potential, but also by 'a Manichean split between a controlling authoritarian government, which was to be mistrusted and resisted, and an informed new generation of computer users, who were staking out new territory on the "electronic frontier"' (2019: 642). The dotcom era of the mid-to-late 1990s was accompanied by a neoliberal celebration of market principles and liberal entrepreneurial freedom.[5] 'Openness', 'sharing' and 'connectivity' were still important signifiers – this time, however, largely in the service of free market capitalism. As Barbrook and Cameron (1996) observed, the internet during the dotcom era was seen to 'empower the individual, enhance personal freedom and radically reduce the power of the nation state', giving rise to a time of great optimism and belief in internet start-ups.

What followed the inevitable burst of the bubble around 2000, given that many of the start-ups lacked a viable business model, was a kind of rebranding exercise for the Web. In 2004, publisher Tim O'Reilly coined the term 'Web 2.0' to describe the sort of companies that had survived the burst by embracing a collection of ideas, including 'the Web as a platform', 'collective intelligence', data openness, iterative software development, user-generated content and 'software as a service' (Marwick, 2013; O'Reilly, 2005).[6] While largely a marketing stunt, the term 'Web 2.0' stuck, as did the collection of ideas associated with it. The Web 2.0 ideology promised freedom from large corporations, a return to the democratic principles of early networking through easy access and a communal spirit, and a better user experience thanks to the development of new networking technologies such as AJAX and blogging software. As O'Reilly put it, '"the 2.0-ness" is not something new but rather a fuller realization of the true potential of the Web platform' (2005). Openness and sharing, again, played a key role in the discursive formation of this 'new' version of the Web. Unlike the pre-Web or Web 1.0, it wasn't code or information that was shared, but data about people's lives. This was not the Web of information but of participation (Song, 2010). Early Web 2.0 discourse became infused with terms such as 'user-generated content', 'empowerment', 'democratization' and 'participatory culture', both by intellectuals eying up hopes for the democratic potential of the internet to be realized and the many new technology and social media start-ups seeking to capitalize on those very hopes and promises.

It is against this background that the normative values and cultures of social media platforms like Facebook must be understood. As Streeter suggests, the 'internet is open, not because of the technology itself or some uniquely democratic potential hidden inside the technology, but because we have narrated it as open and, as a consequence, have embraced and constructed it as open' (2011: 175). The same is certainly true for Facebook. The narrative construction of the democratic potential of the internet is reflected in the way that Mark Zuckerberg has talked about Facebook from the very beginning. When announcing the 200-million-user mark in 2009, Zuckerberg recalled how he started Facebook to 'create a richer, faster way for people to share information about what was happening around them ... which would then give them even greater power to change the world' (Zuckerberg, 2009). While Zuckerberg maintains that he created Facebook to connect friends and classmates, part of the origin story includes a fundamental belief in the democratic power of the internet. In a 2010 interview, Zuckerberg told the reporter how he and his college friends at Harvard were inspired by the internet's potential to bring forth a more open and informed society. More information, Zuckerberg reasoned, would lead to a more informed and democratic society, and essentially make people more understanding and tolerant (Zuckerberg, 2010). More fundamentally, 'the need to open up and connect is what makes us human. It's what brings us together. It's what brings meaning to our lives' (Zuckerberg, 2012a). Indeed, Facebook's entire mission of 'making the world more open and connected' should be understood as part of this ideological lineage.

Move fast and break things

Facebook famously cultivates a culture and management approach they call 'the hacker way'. The hacking culture is such an integral part of Facebook that it has become the principal way in which the company presents itself, internally as well as externally. As described in a letter penned by Mark Zuckerberg and included in Facebook's IPO registration statement, the hacker way is an approach to building that 'involves continuous improvement and iteration' (Zuckerberg, 2012b). The hacker, Zuckerberg suggests, has typically been portrayed unfairly in the media. In reality, 'hacking just means building something quickly or testing the boundaries of what can be done'. The Facebook hacker is not like the university hackers of the 1960s described by Steven Levy (2010) in his book *Hackers*, nor anything like the underground hackers described in Gabriela Coleman's (2014) work on Anonymous. The Facebook hackers specifically 'believe that something can always be better, and that nothing is ever complete. They just have to go and fix it – often in the face of people who say it's impossible or are content with the status quo.' For all its heroic rhetoric, hacking has moved from the margins to the mainstream (Gregg, 2015). The hacker has come a long way from their subversive origin, seen as someone who attacks and works to disrupt existing systems. As Sarah Davies suggests, today, the figure of the hacker is 'entrepreneurial, libertarian and independent, influenced by the Californian ideology of individual freedom and creativity enabled through technology' (2018: 356).

It is in this sense that Mark Zuckerberg personifies the hacker with his youthful appearance and the washed-out grey T-shirt or college sweater that he always wears when appearing in public. Whatever imagined gap there might have been between users and the mythical founder figure, the T-shirt does its job of letting the world know that he is just a coder. In one of Facebook's Q&A sessions, Zuckerberg told the audience how the T-shirt eliminated unnecessary choice. Knowing exactly what to wear every day would leave him more time to 'build the best product and services'. The T-shirt, Zuckerberg claimed, helps him dedicate all his time and energy to 'reach[ing] the company's goal and achiev[ing] the mission of helping to connect everyone in the world and giving them the ability to stay connected with the people that they love and care about' (Facebook, 2014). Bolstering his role as the hard-working CEO, the T-shirt came to solidify Mark Zuckerberg's image as the dedicated coder – even long after he stopped actually coding the system.

Facebook's hacker way is characterized by numerous core values, carefully crafted through slogans and popular sayings that pervade not only the company's discourse but also its physical setting and workplace. When I visited the Facebook headquarters located at 'Hacker Way' in early 2018 as part of an invited unconference, I entered exactly what I pictured a Silicon Valley tech company would look like – part playground, part college campus, game consoles and print workshops, vending machines with electronic gadgets, free ice cream and cookies, BBQ and taco stalls, heavy security and tons of motivational posters, all printed with a beige background and bold red text: 'Move fast and break things', 'What would you do if you weren't afraid?', 'Done is better than perfect', 'Think wrong', 'Stay humble.'

The hacker identity, however, has not always been a part of Facebook's brand. The external hacker brand first had to be created. In 2008, cultural and employment branding manager Molly Graham was hired to create and tell the company's story. Graham describes how the defining moment for Facebook's identity came with a blog post by Paul Buchheit, who joined Facebook from FriendFeed in 2009. The post reframed hacking as 'applied philosophy', a way of thinking and acting that 'is much bigger and more important than clever bits of code in a computer' (Buchheit, 2009). In an interview with First Round review, Graham put it like this: 'When Paul wrote that post, he wrote the story of Facebook's DNA' (First Round, n.d.). Unlike real DNA, however, Facebook's DNA had to be written and invented.

The story of the company's cultural DNA, as reiterated on Facebook's career site, accentuates five core values: be bold, focus on impact, move fast, be open and build social value (Facebook Careers, 2020). In an interview with *Business Insider*, Facebook VP of People Lori Goler explained how every new employee should embrace these values, from making bold decisions to building community via radical transparency and collaboration. To make sure that these values are in fact present, the company's DNA is readily 'installed' into every new Facebook employee, as one of Facebook's engineers put it in a blog post (Hamilton, 2010). For example, newly recruited Facebook engineers have to go through a six-week boot camp in which they learn almost everything about the software stack and are exposed to the breadth of code base and the core tools for engineering (Martinez, 2018). As Andrew Bosworth – the inventor of the Facebook boot camp and a long-time Facebook engineer – put it, the boot camp served as a training ground for the camper to be 'indoctrinated culturally' (2011). New employees were told from the very beginning to 'be bold and fearless', an ethos that played an important part in shaping the culture of Facebook engineering.[7]

Moving fast is also an important part of Facebook's infamous hackathons, another cornerstone of the company's self-proclaimed hacker culture. Hackathons are regularly organized and form a core part of Facebook's company culture. Yet, as Antonio Garcia Martinez, former product manager of ads targeting at Facebook, writes in his revealing insider account *Chaos Monkeys,* these hackathons were less about coding and more like 'pep rally-like pageants of Facebookness', aimed at shaping an 'engineering-first culture' reminiscent of 'most tech companies since Google' (2018: 262). For Martinez, Facebook hackathons and other public events highlighting the company's philosophy were really more about the strategic deployment of the hacker ethos for the purpose of company branding and corporate storytelling than anything else.

Hackathons have not just played a central part in conditioning a libertarian culture of entrepreneurialism inside

Facebook. The specific brand of hacking that Facebook has been advocating with 'move fast and break things' has become a popular innovation strategy in the corporate sector more widely. As Melissa Gregg notes, hackathons have become 'emblematic of broader trends in high-tech labour [...] a symptom of a broader transformation affecting career preparation and training as stable paths for recruitment give way to the velocity of dynamic networks' (2015: 184). As a term adopted by the corporate sector in the wake of the global financial sector and the success of a few tech companies like Facebook, the figure of the hacker is now used as an important recruitment tool and a pathway to low-cost development (Gregg, 2015; Irani, 2015).

Company culture is an important aspect of what makes Facebook Facebook. New employees are indoctrinated into the Facebook way from the very start. As Bosworth (2011) proclaimed, '[b]oot camp sets the tone for a successful career at Facebook', while Joaquin Quiñonero Candela, director of applied machine learning at Facebook, said that he loved the culture at Facebook so much that he always gives a talk about it on day one of the boot camp.[8] As Martinez recounts, the on-boarding experience at Facebook seemed almost religious. 'Even in a culture brimming with irreverent disdain', Martinez says, 'I never heard anyone utter a word of cynical trollery about Facebook and its values' (2018: 263). If we are to believe Martinez's account of what the company culture at Facebook was like during the time that he worked there (2010–15), indoctrination seemed rather successful. 'Facebook is full of true believers who, really, really, really are not doing it for the money', Martinez claims, people who truly think of Facebook as the path to a more open and connected world (Martinez, 2018: 285).

While it might be easy to dismiss the strategic use of the hacker ethos as corporate branding only, Martinez's insider accounts also highlights how the 'spirit of subversive hackery' indeed seemed to be a big part of the culture at Facebook

(Martinez, 2018: 284). Having worked at Facebook for five years, Martinez suggests how the right attitude counted for more than mere credentials and training. 'The hacker ethos prevailed above all', Martinez says, as long as 'you could get shit done and quickly' nobody cared about the rest (2018: 284). Facebook is routinely depicted as a cool and cutting-edge place to work, with core staff reiterating this public imagery in an almost evangelic manner whenever they are publicly speaking about the company culture. Yet, as Karppi and Nieborg (2020) point out, in recent years there has also been a tendency for core staff to 'abdicate' publicly when leaving Facebook and to speak out against the company they once worked for.

The symbolism is not just reserved for the motivational posters but is part of the built environment and office design in every sense of the word. As one former employee recalls on Quora, 'you walked into a corner of the building and would see flags hanging that not only represented the inter-national nature of the people we hired, but was a symbol for the global adoption Facebook intended to have' (Johns, 2014). In a *New York Times* article, journalist Quentin Hardy (2014) details the way in which the interiors of the office spaces at Facebook have been carefully designed to reflect the company's culture of openness and change: open-plan offices, of course, where meetings often happen on the fly, and where no one has secrets, and common areas where the couches may be replaced without warning in order to create a space of perpetual change. 'Similarly, design changes to Facebook's home page are known as "moving the furniture around"' (Hardy, 2014).

Taken together, the motivational posters, boot camp, hackathons and office spaces constitute a key material-discursive site for the inscription and 'indoctrination' of a culture, or a spirit of capitalism specific to Facebook. As demonstrated by Luc Boltanski and Eve Chiapello (2005) in their seminal work, managerial discourse constitutes a key site in which the 'new spirit of capitalism' is inscribed. The capitalistic system must convey a message of self-motivation and attractiveness 'to make commitment to it worthwhile' (Boltanski and Chiapello, 2005: 16). The new spirit of capitalism that Boltanski and Chiapello identify in management literature suggests a shift from a hierarchical organization and corporate control to a networked form of organization and individualized responsibility for employment success (Guyard and Kaun, 2018; Veldstra, 2018). At Facebook, responsibility for one's own success is tightly tied not only to the continued success of the company but to an almost impossible aspirational goal of the greater global good. As Chris Cox, former chief product officer and one of the leading Facebook executives before leaving the company in March 2019 after thirteen years, explained in an interview with FastCompany:

> A new engineer gets to decide which team they get to work on, which is pretty unique. The instructions are, go find the place that you're going to make the most impact, and think very, very carefully about what that means for you and for the world. Think about where you're going to have that impact, and go do it. People say all the time when they're starting here, 'That's a really serious set of instructions to receive on my first day.' But it's reflected in the culture of the company. We're here to try and help bring people closer together, and that's what we do. (McCracken, 2015)

While this neoliberal logic works to create a company brand and work identity that hinges on a fun, creative and autonomous image, Facebook's 'hacker spirit' can also be understood as a form of 'cruel optimism' (Berlant, 2011), insofar as it constitutes an ideologically imposed set of positive effects that benefit the bottom line more than perhaps the hacker's quality of life.

When visiting the Facebook headquarters, I couldn't help wondering what it is like to look at those motivational posters all day at work. How does it influence the workplace to live and breathe the Californian ideology? To be happy, cool and fun all day long? Every motivational poster must have its (psychological) limits. Andy Johns, former product manager in the Facebook growth team, describes how banners with messages such as 'Go big or go home' and 'Up and to the right' were a constant reminder at work about the team's mission. Others have spoken out against a work culture at Facebook that felt like too much pressure to remain positive and happy, particularly given the company's performance review system. Based on the 'stack ranking' system introduced by management guru and General Electric CEO Jack Welch in the 1990s, Facebook employees undergo a twice-yearly performance review (Martinez, 2018). Employees are asked to solicit peer feedback from up to five of their colleagues and write a self-assessment report. As explained by former Facebook employee Molly Graham on Quora, 'managers meet to look at the assessments of everyone on their team and ensure that people are rated correctly relative to their peers' (Graham, 2013). Out of seven possible performance measures, only approximately two per cent of the employees can get the highest rating every cycle, and some, no matter how good they are, will have to get the lowest ranking, Graham suggests. Reliance on peer reviews for such performance rankings arguably creates an underlying pressure for Facebook employees to forge friendships with colleagues for the sake of career advancement. As an article in the *Business Insider* put it, the system 'made employees feel the need to participate in after-hours social events, grab lunch with teammates, and remain a positive advocate for the company to remain in good standing with colleagues' (Bastone, 2019).

Bad feelings are at odds with the ethos of passionate work. As Carolyn Veldstra argues, the contemporary work environment of creative and affective labour asks workers 'not only to produce positive affects, but also to subordinate the bad feelings', suggesting that the 'prevalence of positive feeling operates ideologically to normalize precarious working conditions' (2018: 1). Angela McRobbie (2016) has described how the creativity dispositif demands above all an enthusiasm among those seeking success on its terms. Neoliberal work regimes, Veldstra further suggests, 'entail obscuring the bad feelings that issue from a structurally determined cruelty' (2018: 11). While Facebook is routinely attacked for the lack of a dislike button for users to express their disapproval of something, the company's 'Like economy' (Gerlitz and Helmond, 2013) stretches far into the very organizational core of Facebook. In other words, what goes for Facebook content also goes for Facebook employees. Just like the algorithmic logic of the News Feed where all content has to compete for a place at the top, Facebook employees find themselves at the centre of a popularity contest too. Instead of Likes and Shares there is stilted sociality. As Rider and Murakami Wood (2019) suggest, at Facebook you are 'condemned to connection', whether you like it or not.

Metaphors at work

Defining the nature of a technology or service is no small task and requires ongoing work. Is Facebook a media company, a technology company, a community, a network or a platform? Does it resemble a town square or a living room, or is it best described using reference to established communication forms such as public broadcasting or interpersonal commu-nication? Is it more like a phone book, a news reader or a postal service? Or, even more basic, like a door or a chair or any other thing that 'connects us' (Zuckerberg, 2012a)? Definitions and metaphors perform important rhetorical work. In the history of science and technology, metaphors have been used to capture the complexities and polysemous semantic nature of technologies and make them seem more familiar and tangible. The internet, for example, has often been described using spatio-temporal terms such as 'cyber-space' or 'information superhighway' (Sawhney, 1996), while

Microsoft has framed its software in terms of 'windows' and 'menus' that conveniently invoke connotations of choice and transparency (Wyatt, 2004). As Sally Wyatt suggests, 'different social groups use different metaphors to capture and promote their own interests and desires for the future' (2004: 245). Whether the internet has been described as a highway, shopping mall or Web, these metaphors not only shape the way we *see* the internet, they also serve important legal, economic and political purposes. The same can be said of the many competing, conflicting and overlapping metaphors used to describe Facebook.

While different groups may use different metaphors, Mark Zuckerberg himself has notoriously shifted his framing of what Facebook is. In most early accounts, Facebook was described as an 'online directory' and 'utility'. Facebook was simply a place to find and connect with your friends (Zuckerberg, 2006). As people started to flock to and use the site more extensively, Zuckerberg's framing began to focus on the value of sharing. The most important thing for Facebook in its expanding phase was to give people a reason to return to the site as often as they could. Framing Facebook as a site for sharing the things that people cared about was pivotal to this mission. As Nicholas John has argued (2016), the term 'sharing' even shaped up to become an essential keyword for Web 2.0, largely due to its central role in Facebook's discourse. After its initial success was established, Mark Zuckerberg started to accentuate Facebook as a 'core social infrastructure'. Sharing content between friends was still deemed a core activity, but by 2012 Facebook had also become a public company that needed a greater purpose. Zuckerberg wrote posts with titles such as 'The World Perspective' (Zuckerberg, 2012c) and 'The Things That Connect Us' (Zuckerberg, 2012a). The company was rolling out zero-rating mobile phone plans in various parts of the world and delivering connectivity from solar-powered drones. Facebook was on a mission to connect the whole world beyond family and friends. The company invested heavily in the development of artificial intelligence and virtual reality, ventured into new businesses, and launched a plethora of new products and features. Framing itself as a core social infrastructure certainly fulfilled the imperialist aim of global expansion.

Yet, as we are writing in 2020 and following years of political turmoil and privacy scandals, Facebook finds itself on a seemingly humbler route. While the terms are still the same – 'community', 'connection', 'infrastructure' – the expansionist rhetoric has been scaled back in favour of a more comforting and caring discourse, which puts Facebook in the position of a nurturer and protector. Starting with the idea of bringing the world closer together and framing Facebook as a place for communities of social support, through to the current emphasis on the safe and intimate spaces of people's living rooms, Zuckerberg now envisions how, in the future, 'interacting with your friends and family across the Facebook network will become a fundamentally more private experience' (Zuckerberg, 2019a). While Zuckerberg admits to having 'historically focused on tools for more open sharing', the future of communication as he sees it 'will increasingly shift to private, encrypted services where people can be confident that what they say to each other stays secure and their messages and content won't stick around forever' (Zuckerberg, 2019a).

As we have seen, the move to redefine how people think of and use social media comes at a time of much unrest for Facebook. In the wake of the Cambridge Analytica scandal and only two weeks after Mark Zuckerberg testified before congressional lawmakers in April 2018, Facebook launched the largest brand-marketing campaign in the company's history. The PR offensive had major US cities plastered with analogue billboards promising to fight fake news, fake accounts and data misuse. It bought whole-page ad space in a plethora of international newspapers and ran an extensive campaign on Facebook itself. It also ran a major TV campaign called 'Here Together', which was first aired during the NBA Playoffs, one of the most important televised sports events in the US. In 'Here Together', a male voice narrates the tale of a protagonist's challenge to fight off evil and the path to redemption in a rather utopian Silicon Valley manner:

> We came here for the friends. We got to know the friends of our friends. Then our old friends from middle school, our mom, our ex and our boss joined forces to wish us a happy birthday. Then we discovered our uncle used to play in a band, and realized he was young once too. And we found others just like us. And just like that, felt a little less alone. But then something happened. We had to deal with spam, clickbait, fake news and data misuse. That's going to change. From now on, Facebook will do more to keep you safe and protect your privacy, so we can all get back to what made Facebook good in the first place – friends. Because when this place does what it was built for, then we all get a little closer. (Facebook, 2018)

While metaphors work to make the unfamiliar more familiar, 'they can also mislead, sometimes deliberately, because the kinds of experience they purport to connect may be incommensurate' (Wyatt, 2004: 245). Facebook is not a town square, nor is it a living room, but thinking of Facebook as one or the other not only functions as a cognitive structuring device, it also has important political, economic and legal ramifications. As we will see throughout this book, it matters what we think Facebook is or resembles. By no means are the terms and metaphors used to describe Facebook innocent as they perform important legal and regulatory work. Suffice it at this stage to mention that the words used to describe Facebook matter quite a bit.

Concluding remarks

One of the things that makes Facebook Facebook is that it defies easy definitions. The problem is not that Mark

Zuckerberg can't seem to make up his mind as to what his service is or should be, but that this indecisiveness is beneficial. It is not that he can't decide, but that he won't decide. The world coheres around clear definitions, and when something seems to defy classification it shakes up the things with which it comes into contact. When that something is a corporate entity that operates on a global scale its definitional messiness becomes a liability. For all the attempts at speaking in one coherent voice about what the company is, the fact that its ontological status is still so heavily debated and up for grabs is not just fascinating but part of the strategy itself. Framing Facebook one way or the other always happens in a particular historical, political, economic and cultural context. While Facebook might emphasize its similarities to a town square one day, it might dismiss such comparisons altogether the next. As we have seen with Zuckerberg's 'Privacy-Focused Vision for Social Networking', even seemingly stable concepts such as openness and sharing are up for grabs. As the many recent cases of data misuse and other privacy scandals have shown, there have been times when defining Facebook in the service of openness does more harm than good, hence the recent discursive construction of Facebook's future as an encrypted messaging service.

As Bazerman highlights in his study of Thomas Edison and the introduction of electric light, the innovation did 'not just appear through the mute work of a few mute technologists [...] it had to emerge as the drama of human meanings' (2002: 2). In 'selling' the idea of electric light, Edison had to deal with the media, the public, financiers and government agencies alike, by taking on multiple roles and drawing on different communicative genres, terms and metaphors. Making light a common utility was not a preordained development. It 'involved work of publicity and organization on part of those connected to the nascent industry' (Luyt, 2008). In a similar way, we might understand Zuckerberg's efforts to control the symbolic ground over which the battle of definitions is fought. As Tarleton Gillespie has argued with regard to discursive construction of internet architecture, there is much at stake in 'circulating compelling metaphors: metaphors that characterize the technology in ways that elevate' its preferred uses (2006: 450). Thus, we need to think of Zuckerberg's seemingly idiosyncratic attempts at framing Facebook as a calculated attempt to position Facebook in a way that benefits whatever goals and aims the company has at any given moment.

Whether 'making the world more open and connected' or 'giving people the power to build community and bring the world closer together', what these mission statements have in common is above all a declaration of public value. As van Dijck et al. argue in their book *The Platform Society*, corporately owned platforms often claim that their services benefit the 'public' by pushing private interests under the flag of the common good (2018: 23). If 'making the world more open and connected' was strategically linked to the notion of a tolerant and understanding society, the new mission statement of 'bringing the world closer together' works in the service of communal bonds and social support. 'Are we building the world we all want?' Zuckerberg asked in his letter 'Building Global Community' (Zuckerberg, 2017a). The real question, however, is who the 'we' alluded to in Zuckerberg's question is, and whose interests such a Facebook-engineered world really serves.

CHAPTER TWO

Of electricity and chairs: Facebook as infrastructure

> Maybe electricity was cool when it first came out, but pretty quickly people stopped talking about it because it's not the new thing. The real question you want to track at that point is are fewer people turning on their lights because it's less cool?
>
> Mark Zuckerberg (2013)

In an interview with James Bennet, the then editor-in-chief of the *Atlantic*, Mark Zuckerberg makes an interesting analogy (Atlantic Live, 2013). When asked whether Facebook is at risk of losing its coolness among the younger generation, Zuckerberg says that it was never his intention for Facebook to be cool. Instead, he suggests, the goal was to create something that's a basic utility, like electricity. Much in the same way that no one would think of asking whether electricity is cool, Zuckerberg suggests, the real questions and concerns lie elsewhere. 'Our society needs a new digital social fabric', he explained. 'We can help build it.' This was 2013. In the meantime, Facebook has indeed become a new digital social fabric, and what seemed like a far-fetched analogy to electricity has turned out to be surprisingly accurate. For all the metaphors that have been circulating over the years to describe Facebook, they have only added to the perceived complexity and difficulty of knowing how to deal with something that cannot easily be pinned down. Yet, certain metaphors stick and linger more than others. In this chapter I argue that the definitional messiness of Facebook should not be seen as a problem, but as an invitation to explore some of the multiplicity and complexity that Facebook entails. The fact that something cannot be easily pinned down is only a problem if we start from the assumption that there is, or should only be, one definition. As was discussed in the introductory chapter, one of the central assumptions in this book is that Facebook is not just one thing but needs to be understood as multiple. This chapter lays out the theoretical and conceptual framework for this claim, suggesting how Facebook's multiplicity can be effectively studied through the concept of infrastructure. To guide the discussion, I will consider two metaphors used by Facebook itself to describe what it is: electric lighting and chairs. They will each provide a path for grappling with the following questions: What is Facebook? How can we know Facebook? Why does it matter?

Electric light

So, Zuckerberg made an analogy between Facebook and the electric light. Although the message was about the perceived coolness of Facebook and the ongoing concern over a teenage flight from its service, the analogy is far from trivial. What does it mean for something to be like electric light? One obvious answer, to which Zuckerberg also alludes in the opening quote of the chapter, is that it implies that something exists as a basic utility. Something you cannot do without. This understanding of Facebook corresponds to seeing it as an infrastructure. In the introductory chapter we defined infrastructure as something ubiquitous and widely shared, a platform for others to build upon, across time and space. The concept of infrastructure owes much of its intellectual history to science and technology studies (STS), where it has been theorized as a topic of research for at least four decades. According to the pioneering work by Susan Leigh Star, Karen Ruhleder and Geoffrey Bowker, an infrastructure is not something absolute, but relative to working conditions. There is thus a relational quality to infrastructures, suggesting an understanding of the term as both 'that which runs "underneath" actual structures' and 'that which is between' (Star and Bowker, 2006: 230–1). For anthropologist Brian Larkin, 'infrastructures are matter that enable the movement of matter' (2013: 329). They are simultaneously things and the relations between things. Electricity, then, is both a physical phenomenon and an enabler of many other things. It allows engines to work, food to be cooked, things to be seen, people to gather.

Importantly, technology is never just a technical thing but contains a rich mixture of economic principles, political forces and social concerns. The complex history of making electric light matter, or 'gaining momentum' as Thomas Hughes (1983) would call it, is not just the work of one genius inventor, but that of many forces and strategic negotiations (Bazerman, 2002; Hughes, 1983; Marvin, 1988). That is to say that there is nothing 'natural' or inevitable about electricity in the sense that its invention needs to be understood as a complex process. As Carolyn Marvin suggests in her study of how electric light was publicly envisioned, artefacts are 'constructed complexes of habits, beliefs and procedures embedded in elaborate cultural codes of communication' (1988: 8). What these studies suggest about the discursive and material construction of electricity as a technical infrastructure also holds true for Facebook. Facebook is both a thing and an enabler of connections, and movements of and between things. It is both that which runs underneath and that which is in between. For these reasons it is important to unpack what Zuckerberg's analogy to electricity really means and to show that proclaiming Facebook as a basic utility does not necessarily make it such. Rather we must think of the infrastructural claim as partly a fantasy with real social stakes.

Susan Leigh Star famously wrote that infrastructures are 'boring things' (Star, 1999). Zuckerberg surely didn't suggest that Facebook *is* boring when comparing Facebook to electricity, only that such superficial labels like cool or uncool do not make sense when describing something as

fundamental as an infrastructure. For Facebook as infrastructure, coolness is not an issue. As Larkin (2013) suggests,
infrastructures are not just material objects but semiotic ones
too. They are discursively made, maintained and remade.
Bringing this view to bear on Facebook means decentring
technology as the explanatory factor in accounting for
Facebook's ontological status.

   The infrastructural view thus places the system, or an
amalgam of elements making up what we take Facebook
to be, at the centre of analysis. According to Hughes, the
invention of Edison's light bulb can't be understood independently from other objects that, together, made up what we
now think of as the electric light. Every invention necessitates
a network of other elements. In the case of the light bulb, the
other elements entailed other inventions such as the Edison
Jumbo generator and the Edison main and feeder, but also
the holding company and accounting practices that went
with it (Larkin, 2013; Hughes, 1983). The infrastructural optic
of conceptualizing it as a system of substrates allows us to
think about Facebook in terms of the many elements and
more detailed 'inventions' that were needed for it to emerge
as a seemingly unitary and large-scale technical system. A
website, yes. An online directory for college friends, yes. A
news feed showing updates from your friends, true. But also
the many other elements that make Facebook work in the
way that it does, including social plug-ins such as the Like
button, which have helped expand Facebook into the rest of
the Web (Helmond, 2015; Gerlitz and Helmond, 2013), or the
many business tools, such as Facebook Analytics and Pages,
that have helped to sustain Facebook's advertisement-driven
business model. So, there are other 'technical' elements, such
as buttons, protocols and APIs, which need to be accounted
for in order to understand the infrastructural qualities of
Facebook. And there are 'social' and 'financial' elements like
advertising and sharing practices, which are just as important
in making Facebook an infrastructure. Most importantly,

these elements are never 'technical' or 'social' or 'financial' only, but all of these and much more besides.

Let's take the famous Facebook Like button and the Open Graph project as cases in point. In 2010, at their annual developer conference f8, Facebook launched a stack of new products and features, under the umbrella of the Open Graph. Designed to facilitate connections between people and things, Open Graph consists of a protocol, an application programming interface (API) and social plug-ins, including the now pervasive Like button (officially launched a year earlier, in 2009). The Open Graph protocol describes a way of building a semantic map of the internet, by offering a standardized means for external websites to integrate and exchange data with Facebook using simple markup language and tags. Technically, Open Graph is implemented through RDFa, a data model and W3C standard for mapping that allows Web page owners and application developers to mark up human-readable data with machine-readable indicators (see http://ogp.me). For instance, a website such as the Internet Movie Database (http://www.imdb.com) can be semantically linked up to Facebook's core service by adding some meta tags to the html of the IMDb site. This markup code turns external websites and digital objects into Facebook graph objects.

The Open Graph protocol allows Facebook to track and process user data across the Web with the use of social plug-ins. These plug-ins function as small 'hooks' that provide meaning to nodes (i.e. Web pages, movies, books, etc.) that were not meaningful to Facebook before being linked to the larger infrastructure provided by Open Graph. With the help of these hooks, all kinds of entities can be given a social network presence. The purpose of the Open Graph is thus to create links between various nodes that extend beyond the core site of Facebook, whether the link is established between two users or between a user and a web page. Importantly, this map of connections allows the data that flow between actors to be tracked and processed more easily, since all the data created in and through these articulations are fed back to Facebook. Essentially, Open Graph constitutes a centralized infrastructure that generates value by decentralizing social action. This data-intensive infrastructure is powered by the implementation of the Like button, which enables the registration and tracking of user actions tied to external sites.

The Like button is deceptively simple. All that anyone administering a website has to do in order to integrate with Facebook is to embed a piece of JavaScript code into their website, and voilà, a connection to Facebook's database is established. Anne Helmond's work shows how the Like button is emblematic of the dual logic of platformization, the idea that Facebook 'employs its platform as an infrastructural model to extend itself into external online spaces and how it employs these extensions to format data for its platform to fit their economic interest' (2015: 7–8). This dual logic of platformization speaks to the extendability of infrastructures, the way in which digital media platforms 'are designed to be extended and elaborated from outside' (Plantin et al., 2018: 298). By allowing third parties to use a small piece of Facebook in the form of a Like button or other plug-ins, Facebook scales and grows. As Helmond (2015) writes, social plug-ins enable the decentralization of platform functionality and data, while at the same time working to recentralize the data produced outside of the platform. Social plug-ins thus enable the continuous flow of data between external websites and Facebook's database, which in turn contributes to the expansion and continued growth of Facebook.

If Facebook Inc. can be likened to the Edison General Electric Company, the Like button can be regarded as Facebook's light bulb, an application of the core invention of a social network site that contributed to the diffusion of Facebook into other Web spaces in the same way that the light bulb provided the application of electric light. If we go with this analogy for just a while longer, notwithstanding its limitations, we might further think of the Facebook APIs as being akin to the sockets that connect the light bulb to electric power currents, and the Open Graph protocol as the voltages and frequencies of the electrical power distribution. That is to say that neither the electric light nor Facebook grew *de novo*. They developed amid a stream of technical antecedents, social conventions and practices, and had to be adaptive to new technologies and cultures. There were many things that had to be in place, and work in parallel with, and be developed to enhance the possibilities of the core invention, to make it work.

As Star and Bowker suggest, infrastructures are built on structures that are already in place, meaning that they have to 'wrestle with "the inertia of the installed base" and inherit strengths and weaknesses of that base' (2006: 231). While the Like button and the Open Graph protocol were introduced as novel inventions at the Facebook developer conference f8 in 2010, they did not just emerge out of the blue. Facebook's data exchange with third-party websites and apps dates back to 2006 when Facebook introduced its Facebook API that enabled the structured exchange of data between its users and other sites and services. In 2007, Facebook further launched Facebook Platform for developers to build apps on top of Facebook's social graph. The Facebook Platform API also opened for beneficial connections in terms of higher revenues (e.g. ads sold) and user growth to Facebook's platform. In 2008, Facebook Connect was introduced, making it possible to use Facebook profiles as authentication across the Web (Gerlitz and Helmond, 2013).

Often, when the term 'infrastructure' is used more colloquially, the focus is on material infrastructures – railroads, water supply or cell towers – and the ways in which technologies work in a material sense. Yet, as much work in infrastructure studies and STS attests to, material infrastructures emerge, and are supported by a vast matrix of social arrangements. Indeed, as Star and Ruhleder say of infrastructure, one of its defining features is embeddedness, the way in which it is 'sunk into, inside of, other structures, social arrangements and technologies' (1996: 113). Just as Facebook becomes part of other structures, governments, organizations, businesses and life worlds, the pre-existing environment on which Facebook was built is far from just technological. Facebook's 'installed base' is just as much about the different communities, cultures, locations, organizations, ideologies and imaginaries that Facebook's existence is indebted to and builds upon as it is about the concrete technologies enabling the development of the platform.

The infrastructural optic helps to see the matrix required for something like Facebook to appear and work as a seemingly stable and unitary thing. Just as electric light didn't emerge or work in a vacuum, as it required many other inventions, interests and stakeholders for it to be realized and materialized, Facebook and its many products, including the Like button, need to be understood as a nested and interconnected assemblage of inventions and relations. Examining the rhetorical shaping of Edison's electric light, Bazerman argues how technologies emerge into the social configurations of their time. In order to understand the world that shaped the conditions of possibility for Edison and his colleagues, Bazerman examines a range of arrangements and contexts deemed necessary for something like the electric light to emerge and gain momentum as a core invention, including: the American patent system, the emergence of large cities, new communication infrastructures, national markets, large-circulation newspapers and new technological professions. Extending this to our understanding of Facebook, we might ask what the kinds of arrangements and circumstances of the contemporary world are that have helped to shape the actions of Zuckerberg and his friends.

Certainly, the world of Zuckerberg and his friends is made up of too many things to be counted, but we might attempt a short list nonetheless, based on some of the things already discussed in previous chapters, some of the things to be discussed later on, and some of the things that might not make it into the book but are too important to be left unmentioned: modern neoliberal capitalism, the start-up culture, entrepreneurship, venture capital, the financial crisis, elite universities, Web 2.0 discourse, the ethos of sharing, the participatory culture, data science, machine learning, statistics, network science and graph theory, the hacker culture, datafication, solutionism, self-regulation, the US Communication Decency Act, the EU E-Commerce Directive, GDPR, privacy norms and values, personalization, targeted advertising, the next billion users, digital divides, emerging markets, global politics, election campaigns, fake news, disinformation and surveillance. And the list goes on. All of these elements somehow participate in setting the scene for something like Facebook to emerge and to develop. More than simply part of an historical backdrop, these and many other things are sunk into the very infrastructure of Facebook, while at the same time displaying infrastructural qualities themselves, insofar as they form part of the underlying base or foundation for the operation of Facebook, at various stages and in varying degrees. That is not to say that Facebook would not have existed without the US Communication Decency Act or machine learning, for example, but that these elements have helped to shape the condition of possibility for Facebook and structured how the company and its products have evolved over time. While modern neoliberal capitalism and start-up culture can be said to be part of Facebook's installed base, or providing the grounds on which Facebook was built, other elements such as fake news and disinformation have only later emerged as part of Facebook's infrastructural drama, adding to the complexity of Facebook as an evolving socio-technical system.

Chairs

Taking a cue from infrastructure and media studies, Facebook can be conceptually situated within a 'broader landscape of related, and often unnoticed or invisible, material things, such as filing cabinets ... telephone poles ... or wireless bandwidth' (Boczkowski and Lievrouw, 2008: 954). While it might seem like a bit of a stretch to suggest that chairs belong to these related things, if we are to believe Facebook's first ever TV ad, they do. On 4 October 2012, Facebook released a rather grandiose ad entitled 'The Things That Connect Us', produced by the advertising agency Wieden + Kennedy, and directed by the Oscar-winning Mexican director Alejandro Iñárritu.[1] The ad begins with an image of a floating chair in the woods, and continues by depicting the many mundane scenes involving different kinds of chairs and people, set in cities ranging from Los Angeles and New Orleans to Buenos Aires. The scenes depict people sitting on chairs, people sitting together on chairs, people reading books and relaxing on chairs, elderly people taking a break on chairs, children playing on chairs, young adults sitting around a table, sharing a meal and laughing. While chairs are the heroes of this ad, it doesn't stop there. Against a throbbing soundtrack, a female voice-over explains how all the seemingly mundane things of the world – doorbells, aeroplanes, bridges, dance floors – are the things that glue the human kind together:

> Chairs. Chairs are made so that people can sit down and take a break. Anyone can sit on a chair, and if the chair is large enough, they can sit down together. And tell jokes. Or make up stories. Or just listen. Chairs are for people. And that is why chairs are like Facebook. Doorbells. Airplanes. Bridges. These are things people use to get together so they can open up and connect about ideas, and music, and other things people share. Dance floors. Basketball. A great nation. A great nation is something people build, so that they can have a place where they belong. The universe is vast and

dark and makes us wonder if we are alone. So maybe the reason we make all of these things is to remind ourselves that we are not.

'Chairs are like Facebook.' Chairs, one of the most basic things used by people around the globe, the ad suggests, are like Facebook because they are made for people. No more, no less. Or so it seems. Things are never that simple. We know that things carry weight, meaning and affordances. Things talk, Lorraine Daston suggests, they 'communicate by what they are and by how they mean' (2004: 20). There is nothing innocent or neutral about a thing or collection of things.

So what is it with things? Why these things and not others? There has been much philosophical, sociological and anthropological treatment of the status of things, from the pre-Socratic Greek philosophers such as Anaximander, the philosophy of technology, material culture studies' interest in 'the social lives of things' (Appadurai, 2006), the notion of 'thing theory' (Brown, 2001), through to new materialism, and Jane Bennett's (2010) concept of 'thing-power'. For all their differences and historical and disciplinary contexts, these theories and conceptualizations have in common an interest in the ways in which things (often to be distinguished from mere *objects*) have value, agency and power beyond their relations to human subjects. Jane Bennett's vibrant materialism, for example, suggests that things do stuff, that they make a difference, and 'become the decisive force catalyzing an event' (2010: 9). The idea that things have the capacity to make a difference is also one of the core tenets of actor-network theory. According to Latour, '*any thing* that does modify a state of affairs by making a difference is an actor' (2005: 71). Writing about the sociology of door closers, seat belts and speed bumps, Latour sees them as designed artefacts that constrain or shape the actions of individuals on behalf of society as a whole (1999). For example, the speed bump can be read as scripts and delegations. Rather than having a human policeman standing by every road to enforce certain speed limits, the speed bump acts as a sleeping policeman. Latour would say that we have delegated the policeman's social and legal effects to a speed bump, and by making a difference to the state of things (e.g. forcing cars to slow down) they gain agential capacities.

Chairs do things too. The Facebook ad tells us that chairs afford relaxing, taking a break, playing, having a good time, learning, socializing and, most importantly, connecting to other people. Unlike the many metaphors used to describe Facebook, with this ad Facebook itself is turned into a metaphor. This time it is not Facebook that is explained by analogy to something more familiar, but in a peculiar sense Facebook that is used as an explanation for one of the most familiar things in life: chairs. However, the ad also suggests that chairs are only like Facebook *if* they support people. People and chairs go together. If anything, Eugene Ionesco's absurdist tragic farce *The Chairs* conveys the vast sadness and disenchantment created by a collection of empty chairs. Chairs are nothing without humans, then, which we might extend to the idea that Facebook wants to convey with its ads. Humans make Facebook meaningful but, according to the ad, Facebook enables human connections in the first place – not unlike the chairs around a dinner table. Chairs invite conversation and sociability. Chairs facilitate and motivate. They invite and incite.

The primary function of a chair is to allow for sitting. As a cultural technique of sorts, chairs *seat* people. Architectural theorist Galen Cranz (1998) suggests how chairs are true cultural artefacts insofar as they furnish everyday life. Much in the same way as chairs can be found everywhere from dining rooms and waiting rooms to cars, subways, cinemas, meeting rooms, schools and restaurants, Facebook furnishes everyday life too. When we wait for someone in a restaurant or travel on the bus, the chances are high that we check Facebook. How many students do not talk to each other on

Facebook while seated in a classroom, or like their friends' posts while sitting around the dinner table? Because chairs support seating, and ideas of seating are culturally distinct and evolving, understanding the social history of chairs might be a useful exercise for an appreciation of the ways in which they organize the environment. As Cranz (1998) sees it, chairs convey social status and style. Ancient chairs, she writes, 'reflected the relationship of power between rulers and ruled', while chairs in today's offices still demarcate the social hierarchies between bosses and employees (Cranz, 1998: 23).

Chairs can also have profound social and communicative impacts. Organizing chairs, say, in a row, all facing one direction, has very different implications for social interaction compared to arranging them in a circle. Who hasn't considered what seat to take on public transport to avoid having to face a stranger? Some days it's OK, even exciting, to sit down opposite someone in a bus, but more often than not, sitting next to someone facing the same way seems like the preferable option. In pandemic times, we are explicitly asked not face each other and always to leave at least one seat empty before sitting next to someone. Moreover, chairs can be comfortable, like cinema chairs, or quite uncomfortable, as is the case in places where they do not want people to linger for too long. Most laptop-friendly coffee shops, or 'coffices', do not provide the most comfortable chairs as a way to ensure greater circulation of people (and more coffees sold). Indeed, what kind of chairs a café or restaurant chooses says a lot about the kind of sociability it envisions and is designed for. The absence of chairs furnishes spaces and organizes sociability too. Some concert halls have chairs, others do not. Just like attending a rock concert while seated seems a bit off, so does attending a classical symphony concert without chairs.

Chairs are not as universal, then, as Facebook would like them to be. According to the ad, chairs are like Facebook because they connect people in much the same ways as doorbells and aeroplanes do. Far from universal, disability and design scholars have pointed out how chairs indicate the 'outline of the body meant to use them' (Hamraie, 2017: 19). Thinking about all the ways in which chairs can also be excluding, even discriminatory, would surely not fit the picture that Facebook tries to create. Of the many chairs missing in the ad, the wheelchair was perhaps the most noticeable. While chairs are indeed 'made so that people can sit down and take a break', as the ad tells us, some people do not have this choice but are more or less confined to a chair.

The wheelchair, arguably the quintessential symbol of disability, is not just curiously missing from the ad but something that illuminates the relationality of infrastructures. As Star has said, 'one person's infrastructure is another's topic, or difficulty' (1999: 380). This now famous statement on the relationality of infrastructure explicitly uses the wheelchair as an example of how infrastructures are never static entities but need to be understood relative to their use. Infrastructures provide access, but not for everyone, or at the same time. Infrastructures become visible upon breakdown, such as when a building isn't rigged for wheelchair users. How the built world is rigged becomes apparent in situated practices. Thus, infrastructures materialize differently, depending on the people they support or disavow.

Yet, the world tends to convene around a rather limited conception of what the average body looks like and how it works. Disability scholar Aimi Hamraie offers the term 'normate template' as a way to conceptualize how the 'world was designed with the normate inhabitants in mind' (2017: 19–20). It should come as no surprise that the white, masculine and non-disabled citizen constitutes the ideal Western body, acting as the normate template for the built environment. This ideal body provides such a pervasive template that it figures in almost everything from how we think of access to knowledge, culture and communication.

The hopelessly naive ad notwithstanding, its missing

wheelchair allows us to attend to the complicated relation-alities created by infrastructures and media environments. The breakdowns and invisibilities offer a way to 'examine the situations of those who are *not* served by a particular infrastructure' (Star, 1999: 380) and to grapple with regimes of 'access knowledge' concerning 'what kinds of people are likely to be in the world' (Hamraie, 2017: 5). The question then becomes: Who are the people not served by Facebook's seemingly universal connective paradigm and design? Whose voices and concerns are deemed less important or (in)effec-tively silenced? Indeed, what is Facebook's normate template?

What the missing wheelchair does for us in answering these questions is open a way of thinking through issues of access, normalcy, design choices, configured environments, inequalities, invisibilities, usage, labour and universalisms. It points us in the direction of distinct but related discourses and scholarship on disability studies, critical access studies, crip technoscience, digital divides, social inequalities, govern-mentality, standards, inclusive design and affordances. If we begin from the latter, we might ask what Facebook's design and affordances suggest about the ideal user. Consider, for example, the ways in which gender is baked into Facebook's profile templates (Bivens, 2017; Bivens and Haimson, 2016), the impact that Facebook's real-name policy has for margin-alized people (Guynn, 2014), or what Matamoros-Fernández (2017) terms 'platformed racism', the ways in which Facebook's design, affordances and policies amplify new forms of racism and help to shape social inequalities. For example, Facebook offers an 'ethnic affinity' marketing solution, which allows brands to segment their audiences. Within the housing category, marketers up until recently were offered the option to exclude users with an African-American or Hispanic 'ethnic affinity' (Matamoros-Fernández, 2017: 933). After policymakers and civil-rights leaders expressed their concern at the discriminatory potential of such segmentation options, Facebook went public to disable ethnic affinity, at least for certain types of ads, including housing (Egan, 2016). In terms of gender categories, during the first decade of its existence, Facebook offered only a very limited and binary understanding of gender, until it radically expanded the options by going from two – 'male' and 'female' – to sixty potential categories (Bivens, 2017). Furthermore, Facebook's obsession with 'authenticity' and 'real' state-validated identity assumes that 'being in public carries little or no risk' (Cho, 2018: 3184), often at the expense of people already at risk of being further marginalized (boyd, 2012; Haimson and Hoffmann, 2016). From LGBTQ youth to religious minorities, Facebook's public by default settings may have real-life consequences in ways that often seem far removed from the purview of the everyday realities of the average Silicon Valley developer.

As with any great PR stunt, 'The Things That Connect Us' was designed to tell a specific story. To celebrate the occasion of having reached Facebook's one billionth user, this video was meant to leave no doubt as to Facebook's global role as a social infrastructure. In order to translate the rather abstract idea of a social infrastructure, Facebook's first-ever brand-video reworked 'this expansive, invasive, insatiable network into an innocuously quotidian object' (Mattern, 2017). The move was not simply to turn Facebook into a familiar object but to suggest that Facebook itself has become quotidian. What the video seems to suggest, then, is that Facebook furnishes everyday life. Like chairs, doorbells and dance floors, Facebook supposedly ranks among the normal things that connect us. Whether or not this is true is not the point. To suggest that something has become so commonplace that it no longer needs explaining but can serve instead as that which explains is the subtle but more powerful statement this video seeks to make.

Concluding remarks

If we are led to believe that Facebook is like electric lighting and chairs are like Facebook, there is also a way in which these seemingly separate statements are related. Going back to Edison, what the history of his success demonstrates, is not the journey of a lone genius but of a 'strategist, a researcher, a public relations man' (Akrich et al., 2002: 215). Like Facebook, the innovative potential of the electric light was not self-evident but had to be invented and strategically formulated. As we have seen in this chapter, the history of electric lighting is essentially a story of 'infrastructuring', of the socio-technical formation of complex systems (Star and Bowker, 2006). There is much to be learned from this history for an understanding of Facebook and other media infrastructures.

First, the history of 'Edison's light' (Akrich et al., 2002; Bazerman, 2002; Hughes, 1993; Marvin, 1988) highlights how infrastructures are relational entities. If anything, the strange conflation of Facebook and chairs conveys this multi-dimensionality. Both material and symbolic, functional and affective, understanding the infrastructural dimensions of Facebook means above all to analyse the work that goes into making things appear to hang together, even when they don't. What does it take for something to appear as unitary and stable, who is involved in shaping this appearance, and for what purpose? It also entails asking for the things that might not be part of the public appearance, including the missing wheelchair. If chairs, like Facebook, connect, then what about the prospect of empty or otherwise 'problematic' chairs? Now that empty chairs have become a prevalent symbol of the pandemic, does Facebook still want us to think of chairs as being like Facebook? The analytic task is thus to enquire into the limits of such metaphors, their potential disruptions and breakdowns.

Second, the infrastructural optic extends the focus from mere technology and directs attention towards the organizational and social dramas that accompany its formation and maintenance. As such, knowing Facebook is as much about analysing its 'symbolic engineering' (Bazerman, 2002) as it is about the product itself. If the 'electric light was the great late-nineteenth-century medium of the spectacle, dazzling its audiences with novel messages' (Marvin, 1988: 6), we might think of Facebook in similar terms. Attempting to dazzle its audience with seductive metaphors of chairs, dance floors and basketball, Facebook indeed seems like an early-twenty-first century medium of the spectacle. As was the case with Edison's light, the success of Facebook has as much to do with its ongoing discursive and rhetorical construction, as it has with any of its technical functions.

Third, when inverted and picked apart for analytical reasons, infrastructures reveal a much messier reality of ongoing negotiations and processes of stabilization. The light bulb, the chair, and Facebook, may all seem like more or less stable things. Yet an 'infrastructural inversion' (Bowker, 1994) directs attention to the processes and elements that both enable and are enabled by them. Whether we consider the modularity and interoperability of technical elements (e.g. Like button and the Open Graph) or the social practices that condition and are conditioned by such material constraints and conventions (e.g. practices of liking and the processes of datafication that such liking affords), infrastructures need to be seen as manifestations of power relations (Plantin and Punathambekar, 2019). To know Facebook, or any other platform for that matter, entails grappling with 'entire swaths of infrastructural activity' (Ribes and Lee, 2010: 238), including: its planning, implementation, technical operation, standards, allies and spokespersons, users, workers, symbolic engineering, semiotic registers, moments of breakdown, repair, regulation, organizational embeddedness and social drama. The point, however, is not that the analyst needs to uncover the entirety of elements that go into its assembly. Rather, the task seems much more modest: to acknowledge the messiness and multidimensionality in things that appear stable and uniform, and to enquire into such world-making in the first place.

CHAPTER THREE

Grounded in reality: How Facebook programs sociality

Being grounded in reality has always been a very foundational element of what makes Facebook, Facebook.

Mark Zuckerberg (2011)

It can be hard to remember what Facebook felt like and what the site signified when first becoming a member. For an astonishing number of people around the globe, Facebook has become such a common part of everyday life that they barely stop to think about its role. These days, when we hear about Facebook, it is often in terms of the many privacy scandals surrounding the company, its role in global politics, or its entanglement in the increasingly problematic 'fake news' and disinformation. There is no doubt that these are extremely important matters. Yet, for a long time, Facebook was primarily understood and experienced as a social network site. Consider this mundane account of a Canadian blogger's early encounter with Facebook:

> I was reluctant to join Facebook because I don't like social networking. It feels contrived (because it is) and it feels empty and I am not a big fan. But I joined and I created my profile and sweet merciful crap people started to poke me all over the place.
>
> And ohmygod, it's fantastic. It's fantastic because these little blips of conversation and 'how have you BEEN these past 20 years?' are exactly the same connection I felt while sitting in the cafeteria in the mornings or walking to classes. They're quick and connecting and don't require a big investment of time – all while making me feel like I'm part of a group of friends again. (MiserableBliss, 2007)[1]

Facebook was, and still is, a place to connect with friends, family and acquaintances. As the Canadian blogger's experience of joining Facebook encapsulates, to some, Facebook offers a space for effortless socializing and the feeling of being part of a community of friends. As Facebook evolved from a closed Web-based 'social directory' into a 'social infrastructure' for building a 'global community', it grew into an omnipresent and powerful part of people's everyday lives. How did this company that was once merely a website designed to support distinct college networks grow into a global social infrastructure with a monopoly over people's social connections? This chapter explores the meaning of Facebook for social life, how the platform became a core site for sociality, and how that sociality is essentially engineered around the ideology of authenticity as materialized through Facebook's real-name policy. Understanding Facebook's role in connecting people is not just about understanding sociality or interpersonal relations, but is intrinsically linked to understanding the ways in which Facebook's technological and economic architecture steer user interaction in particular configurations and how those engineered conditions for interaction also help to shape social norms (Bucher, 2013; van Dijck, 2013a; van Dijck, Poell and de Waal, 2018). In this chapter we will move between the front end and the back end of Facebook, so to speak, in order to take seriously the felt experience and the often mundane ways in which Facebook comes to matter for different people in their everyday life, while not losing sight of the technological and economic back end designed to organize interactions between users.

Throughout the chapter, quotes by random users will be dispersed in order to add textual flavour to the kinds of ordinary affects (Stewart, 2007) generated by Facebook. These accounts, taken from various blog posts, social media posts, research projects, interviews and other discursive materials encountered on the Web, are meant to function as vignettes and explorations of the affective landscape that

Facebook seems to generate. The quotes are not meant to be read as generalizable statements about Facebook. They have not been collected in any methodological consistent or systematic way. Rather, these quotes are meant to provide a sense of Facebook's ordinariness that are still a big part of how Facebook is felt, despite much public reporting on more sensational matters concerning Facebook. Similarly to how Kathleen Stewart collects series of everyday happenings in *Ordinary Affects* (2007) as a way to explore what it feels like to live in contemporary America, we might think of the different quotes dispersed in this chapter, including the opening quote by the Canadian blogger, as atmospheric blips that come together to tell a story about what Facebook variously feels like. The unsystematic placement of these scenes and quotes is intentional, as there is no coherent story to tell, nor do these scenes necessarily add up. Sometimes these quotes may feel disruptive and misplaced in the usual narrative flow of things, a feminist intervention à la Sara Ahmed (2017), if you will. Ahmed's writing on the feminist killjoy suggests the inconvenience of those who disrupt or change the smooth flow of communication. The figure of the feminist killjoy, by not necessarily adapting to the social norms that demand an uncomplicated social situation, helps to make social scripts visible and subject to critical reflection to begin with. Other times, the quotes align better with the narrative of the chapter and the different subheadings.

These are not just narrative sprinkles, however, but offer a way of writing about Facebook that matches the disruptiveness and attention-grabbing techniques of its operation. Usually verbatim quotes are used by researchers reporting from an interview study in order to provide evidence for their interpretations, as an illustration for themes and findings, to give participants a voice, to offer readers greater depth of understanding and to enhance the readability of the text. While some of these reasons apply to this chapter as well, the quotes also function as a form of non-representational

method, understood 'less as a way of articulating a set of
practices that are forced to stand up in a particular epistemo-
logical theatre of proof, and more as a way of going on in the
world that allows its different modes of making difference
potentially sensed' (McCormack, 2015: 93). If everybody has
a Facebook story, then these scenes constitute one more
modality to that story. As random and carefully crafted as any
other Facebook status update, these quotes may both add and
subtract meaning, they may infuriate and amuse, they may
bring you back on a memory lane or not resonate with your
own experiences at all.

> I started thinking about what Facebook means to me because
> of a series of articles in various media and posts on Facebook
> [...] Facebook had me at 'hello'. At its best, Facebook is
> like the International Departures Lounge at an airport in
> Marrakesh. I have conversations that are amusing and pull
> in friends from around the corner, from high school, from
> college and from jobs long gone [...] At its worst, Facebook
> slides south in the direction of a parking lot carnival redolent
> of hot grease and musk. (Imagineannie, 2009)[2]

One of the first things to note about sociality in the context
of Facebook is the way in which Facebook is 'grounded in
reality'. Unlike the early Web or any preceding and competing
social network sites, Facebook made a strategic business
decision from the very start to rely on people's real names
and identities. Gone were decades of (apparent) anonymity
in cyberspace in favour of 'real friends and family'. As Mark
Zuckerberg regularly emphasized in lectures and interviews
during Facebook's early days, his original intention was to
design a platform that helped to map out people's connections (f8, 2008; Harvard University, 2005). The core idea
was to build a site that would let people know to whom they
and their friends were connected. In the first chapter, the
argument was made that Facebook is Facebook by virtue
of having grown into a phenomenon too vast and complex
to be described by metaphors or pinned down using other

descriptive markers such as social media or social network site. In order to appreciate how Facebook grew into Facebook we also need to consider the times when Facebook was not yet a ubiquitous feature of society, when indeed it was most commonly described in terms of merely being a social network site. In the following sections, we will take a close look at the ways in which networks became 'social' and how Facebook's identity is shaped around its real-name policy, address the research literature on Facebook as a social network(ing) site and social media platform, consider its specific conception of friendship, and take a closer look at Facebook's technological and economic architecture that helps to construct a particular configuration of sociality and social norms.

How networks became social and online identity grounded in reality

At the time of Facebook's launch in 2004, social network sites (SNSs) were already a very prevalent feature of society. Remember the first message on my own Facebook feed posted in autumn 2006, mentioned in the introductory chapter. It came from one of my closest friends telling me she would give Facebook a try, despite having already signed up for so many similar sites. In their seminal article defining social network sites, danah boyd and Nicole Ellison begin from the premise that 'there are hundreds of SNSs, with various technological affordances, supporting a wide range of interests and practices' (2007: 210). What sites such as Cyworld, MySpace, Dodgeball, YouTube and Facebook have in common, is that they 'enable users to articulate and make visible their social networks' (boyd and Ellison, 2007: 211). The authors further note how one of Facebook's defining features is the ability for outside developers to build applications on top of the platform, but also the way in which the site primarily encourages users to maintain existing offline relationships as opposed to meeting new people.

It seems almost strange to write, but fifteen years ago, Facebook was just one of many similar sites. Today, it has become *the* social network site par excellence, to the extent that, as with any monopoly, leaving the site is not always a viable option. As Zeynep Tufekci (2018) writes, 'in many countries, Facebook and its products simply *are* the internet. Some employers and landlords demand to see Facebook profiles, and there are increasingly vast swaths of public and civic life [...] that are accessible or organized only via Facebook.' Leaving Facebook might be an option for those of us fortunate enough to not have our job prospects, social support or safety depend on having a Facebook profile, but this indeed is a privilege reserved for the few.

More than that, one hardly ever speaks of social network sites any more. It is not necessarily a class of objects in the same way it used to be. While Facebook is still a site for social networking and for displaying a user's social network, this is not its primary feature any more. In fact, by arguing that Facebook is Facebook, what I want to highlight is the importance of not relegating its definition to that of a social network site, or even social media platform. While I will continue referring to Facebook as a social network site in the sections below, this is only to show how Facebook was indeed designated and imagined as such in the academic and popular discourse of the 2000s and early 2010s.

If the kinds of social network sites that emerged in the mid-2000s were mostly designed around the idea of a public or semi-public personal profile, along with a visible list of connections, social networks, or the conception of networks *as* social, were far from new. Long before the advent of Facebook, people were already socializing over computer networks. Remember some of that history from Chapter 1, including the early uses of ARPANET, the hobbyist uses of the personal computer and the new communalists. Computer networks were never just used for file sharing or the transmission of data, but for communicative and social purposes as well. According to Esther Milne, for example, the success of the internet was largely due to email (Milne, 2012). Although early email addresses in the 1970s and 1980s were linked to institutional accounts, the advent of personal computers and service providers like CompuServe made it possible to create personal email addresses that allowed for the creation of usernames and personas that were decoupled from a work context and real-life identity (van der Nagel, 2017). Long before Facebook, then, people used the internet to socialize through messaging systems, bulletin boards, chat forums and online games (see also Driscoll, 2016; Turkle, 2011).

Online sociality in the early days of the internet was defined to a large extent by anonymity and pseudonymity. Research on 'cyberspace' and 'virtual community' highlights how the internet was used to facilitate social interaction and community building based on identity play (Rheingold, 1993; Turkle, 2011). The internet of the 1990s was often portrayed as a virtual space that allowed communities to form on the basis of interests, not identity. In his seminal book *The Virtual Community*, Howard Rheingold took his experiences with the WELL bulletin board system (BBS) as a case in point to argue for the virtues of supportive online communities based on 'a syntax of identity play: new identities, false identities, multiple identities, exploratory identities' (1993: 152). The social networks people formed and maintained on text-based channels such as Multi-User Dungeons (MUDs), Internet Relay Chat (IRC) and Usenet were explicitly framed as spaces for identity exploration, distinct from the constraints of the physical or real world. People socialized and communicated without knowing the 'real' identities of their interlocutors.

Some scholars, like Sherry Turkle, questioned the usefulness of using real-life identity as a benchmark, arguing for a decentred and multiple self. More than simply playing different roles in life, Turkle argued that the self exists in many worlds at once, and that real life was 'just one more window'. 'Why grant superiority to the self that has a body', she wondered, 'when people can play at having different genders and different lives?' (Turkle, 2011: 14). Yet, as others have argued, the idea of a playful identity game based on anonymity, free of power relations and hierarchy, is a utopian one at best (Baym, 2010; Dibbel, 1994; Herring, 2000). As Susan Herring (1996, 2000) has shown, anonymity notwithstanding, people's communicative style and tone of language in textually oriented computer-mediated communication may already reveal important clues about their gender. Something as simple as email addresses may also work to maintain traditional hierarchies of power. Judith Donath (2002) has documented how, despite the syntax of identity play associated with virtual communities, institutional email addresses were associated with a greater degree of authority than their personal counterparts. Regardless of how democratic and anonymous the early Web may have seemed, some things, such as racism and sexism, run much deeper than knowing what someone looks like.

> When I received the same 'authentic name' message from Facebook, I informed them that I am a victim of abuse, that I would not be providing them with my information, and asked them to delete my account. I received an email from Facebook, saying that my account had been deleted, although I continue to receive notifications from them for friends' birthdays, upcoming events and people whom they think I should 'like'. (#MyNameIsCampaign, 2015)[3]

One of the things that set Facebook apart from its predecessors was the introduction of a real-name policy. In a closing conversation at the E-G8 Forum in 2011, Zuckerberg was asked about the magic formula that made Facebook such a success. 'What we focused on from the beginning', Zuckerberg said, 'is that people had their real identity there and were sharing with people who were real friends and family.' As the epigraph suggests, the success, according to Zuckerberg, came from 'being grounded in reality', which was a 'foundational element of what makes Facebook Facebook'

(E-G8 Forum, 2011).[4] In contrast to other social media sites that did not focus on 'creating networks where everyone is who they are', Facebook's advantage, according to Zuckerberg, was doing the exact opposite. This 'administrative identity', as Haimson and Hoffmann (2016) call it, works to reinforce the notion of Facebook as somehow more authentic or trustworthy because the identities of its users have been institutionally supported and verified via existing school networks and similar stamps of approval. At least in theory.

In practice, we know that the idea of a 'real' authentic self is a bit more complicated than a verified student card, that users sometimes hold several user accounts, and that some people's identity may not even register in someone's else's frame of mind. As Lingel and Golub argue, Facebook 'tends towards a design ethic of singularity and simplicity, fundamentally at odds with technological preferences (or needs) for complexity and mess' (2015: 537). Despite recent developments in political propaganda and the proliferation of so-called 'fake accounts' and the spread of disinformation, the legacy of Facebook's real-name policy still looms large. As Haimson and Hoffmann show, 'real names' perform multiple functions for Facebook. First, the idea of real names has been thoroughly entrenched into the core material and symbolic registers of Facebook. Real-name identities are not just a vital part of Facebook's origin story but are regularly credited with generating a sense of trust and security on the platform. For Zuckerberg (2011), the fact that people had to sign up with their real names and identities 'made it easy for people to feel comfortable sharing things about their real lives'.

However, as Haimson and Hoffmann note, the equation between real identity and real accountability is far from unproblematic. As they write, the real-name policy 'leaves little room for alternative conceptions of safety that may hinge on obscurity and invisibility' (2016: 8). The policy reflects a discrepancy between the kind of normative assumptions baked into Facebook as a social directory for elite college students, and the lives of marginalized groups and people at risk. While real-name identities may not seem to pose an immediate problem for Zuckerberg and his privileged peers, the policy is far less accommodating to those with non-normative identities, such as trans people, and others whose name might pose an actual threat to their security, including activists and dissidents. One of the most publicized controversies surrounding the real-name policy happened in September 2014, when hundreds of transgender people and drag queens had their Facebook accounts shut down after they were reported as fake. The 'My Name Is' campaign collected thousands of stories by people affected by Facebook's real-name policy, gathering more than 75 human rights, LGBTQ and women's rights advocacy groups to petition against the dangers of 'authentic names'. In 2015, after almost a year of stories from affected people, incidents involving the difficulty of having non-Western names and cases of abuse, Facebook publicly recognized that the policy didn't work for everyone (Osofsky, 2015). While Facebook was not willing to change the real-name policy itself, the company did roll out a new system for reporting and appealing to false-name accusations that was seen as a step in the right direction.

The real-name policy is an emblematic case of how systems embed values in their design. As scholars in science and technology studies have shown, values and ethics intertwine with technology development and use (Shilton et al., 2013). Literature on values in design (Flanagan, Howe and Nissenbaum, 2008; Friedman and Nissenbaum, 1996) holds that all technologies have values that were integrated by designers and subsequent use practices, whether consciously or unconsciously. Building on from Langdon Winner's (1986) notion that artefacts have politics, the concept of values in design emphasizes the shaping aspects of technology. Accordingly, technology not only has the power to enable certain practices but is also generative and constitutive of new realities and social norms. In the previous chapter, we discussed the notion of the normate template and how the world is designed with a rather limiting and conformist view on what the universal body looks like. It is useful here to be reminded that Mark Zuckerberg's notion of authentic identity is not a universal kind of authenticity but reflective of a white, middle-class, affluent and liberal life trajectory.

Whose authenticity?

Authenticity lies at the centre of Facebook. Usually 'associated with qualities such as truthfulness, genuineness and realistic' (Gubrium and Holstein, 2016: 124), pretty much everything on Facebook is made to signify the importance of such qualities. Social media in general, especially its notion of user-generated content, is premised on the idea of authenticity. In a study of the promotional language and visuals used by eleven different social networking sites between 2002 and 2016, Salisbury and Pooley (2017) found that nearly all of these sites invoke authenticity as a key marker. From YouTube's early slogan 'Broadcast yourself' to Twitter's small snippets of everyday aphorisms and Facebook's prompts to share what's on users' minds, these companies all claim to promote a more authentic or realistic picture of how people live their lives. These claims, Alice Marwick (2013) suggests, were largely influenced by the DIY culture of the early internet and its role in the discursive celebration of tech entrepreneurialism (see also Chapter 1). As Marwick writes, 'zines, blogs and personal home pages created opportunities for people to earnestly and honestly discuss their experiences with work, parenting, illness, politics and other intimate topics' (2013: 248). From the very beginning, then, online content created by individuals was seen as more authentic than its mass media counterpart (Marwick, 2013: 247). Yet, as Gunn Enli (2015) usefully shows, the mass media has always been engaged in the construction of reality through mediated forms of authenticity. As Enli reminds us, mass media critiques propagated by the Frankfurt School and later on by postmodernism and semiotics were essentially about the betrayal of the public by the culture industry and television 'presenting a phony version of reality' (Enli, 2015: 7–8). In contemporary media culture, Sarah Banet-Weiser asserts, authenticity is itself becoming a brand (2012: 14).

> I want to disconnect entirely from the divisive, egocentric and artificially idealized culture Facebook has fostered, but not at the price of being disconnected from the people I care about. (Chandler)[5]

What constitutes authenticity, however, is highly contested. Ranging from social theory (Taylor, 1992; Trilling, 2009) to critical theory (Adorno, 2013; Benjamin, 2008), popular music studies (Barker and Taylor, 2007; Grazian, 2005) and tourism studies (MacCannell, 1973; Wang, 1999), authenticity is variously understood as, for example, a moral imperative to be true to oneself (Taylor, 1992), a mistaken search for proprietary origins (Adorno, 2013) or an idealized representation of reality that is socially constructed (Grazian, 2005). The idea of an idealized representation, or the performative aspect of authenticity, has been particularly influential in the study of social media (see Abidin, 2018; Duffy and Hund, 2019; Marwick, 2013). Although there is no consensus on what authenticity means in the context of social media, researchers seem to agree on the contextual and malleable understanding of the term. Being authentic, in this body of research, may connote everything from transparency, truthful self-expression and realness to self-branding, relatability and much more besides (Abidin, 2018; Banet-Weiser, 2012). Importantly, being truthful or more real does not happen in a vacuum. How one expresses and presents oneself online is configured by the technical affordances and social norms, as well as the economic and political governance and constraints of platforms (Uski and Lampinen, 2016; van Dijck, 2013a). This is no different on Facebook, where what it means to be grounded in reality is highly intertwined with the technological architecture, designed affordances, social norms, economic concerns and platform governance.

On Facebook, the ideal of authenticity permeates everything from its terms of service, real-name policy, central features such as the personal profile and the timeline, and the algorithms matching people's friends, through to its ad infrastructure. The personal profile, for example, is built around the original idea of a social directory emphasizing demographic information, including relationship status, education and current workplace, while the timeline privileges a linear view of life trajectories assembled around the kinds of trajectories that are typical of affluent societies (Haimson and Hoffmann, 2016). Organized as a narrative biography, Facebook's timeline chronicles 'how life has been up to the present day by rearranging bits and pieces uploaded previously' (van Dijck, 2013b: 204). The retroactive ordering principle around major life events such as graduations, marriage and new jobs works to promote a specific idea of what an authentic life looks like. What information belongs in the personal profile or what the possibilities are for posting updates are not merely configured by technological affordances or design templates, but are also socially configured. In their research on what they term 'profile work', the strategic self-presentation on social network sites, Uski and Lampinen (2016) found that Finnish Facebook users in their early twenties expressed the ideal of having a Facebook profile that came across as naturally as possible. The pursuit of being real, they found, was guided by a set of social norms around practices of sharing and expectations of presenting oneself 'in the right way' (Uski and Lampinen, 2016: 460).

However, as Pooley reminds us, 'all interaction is performative; there is no such thing as a non-performative, "authentic" self-disclosure, on Facebook or in person' (2010: 83). Even if Facebook would like us to think so. Indeed, this insight is reminiscent of both Goffman's (1959) decentred theory of the self and Adorno's (2013) critique against the 'jargon of authenticity', which he saw as an ontological fiction of absoluteness. For Adorno, this jargon is not just anti-intellectual as he puts it, it is also politically and socially harmful. Levelling his critique particularly at the fascist philosopher Heidegger, whose theory on being is fraught with notions of the authentic, Adorno (2013) highlights how claims of genuineness and authenticity are used to legitimize proprietary origins that privilege settlers over any latecomers and alleged outsiders.

As we saw in the previous chapter, Facebook's 'normate template' (Hamraie, 2017) is built around the ideal of the white, westernized, universal average body. This normate template tells us to have important life events, networks of friends (as many as possible) with whom we may celebrate so-called 'friendversaries' and wish happy birthday to on a (hopefully) daily basis, socialize by habitually sharing stuff and liking other people's stuff, and upload pictures that we want others to see and that can be repurposed as happy moments and nice memories at a later stage. However, as Cho points out, Facebook's 'steroidal version of publicity' whereby everyone is expected to communicate openly and across dispersed networks ignores the notion that 'at least in the United States, the state of publicness is thickly encrusted with centuries of policy, violence and cultural mores' (2018: 3184). Cho found in his study of how US queer youth of colour experience social media that all informants viewed Facebook as a dangerous space. Two of the informants told Cho (2018) that they had been disowned by their families due to having been outed by the default publicness of Facebook. Some of these informants had developed elaborate worka-rounds to express their identity 'truthfully', for example by having multiple profiles or 'fake' profiles.

Certainly, marginalized people (whether it is because of race, socio-economic status, gender, orientation or their inter-section) are disproportionally affected by policies and systems

that purport to support 'the ideology of having one transparent self or one identity' (van Dijck, 2013b: 212). As much
scholarship in queer/Black studies shows, authenticity is a
highly normative and contested matter (Bailey, 2011; Strings
and Bui, 2014). To many, 'being true to oneself' or 'being who
they are' is more complicated than notions of 'truthfulness'
or 'genuineness' seem to suggest. To some, it is not even
an option. For example, studies on gender/racial 'realness'
in ballroom culture suggest that undoing or unmarking
one's trans/queer identity in favour of a heteronormative
gender identity, as commonly practised, is not evidence of
inauthenticity but a 'necessary strategy by which to avoid
discrimination and violence in the urban space' (Bailey, 2011:
366). The question, then, is not just what it means to be
authentic, or rather to perform shifting forms of authenticity,
but whose authenticity counts and is accounted for.

The big business of friendship

'Authenticity' and 'reputation' do not just serve the discursive
purpose of making people feel more safe and secure, as
Zuckerberg mentions as being the primary reason for
Facebook's real-name policy, but highlighting these values
also has social, political and economic effects beyond their
symbolic register. The whole idea of an authentic identity is,
of course, entirely premised on the commercial need to match
advertisers to real people. Without the real identities of people,
the business model of excessive data extraction could simply
not exist. Far from peripheral, then, Facebook's real-name
policy lies at the centre of its financial and political motivations.

There are three major ways in which the notion of friendship
can be understood in relation to Facebook: in economic
terms as something valuable that can be capitalized on, in
technical terms as something computable and programmable, and in social and affective terms as something that
is culturally universal but variously meaningful to people

regardless of their background. These different aspects of Facebook friendships, however, are not separate but inherently overlapping, which is why friendship constitutes a powerful organizing mechanism. By building an empire around friendship, Facebook capitalizes on one of the most significant concepts we have for describing the close and intimate relations between human beings. As the cultural critic Siegfrid Kracauer wrote in his essay on friendship from 1917:

> There are words that walk through the centuries from mouth to mouth without their conceptual content ever appearing clearly and sharply defined before the inner eye. The experience of generations, inexhaustible life, numerous events are hidden in them, and one marvels only that these word-vessels, which are made to carry such fullness, always retain their old validity, endure and let themselves be filled with ever new content. Our whole life is pervaded by them, we think with them and take them for unities despite the indeterminate multiplicity that quivers within them ... (quoted in Blatterer, 2019: 176)

Friendship, according to Kracauer, is destined to remain unclear. It is a 'concept to which new experience has repeatedly attached itself, unbridled fullness in the paltry form of a word!' (ibid.). Understood as an indeterminate multiplicity contained in a word vessel, it is not difficult to see the attraction and usefulness of the term for organizing a networked business like Facebook. The fact that new experiences continue to attach themselves to the concept of friendship is probably nowhere as evident as in the case of Facebook. If the 'Dunbar number' suggests that we cannot keep social contact with more than 150 people, then Facebook with its doubling and quadrupling of this number has certainly contributed to changing people's conceptions of friendship.[6] This does not mean, however, that thanks to Facebook, people now have *more* or *better* friendships. We might have 500 or 1,000 'Facebook friends', but this does not necessarily mean anything beyond the fact that a company decided to use 'friends' as the strategic name for the connections people form via its site. Building on the idea of strong and weak ties (Granovetter, 1973) and the notion of 'social capital' (Bourdieu, 2018; Putnam, 2000), much social research on social networking online (boyd and Ellison, 2007; Ellison et al., 2007; Valenzuela et al., 2009; Vitak and Ellison, 2013) suggests that people tend to socialize with existing connections and known friends.[7]

> I started out using the platform when I was in college, but moved to Europe in 2007. I used it as a way to keep in touch with my family and friends. Then I became a dance teacher and my online presence there is absolutely crucial to my job, helping me stay in contact with the swing dance community and bringing in future jobs. I have taken breaks, but it sometimes has cost me jobs. I went so far as to create a second Facebook page for just close friends and family where I can post more personal content and feel free to be myself. (Sandy, 2019)[8]

Facebook is not merely for known friends. As Rangaswamy and Arora show, in places like the slums of Hyderabad and Chennai, 'Facebook engagements are gateways to unimaginable opportunities' (2016: 619). Marginalized youth in these slums actively seek 'to connect and expand their networks' by friending strangers, especially people from an elevated social status (Arora and Scheiber, 2017: 413). Similarly, Costa (2016) found in her ethnography of social media use in South-East Turkey that it was quite common to use Facebook as a way of expanding one's social network by connecting to *yabanci* ('strangers'). In line with findings from some of the other ethnographies produced as part of the Why We Post research project (see endnote 3, Costa's was one of them), there are various motivations for connecting to people on Facebook, strangers included. For people in the Indian field site, rural China and South-East Turkey, social media 'opened new, private channels of communication, changing the notion of love and redefining local notions of masculinity and femininity. Women's social networks have expanded, and in some cases those of men have expanded more' (Miller et al., 2016: 123).

Whether people befriend known friends or strangers, a social network site as defined by boyd and Ellison 'enables users to articulate and make visible their social networks' (2007: 211). These articulations and visibilities suggest that friends can be accumulated and used strategically in economic, computational and social terms.[9] As Bakardjeva suggests, 'perceived as a source of social capital, friendship becomes a matter of fact and a matter of calculation' (2014: 375). On Facebook, friendships are for everyone to see (unless someone is very skilled with using their privacy settings). Being able to see with whom people are friends may serve multiple purposes. Computationally, the articulation of friends is, for example, repurposed by Facebook's People You May Know (PYMK) matching algorithm. Based on the notion of homophily, the axiom that individuals tend to associate with similar others, PYMK reinforces a mutual friends' logic.[10] By assuming that people want to be friends with people they already know, Facebook's algorithmic system works by elevating popularity and similarity. Facebook's PYMK, does not simply help users find people they may already know, but helps to perpetuate and reproduce the idea that this is what networks are for – to connect with people we know and to befriend people who are already somehow close to us.

While homophily grounds network science as Wendy Chun (2018) has forcefully argued, it is only important insofar as it helps to generate capital. In other words, more than love of the same, Facebook grounds friendships in the logic of economic efficiency. As stated in a Facebook patent describing the PYMK model:

> Social networking systems value user connections because better-connected users tend to increase their use of the social networking system, thus increasing user engagement and corresponding increase in, for example, advertising

opportunities [...] the friendship value reflects the potential increase in overall engagement of the user with the social networking system due to a given connection. (Schultz et al., 2014: 1–2)

Here, we can see how 'the measure of market success sneaks into the heart of a social relation', as Bakardjieva puts it (2014: 375). For Facebook, friendship is simply a word used for describing people's connections. This flattening of friendship is computationally very useful, insofar as it allows anybody and anything to be considered a friend, as long as a connection is forged. According to another Facebook patent:

the term 'friend' refers to any other user with whom a user has formed a connection, association or relationship via the social networking system. The term 'friend' need not require users to actually be friends in real life (which would generally be the case when one of the members is a business or other entity); it simply implies a connection in the social networking system. (Gubin et al., 2014)

Contrary to the common conception that friendship exists as a relation between individuals, friendship on Facebook is broadly construed to exist as a relation between multiple actors, between humans and non-humans alike. On Facebook, users can be friends with a business, a page, a sports team, books, a movie, celebrities and so forth. While it might seem strange to consider a movie a friend, this conception of friendship derives from the network model of the Web where users and movies are considered 'nodes' in the network (or graph) and the relationship that exists between them an 'edge' or, indeed, a friend.[11]

Communal aspects of friendship

Okay, so, I've read and heard a lot of people say that Facebook is full of drama, that it's stupid, that they're barely on it [...] that they're going to deactivate their account because it's such a time-suck [...]and I just want to say what Facebook means to me, as a stay-at-home mom to three boys under the age of seven.

I get up, I get kids up, I make breakfast and pack lunches. I get the kids dressed and change a diaper [...] I put away dishes and start a load of laundry [...]I take out whatever ingredients I need for dinner to thaw in the sink, and then I log into Facebook. It's true! From almost the very moment I wake up, I am on Facebook!

Yes, I am 'on' Facebook all day. Are my kids ignored? Only so much as an army of pee-soaked, grape-jelly covered, hungry, emotional, needy, loud, interactive, wild, funny and loved clown gorillas could be ignored. So what. I love Facebook. It keeps me connected to my life beyond this house. I get ideas for recipes, activities for my boys, invitations to things I wouldn't otherwise know about. I share and am shared with. I laugh and cry through Facebook. I find out what's going on with family and friends. I can't for the life of me understand why some people have to begrudge me that. (Wee3KidsDisorientAre, 2014)[12]

While calculable and programmable to the Facebook advertising machinery, to many users there are more or less obvious social benefits to using Facebook. Let's just say it: Facebook can be great. It may even feel good at times. It is convenient. It is helpful. Personally, I have found and reconnected with old friends, expanded my network, accepted many event invitations and received a fair share of birthday wishes, Likes and comments in support. Facebook groups have provided me with much helpful advice and tips on everything from travel to health issues and parenting. Being a critical internet scholar, it is tempting to put a caveat in there, to explain these things away, to engage in ideology criticism, but I won't. In fact, I should probably point out the fact that *because* I consider myself a critical internet scholar, this book is already skewed towards a certain side, to certain narrative strategies and critical perspectives. This legacy tells us to give more weight to distrust and exposure, to the fact that Facebook exhorts and exploits. As much as I would have liked to dislike Facebook, I don't. At least not entirely. I could claim that Facebook doesn't really matter any more, downplay its importance and simply say let's move on. I could leave and take my privileged friends with me. But the world doesn't work that way, at least not for many. The truth is that I too have my excuses, my reasons for staying. Whether the excuse is research, curiosity, convenience, support, boredom, habit, or writing a book about it, Facebook connects.

As the above quote from a blog post describing a typical day in the life of a stay-at-home mother suggests, Facebook has not just become part of everyday life in quite habitual ways, but also meaningfully so. While the word 'community', just like the word 'friend', has been annexed and expanded by Facebook's liberal use of it, it is still how many users describe their experience of using the site (Miller, 2011). In the mother's tale about Facebook's role in her daily life with her kids and domestic chores, Facebook might just mean what the colloquial uses of community, friendship and social support usually signify. For her, it is not an escape or flight from daily life, but a way to give added meaning to it. There are many more tales like hers out there, accounts of the mundane and meaningful roles that Facebook plays in people's lives. What Facebook means to people is an empirical question, one that many people have studied in different ways (Miller et al., 2016; Miller and Venkatraman, 2018; Sujon et al., 2018). There is, for example, 'Anne whose interactions are almost entirely based on business connections with her Facebook contacts', and Alice, who 'tends to interact most with people she met when travelling in Australia'. Then there is also Helen who showed a 'strong connection with fellow church members', and Erica, who is mainly friends with the people she works with at the pub (Miller and Venkatraman, 2018: 4–5). While these are merely four specific users encountered by researchers in a British field site, they suggest how Facebook supports social capital. The concept of social capital 'describes the benefits individuals derive from their social relationships and interactions', including social support and exposure to new ideas (Ellison et al., 2010: 873). Whether people are members of dedicated Facebook groups for people with rare diseases, sleep-deprived new parents or climate change deniers, Facebook provides a space for interest groups and communities to form and meet.

Thinking about Facebook's sociality, therefore, is as much about thinking about the real benefits and support that people experience as it is about underlying network models, business models, algorithmic enclosure and administrative identities. Beyond the discourse of social capital, which accentuates the economic logic of friendships as the 'benefit of Facebook friends' (Ellison et al., 2007), perspectives on the domestication of technology (Morley and Silverstone, 1990; Hirsch and Silverstone, 2003) remind us to also consider the ways in which technologies such as Facebook are variously taken up and understood within and beyond the household. Rather than looking at what Facebook offers in terms of beneficial social relations, a domestication framework takes up questions of everyday coordination, communication and family life. As Sujon, Viney and Toker-Turnalar argue, Facebook has 'become both a domestic platform and a domesticated platform' (2018: 6). In a similar way to how Chun (2016) describes networks as habitual, and thus infra-structural, Sujon et al.'s longitudinal study of Facebook use suggests that Facebook has fallen into the background of its respondents' daily lives. This does not imply that Facebook has become unimportant, quite the opposite. While the respondents describe Facebook as a little boring, they also suggest that Facebook has become essential 'for structuring and organizing personal social networks, family connections and personal archives' (Sujon et al., 2018: 9).

Even if the argument is made that Facebook is Facebook, suggesting it cannot adequately be described or labelled as a social network site, social media platform or any other subcategory for that matter, feminist critics also remind us to question the politics of dismissing labels too lightly. As feminist scholars within the sociology of technology and domestic work (Cockburn, 1988; Fortunati, 1995) have argued, there is a tendency to devalue technologies as soon as they are culturally 'tamed' to fit into and help to shape domestic routines. When suggesting that Facebook is no longer a social network site, then, we must also bear in mind, as the blog excerpt above exemplifies, that for many people Facebook is still primarily a means for networking and relational purposes. What is more, as the next section will discuss, relational communication and networking takes both time and work, a form of labour that historically speaking has been highly gendered and framed variously as domestic, relational and emotional (see Jarrett, 2015; Hochschild, 1979; Lai, 2021).

Friendship as work

If friendship is big business it is because people care about friends. Whether we have many or few, friendships connote closeness and intimacy. Friendships are not merely about forging connections – creating new edges in the network, so to speak – but perhaps more importantly about maintaining them. Maintaining friendships takes a lot of work. Importantly, the kind of work that is required – emotional and relational communication – is highly gendered. As Signe Sophus Lai (2021) shows in her ethnographic work on Danish internet users, the kind of communicative and relational labour reinforced by Facebook is often considered to be 'women's work'. Interviewing internet users, Lai found that gendered communicative relations are amplified and intensified in the way in which friendships are performed and maintained on Facebook. For example, women have typically been responsible for writing greetings cards to family and friends, a responsibility and expectation that are very much extended to the digital realm as well. Lai offers the concept of the 'digital shift' to suggest how digital media such as Facebook do not necessarily relieve women of their emotional and relational communicative expectations, but in many cases takes even more time and effort than before.[13] As people upload pictures, write status updates, comment, Like and share, there is also a constant expectation for a fitting response. Writing Facebook birthday wishes, checking in on kids' whereabouts, planning social gatherings and chatting on Messenger all belong to the digital shift. That is, people need to feel loved and appreciated and relationships need to be sustained, and as Lai suggests, 'women, more than men, continue to be the ones responsible for relational communication tasks' (2021: 292).

The literature on digital labour has usefully shown how the invisible and unwaged labour that users perform online is precisely so effective, because it is not framed or thought of as work (Terranova, 2000; Postigo, 2016). In her seminal essay on 'free labour' published during the heyday of the 2000 dotcom bubble, Terranova urged scholars to move beyond the notion that the internet was about escaping reality in order to understand how the internet is a 'network of social, cultural and economic relationships that crisscrosses and exceeds the internet – surrounds and connects the latter to larger flows of labour, culture and power' (2000: 34). For Terranova and many others, the internet is not a separate domain free of the political and economic forces of society, but deeply engrained and connected to the developments of post-industrial societies. Following Lazzarato's notion of immaterial labour as the activities involved in defining cultural standards and norms yet not thought of as work, for Terranova, free labour on the internet encompasses general activities such as 'reading/writing/managing and participating in mailing lists/websites/chatlines' (2000: 42). While 'free labour' as theorized by Terranova is not necessarily all exploitative, the idea of free and immaterial labour has been widely taken up in discussions around the value extraction of user-generated content in social media (e.g. Andrejevic, 2010; Scholz, 2012).

According to the user/worker 'exploitation' thesis, value on social media is primarily extracted by mining individual users' data. As Elmer (2019) points out, corporations like Facebook not only extract value from their users but also from their non-users. Although Zuckerberg claims not to know the term 'shadow profiles', it is widely recognized that Facebook collects enough data about its non-users to be able to create a virtual profile for them even if these users haven't signed up to Facebook yet.[14] One of the ways in which Facebook is able to collect and repurpose data about its non-users is via their friends and contacts who already have a Facebook account. When new users join Facebook they are prompted to upload their phone and email contacts in order to help them connect to people they already know. While friends have always been valuable to advertisers, Facebook automates it by turning everything users and non-users do into a potential data point for the targeting of ads and news-feed content (more on this in Chapter 5).

How people *do* friendship is important, as practices give friendships their meaning. The performative aspect of friendship is made very explicit when considering its constitutive role in powering the underlying economic and operational logic of Facebook. Because friendship is big business, the connections people forge perform important work. Socially and economically, friendships are employed, traded and tested. For example, in the case of social games such as FarmVille or Candy Crush, Facebook friends perform multiple roles: as important recruiters to the game, as game mechanics and as social interaction mechanics (Nieborg, 2015).[15] In a study on the 'free-to-play' commodity form encapsulated by the popular game Candy Crush, Nieborg (2015) suggests that Facebook's political economy cannot be understood without accounting for the value accrued by complementors such as app developers. Facebook users and gamers are intimately tied through friendship connections. In many cases, they constitute both user and player. These relations essentially work to produce the network effects on which platforms so desperately rely. As we will see in Chapter 5 on Facebook advertising, what and how friendship is done is not just a question of interpersonal interaction or explicit communicative acts but how technical configurations and networked communication make friends work in an implicit and automated fashion.

Facebook identity – what's in a name?

If, as Zuckerberg says, Facebook's real-name policy made it easier and more comfortable for people to share things about their lives, the network model of homophily and friendships made it easier for people to trust those connections. This combination proved not just socially and culturally valuable, but a strategic way to grow and expand Facebook's infrastructure beyond its core site. As Wendy Chun points out, "real names' or unique identifiers lie at the heart of big data analytics, for they are crucial to synching disparate databases and calibrating recycled data' (2018: 61). In other words, Facebook's real-name policy is not just a symbolic act but one that has real material and infrastructural repercussions and uses. This becomes evident when considering the wide range of Facebook-enabled and interoperable third-party apps. Take, for example, the dating app Tinder, which is built on top of the Facebook platform. On Tinder, strangers are made more familiar by providing information about mutual Facebook friends. More than that, Facebook *is* Tinder's safeguard against the potential uncertainty of dating strangers. After all, as Zuckerberg claims, Facebook is 'grounded in reality'. In its FAQ section, Tinder states: 'We use Facebook to make sure you are matched with real people who share similar interests and common friends' (Duguay, 2017: 356). As Duguay (2017) suggests, Facebook is used to verify that people are 'real', indeed authentic.

The uses of Facebook's 'administrative identity', as we might call the Facebook ID authentication login, stretches far beyond the boundaries of the platform. Today, a Facebook identity has become an important token for trust and authenticity in and of itself. Whether Tinder, or the house-sharing platform Airbnb, or local childcare/nanny matching sites, Facebook profiles are repurposed as an important verification mechanism and main token of trust. More fundamentally, however, Facebook identity is deemed so trustworthy it has become what is called a 'federated identity'. In information technology, a federated identity refers to the ways in which a person's electronic identity can be used as identity tokens across multiple sites. For example, when a user wants to log in or sign up to a new website, app or free Wi-Fi, they are often given the option to do so using their Facebook or Google account credentials, rather than having to create a whole new account with a new username and new password. In other words, instead of authenticating the user themselves, it has become common for different online service providers to offload their authentication to Facebook or Google. This is no trivial task.

Using a federated identity not only establishes a relationship to the service provider, but importantly exposes data back to the identity provider (e.g. Facebook). Facebook Connect, as Facebook called its suite of products that allowed for such data portability, was launched in 2008, and was described as allowing 'users to 'connect' their Facebook identity, friends and privacy to any site' (Morin, 2008). At the outset, the goal was to transform the Web into a more social space, rather than necessarily offering an electronic identity for the whole Web. Yet, in 2013, Facebook Connect was rebranded to Facebook Login, and explicitly promoted as an authentication service for mobile apps. Facebook Login became a cornerstone in Facebook's efforts to become a mobile-first company. As Zuckerberg proclaimed during the company's fourth-quarter earnings conference call in 2013: 'If 2012 was the year we turned our core product into a mobile product, then 2013 was the year when we turned our business into a mobile business' (Facebook, 2014).

More than simply verifying the authenticity of users and their friends, Facebook identity is a fundamental infrastructural issue with important social and political implications (see also previous chapter on infrastructure). Questioned in an interview that same year on why Facebook didn't think about launching its own phone now that it was aggressively pursuing the mobile route, Zuckerberg revealingly responded that the company's ambition was to go beyond this to instead get 'as deep into the system as we want' (CNN Money/ Fortune, 2013). For users, getting 'as deep into the system' basically means a greater risk of being locked in. A phone you could always replace, but the switching costs associated with deep system integration and data lock-ins are far more difficult to escape. In addition, as Jessica Schroers (2019) points out, there is also the risk of lockouts. If Facebook should decide to terminate or delete someone's user account, that user would not just lose their Facebook data but also access to the multiple apps, websites and services where they've registered using their Facebook credentials. This might seem trivial to some, but if you belong to the subset of the world's population that came to Facebook (and the internet) via a pre-installed data plan, like the many users in Myanmar described in the introductory chapter, a potential lockout may be quite consequential.

Concluding remarks

Technically, there is no reason for calling Facebook connections, friends. Symbolically, emotionally and economically, however, it makes all the difference. There is something inherently challenging about making sense of the convoluted aspects of friendships on Facebook. There is the stay-at-home mom who uses Facebook all day to feel connected while doing the laundry and caring for her kids. There is the long-lost friend whom you suddenly reconnect with. There is the annoying acquaintance from high school who spams your news feed with political stuff you don't agree with. There is the migrant worker whose only sense of intimacy and family life happens on Facebook after a 17-hour work shift. There is the unwaged labour and exploitation of user-generated content. There is sharing as caring and the cultural norms that make friendship such an effective target for capitalism. There are the Facebook groups for the chronically ill, the cancer patients and radicalized youth. How does one reconcile such diverse, disturbing and contradictory facets? How far does the notion of exploitation take us, and where does pleasure start?

If a foundational element of what makes Facebook Facebook is that it is 'grounded in reality', it implies that Facebook must be very messy. For Zuckerberg, being grounded in reality means using real names as tokens of trust and willingness to share – an antidote to the messiness that supposed anonymity brings with it. From an infrastructural perspective, Facebook's real-name policy makes the social traceable and transactional by turning friendships into effective verification mechanisms to ground everything from love to commerce. But, if anything, reality is a messy place. It can be both problematic and unpleasant, and nothing like the 'promise of happiness' or communal feelings engendered by Facebook. As this chapter has shown, for every authenticity claim there is someone who is deemed inauthentic, unreal, excluded and forgotten. Someone's 'real' is always someone else's 'fake', and these notions are already deeply problematic, gendered and racialized. As we've seen in the controversies around Facebook's real-name policy and transgender people and ballroom culture, what it means to be 'true to yourself' and 'being who you are' is far from universal. To some it is not even a real possibility.

Perhaps more than anything, this chapter shows that there is a deep ambivalence to Facebook and the kinds of friendships and sociality it supports and encourages. On the one hand, we are confronted with a platform that once started out as a hot-or-not site by hacking into the databases of college houses to steal pictures of women, only to turn into a global identity provider trusted by millions of websites and services for its ability to provide a secure authentication process. Quite a feat if we think about it. On the other hand, we are reminded of all the ways that Facebook provides meaning to social relations. For example, how using expressions such as 'Facebook friends' or 'making it Facebook official' both says something about the meaning of friendship and relationships today, and how Facebook lends these practices and relations a certain flavour. Facebook's deep ambivalence creeps up at every corner, in various blog posts and comments, in the many disparate attempts to leave and disconnect, in research findings and everyday encounters. Facebook is both time thief and lifeline, a tool for self-promotion and a conduit for self-deprecation, both friend and enemy, and much more.

CHAPTER FOUR

Engineering a platform: Facebook's techno-economic evolution

[T]here's nothing magical about the number one billion. If your mission is to connect the world, then a billion might just be bigger than any other service that had been built. But that doesn't mean that you're anywhere near fulfilling the actual mission.

Mark Zuckerberg (2014)

If the first decade of Facebook was all about getting people to start using Facebook, the second decade (in which we are still in the midst) saw Mark Zuckerberg aiming at world domination. As he somewhat laconically suggested in an interview with *Time* magazine in 2014 (quoted above), what do one billion users matter if all you are really trying to do is to connect the whole wide world (Grossmann, 2014)? In this chapter, we will take a look at Facebook's career, and how Zuckerberg could even arrive at a point from which it seemed realistic to be taking over the rest of the world. Just like any other company, Facebook had to find its way, develop its product, fail and succeed and, most importantly, find a viable business model. In this chapter we therefore take a look at some of the most important developments in terms of product and business strategies, including platform programmability, becoming a mobile company, and key innovations such as the News Feed and its personalized algorithms. These are by no means meant to signify an exhaustive list of events and features explaining how Facebook became an empire. Surely there will be important omissions, missing features, incomplete narratives and partial accounts. However, it is not my intention to provide a complete overview.[1]

Rather, this chapter is meant to give readers a primer into a few important Facebook features and business strategies, and provide a background for understanding how Facebook evolved into an ad tech surveillance complex (Chapter 5) and data-intensive political testing ground (Chapter 6). If the next chapter focuses on Facebook's technologies and economics in terms of its advertising infrastructure in particular, this chapter focuses on some of the techno-economic steps that helped shape Facebook into an ad company. Part of the narration in this chapter stays true to the linearity of those steps, of telling them in a chronological order. But as for most things, even if they happened at a certain point in time, they seldom fit neatly into a chronological timeline. Arguably, this is particularly the case with the things that we want to highlight in our stories. Where do those particularly important things belong?

There are many possible answers to the question of structuring stories. In keeping with the narrative strategy of the previous chapter, here again I take my cue from Facebook itself. While the last chapter sought to illustrate the feed-like experience of sociality on Facebook by disrupting the narrative by inserting (sometimes random) user quotes, this chapter follows the logic of the News Feed in organizing the narrative flow (for better or for worse). This logic refers to the algorithmic organization of the News Feed that works by putting the 'most important' stories first. This logic also borrows from the world of journalism on which the feed is modelled. The principle of the 'inverted pyramid' is a narrative strategy often used in journalism that works by communicating the most essential or important information about the topic before getting into the details. I am highlighting these narrative decisions for two reasons. First, it will hopefully make the chapter more readable, explaining why it is structured in the way it is. Second, it also serves to explain how the News Feed and its algorithms work by enacting them in practice. By making the structuring principle of this chapter very explicit, I also hope to highlight how narrative choices about what counts as 'most important' are just that – choices based on certain assumptions and values. This is no different from how Facebook's News Feed works.

Facebook's News Feed is powered by an algorithm – or in fact several, to be precise – that determines which stories are shown in which order. The order is dynamically changing, depending on the viewing subject, the network of that subject user and time. The goal of the News Feed as of August 2013 'is to show the right content to the right people at the right time' (Kacholia, 2013). Over the years, how Facebook determines what is right has changed. As in the case with machine-learning algorithms like the ones driving the Facebook News Feed, they respond to the constant incoming data streams generated by users. This means that the algorithms themselves are composite creatures that respond to user engagement by changing how they perform and do work in the world. In other words, even if the overall logic of the algorithms determining the ranking of stories in the News Feed is that of perceived importance and relevance, how these parameters are defined is not a constant. Thus, the narrative ranking in this chapter should be understood metaphorically, as it does not in any way mirror the actual operational logics of the News Feed algorithm, to which we will get back in more depth later in this chapter.

Another caveat has to do with my slight reluctance to commit fully to the argumentative implications. Just because this chapter begins with the 'magic sauce' of Facebook – the News Feed and its algorithms – does not mean it is the most important story about Facebook. Yet, if the feed is constantly changing the way it is, offering a new view of incoming stories every time a user visits it, then this chapter should be read as offering one such view. That is, the ranking in this chapter looks as follows: the 'top story' is that of the News Feed and its algorithmic logic. What comes after is a more general story of Facebook's claim to fame, of the many business decisions, product developments, and twists and turns that Facebook faced in turning itself into an empire. Taken together, they present not just a feed of stories about Facebook, but stories about some of the things that arguably make Facebook, Facebook – the News Feed, its algorithms and the platform.

News Feed: Your personal newspaper

One of the most important features on Facebook is the News Feed, which was introduced alongside the so-called 'Mini Feed' (now called 'Timeline') on 5 September 2006. The News Feed was by far the most complex project that the company had tackled until that point (Kirkpatrick, 2011). Not just technically complex but socially daunting as well. The News Feed had been long anticipated and celebrated by its engineers and the tech community. Mark Zuckerberg had first mentioned the prospect of building a 'personalized newspaper based on users' social activity' in 2005. From the very beginning, News Feed was conceptualized as Facebook's killer app, the thing that would potentially be Facebook's business case and claim to fame.

While highly anticipated by the engineers and executive team, users revolted. Everybody seemed to hate News Feed. After its launch, comments from users immediately poured in, nearly all of them negative. In the public's eye, Facebook had turned into 'Stalker-book'. Only a day after the launch of its highly anticipated killer app, Mark Zuckerberg (2006) wrote a blog post entitled 'Calm down. Breathe. We hear you', addressing the massive public outcry and privacy concerns in response to News Feed. Described in a *Time* article as a 'glitzy laundry list' and a tracking feature that monitored 'friends' Facebook movements by the minute', News Feed was essentially received as being extremely intrusive (Schmidt, 2006). In a Facebook post commemorating News Feed's tenth anniversary, Ruchi Sanghvi, the original product manager of News Feed, recalled the stark disconnect between the team celebrating and popping champagne and the tsunami of outraged users that hit them immediately after launching the feature. 'A lot of folks wanted us to shut News Feed down', Sanghvi wrote, 'but we didn't ... News Feed was actually working.' And she went on: 'It seems crazy to think that four people who had just graduated/dropped out were able to build a personalized newspaper for over 10 million users – in other words, one of the largest, real-time, distributed systems ever built' (Sanghvi, 2016).

Sanghvi was at least right about one thing: it is crazy to think about how Facebook became this huge. It is crazy to think about how, as we put it in the closing of the previous chapter, something that started out as a hot-or-not site hacking into the databases of college houses to steal pictures of women turned into a global identity provider trusted by millions of websites and services. It is crazy to think about how fast we, the global audience, became accustomed to being 'unwillingly inundated with each friend's latest Facebook antics', as the *Time* article put it (Schmidt, 2006). Before the introduction of the News Feed, Facebook users had to actively visit their friends' profiles to get new updates. Removing this modality of intentionality by offering an automated stream felt both intrusive and strange at the time. Yet, this process of automation became surprisingly quickly utterly habitual and normalized, turning Facebook into the 'wonderfully creepy' (Chun, 2016) experience of having friends' whereabouts and lives broadcast to you and ready at hand with a simply scroll.

The News Feed would indeed reinvent Facebook and 'become the "epicentre" of the corporation's revenue success' (Zuboff, 2019: 459). Today, it is hard to imagine Facebook without the News Feed providing a constant stream of updates. From the beginning, the News Feed offered new ways of sharing information about friends, in part through the status updates users themselves provided, and partly through system-generated updates (e.g. information about friends' commenting on someone else's post). At first, Facebook was mainly a place for people's immediate circle of friends and classmates. As the site grew, people added more friends and friends of friends. Then came former school friends, colleagues, acquaintances, family, even strangers. Facebook became a place where users habitually shared their thoughts, pictures and updates, shared videos and news, engaged in conversations, and commented on and liked each other's posts. As the user base of Facebook grew, the number of possible stories for each user's News Feed quickly outgrew the available space. Announcing new changes to the home page design in 2009, Zuckerberg (2009) suggested that people were no longer coming to 'Facebook to consume a particular piece or type of content, but to consume and participate in the stream itself'. This was not a trivial observation, as it seemed to indicate a firm stance in what Facebook regarded as its main product.

Considerable efforts went into deciding what the logic of the stream/feed would be. As Steven Levy (2020) writes, some people thought that it shouldn't be the most interesting stories that should be displayed first, 'based on the premise that people would keep scrolling until they got to them'. Zuckerberg, however, 'decided that even at the risk of satisfying users too quickly, the cream should rise to the top' (2020: 262).[2] With more friends than the News Feed feature would allow for if one were to display all content, Facebook essentially built its own algorithmically driven monitoring and measuring system that worked by weighing people against each other, ultimately turning the News Feed into a popularity contest based on who posted, commented, shared and liked the most. Organized and driven by ever more complex algorithms, the News Feed displays a heavily edited view of what friends, groups and pages are up to in an order of calculated importance with the most important updates at the top of the feed.[3] As described in the News Feed patent document:

The news feed may be continuously updated by adding news items about new activities and/or removing news items about previous activities. Accordingly, the viewing user may be better able to follow the 'track' of the subject user's 'footprints' through the social network, based on the news feed, without requiring the subject user to continuously post new activities. (Zuckerberg et al., 2010)

The patent clearly shows how the News Feed was conceived as a service to users. Instead of having to actively consult the news, or post updates yourself, Zuckerberg et al. (2010) posited the News Feed as a service providing a constant stream of new information. This idea was also reflected by Facebook's Help Centre at the time when describing the News Feed: 'It's like we started delivering the mail to you instead of forcing you to pick it up on your own' (DeRuiter, 2016: 23). Not only did the News Feed provide a service, it seemed to be providing a news service. This is important because it shows how the News Feed was designed to mimic the logic of a newspaper from the very beginning. Just as one would read a newspaper to get not just the latest updates about the world but also the most significant ones, Facebook conceptualized the News Feed as a personal newspaper focusing on the most important stories from a user's network. Software features are often designed to emulate known things and familiar practices in order to seem more intuitive and easier to use. This means that the history and operational logics of features such as the News Feed necessarily also contain the history and values of that which it tries to mimic, which in this case entails the world of journalism and news.

News journalism as the model

The analogy between Facebook's News Feed and a newspaper runs deep. It was already present in the way that Zuckerberg proposed the feature in his 2005 summer project brief, and has been a regular feature ever since of how the News Feed is presented and talked about in press releases and other company speech. When first introducing the News Feed to the public, Ruchi Sanghvi described the updates as 'headlines'. In a post on Facebook, she wrote: 'Now, whenever you log in, you'll get the latest headlines generated by the activity of your friends and social groups' (Sanghvi, 2006). The analogy was also a frequent feature in government hearings, policy papers and media reports about Facebook. Martinez describes the narrative seduction involved in defining Facebook at public events. Recounting a PR event he attended in 2011, Chris Cox enters the stage asking the crowd: 'What is Facebook, define it for me.' 'A social network', someone says. 'Wrong! It's not that at all.' Then, a young intern shouts: 'It's your personal newspaper.' 'Exactly!', Cox says, 'It's what I should be reading and thinking about, delivered personally to me every day' (Martinez, 2018: 260). Not only is it a personal newspaper, but as Zuckerberg tellingly proclaimed at a news conference in 2013, 'the best personalized newspaper in the world' (Sengupta, 2013). Zuckerberg was right about Facebook turning into a major news source. In a Pew research study in 2016, the findings showed that the US general public increasingly considered Facebook to be a prime source of news (Gottfried and Shearer, 2016). More alarmingly, as we will discuss in Chapter 6, the News Feed has since also turned into a prime distributor of polluted information.

If modelling the News Feed on existing conceptions of news formed an important part of developing its business model from the very beginning, Facebook was careful about not defining itself as a media company, despite the company's ongoing investments in media services with Facebook Live, TV shows, VR, Instant articles feature etc. (Poell, Nieborg and Duffy, 2021). Shortly before Facebook's IPO, Carolyn Everson, VP of global marketing solutions at Facebook, refuted questions about their business model, saying: 'We actually define ourselves as a technology company

[...] Media companies are known for the content that they create' (Fiegerman, 2016). This line of argumentation has been consistently maintained. During the 2018 congressional hearings following the Cambridge Analytica scandal, Zuckerberg said: 'I consider us to be a technology company because the primary thing that we do is have engineers who write, code and build product and services for other people' (Castillo, 2018). Of course, as Napoli and Caplan (2017) point out, appealing to computer science or technical expertise as a reason for not being a media company is ill informed at best. Technology and media are not separate endeavors, but intimately intertwined.

It is somewhat ironic, then, given Facebook's continued reluctance to define itself as a media company, that the concept of news plays such a central role. On the one hand, Facebook insists on simply being a conduit for news. On the other hand, the company participates in shaping, presenting and packaging content in ways that seem startlingly similar to news work. More than simply displaying the explicit actions of its users as news, Facebook also makes the news. That is, Facebook not only selects a series of news items from a list of explicit actions but takes an active part in manufacturing the news. User action on Facebook, such as someone adding a friend to their network or uploading a picture, isn't strictly speaking news until Facebook defines it as such. Facebook could just as well have chosen to let actions like these go unnoticed by not reporting on them. Nevertheless, it is exactly the kind of mundane reporting that generates value and engagement on a social platform. Being informed about someone uploading a new photo album is the type of 'news' that might make the viewing user curious enough to engage with the News Feed. As the News Feed patent (Zuckerberg et al., 2010) exemplifies, Facebook 'news' of the kind just described above may also be accompanied by various links that may offer additional information or prompts for further action.

That said, we should be wary about reading patent documents too literally, as patents are not evidence of how technologies actually work. Patents are usually filed as early as possible in the lifespan of an idea in order to protect the idea from potential competitors (Eveleth, 2019). In the case of the News Feed patent above, it was filed as early as 11 August 2006. This means that we cannot assume this is how News Feed works in 2020, nor even how it worked at the time the patent was actually granted on 23 February 2010. When reading patents, the value does not necessarily stem from their empirical accuracy but from their imaginary anticipation and assumptions. The fact that Zuckerberg and his team filed a patent for 'dynamically providing a news feed about a user of a social network' that claimed a plethora of methods for displaying a news feed comprised of various activities provides evidence of how the News Feed was ideally conceptualized. While some of the claims persist, others were discontinued or never even realized. As Allen Lo, a Facebook vice-president, told the *New York Times*: 'Most of the technology outlined in these patents has not been included in any of our products, and never will be' (Chinoy, 2018). The timescales between patent application processing and software development mean that most likely the product has changed significantly by the time the patent is granted. This also means that patents are not the best predictions of what companies will do in the future, but should rather be read as indications of the kinds of problems that they are working on.[4]

We may find another good indication of the conceptualization and manufacturing of news in another prominent Facebook patent on 'providing a newsfeed based on user affinity'. In it, Bosworth and Cox describe a 'media generator component' used to 'select and/or generate one or more items of media' (2013: 6). This means that any user action could potentially be translated into a 'story' on a friend's News Feed. In a similar way to how journalists frame stories, write headlines, highlight certain aspects of the story according to journalistic principles and news values, Facebook intervenes in designing and informing the stories that get published on the feed. That is not to say that Facebook works just like news, or that Facebook shapes content according to the same criteria as those utilized in journalism. Far from it. What they do have in common is wanting to publish compelling stories in ways that make people engage with them. How and for what underlying purpose they do this, however, differs.

Journalism and news are also not just *one* thing. There are different kinds of news outlets and different kinds of news. In their most basic form, journalism studies have long distinguished between 'hard' news, defined as news with a high level of newsworthiness, and 'soft' news, stories that are primarily entertaining and do not require timely publication (Tuchman, 1978). Whereas soft news typically refers to time-agnostic human-interest stories, hard news dealing with economics or politics is often considered more timely and important (Lehman-Wilzig and Seletzky, 2010; Reinemann et al., 2012). In the same way that 'hard' news demands immediate reporting and publishing due to its perceived importance, Facebook's News Feed displays 'top news', or the most relevant and time-sensitive (according to Facebook standards) news first. Unlike journalism, however, Facebook's curatorial practice does not follow any strict organizational logic.

To Facebook, it does not matter whether a story is considered hard or soft news. As long as its algorithms have determined a story to be important, it does not matter whether it concerns gossip, lifestyle or economics. Yet, applying these categories as an analytical lens reveals how Facebook's News Feed seems to turn soft news into hard news, or at least change the conditions and definitions of those traditional categories. Whereas 'soft news' is usually seen as having 'little or no intrinsic social or personal importance, so that it can be reported on at any time (if at all)' (Lehman-Wilzig and Seletzky, 2010:

38), Facebook's top news seems to prioritize soft news that shares many affinities with the timeliness and importance categorized as properties of 'hard news'. That is, Facebook's top news is comprised of as much intrinsic social or personal importance as possible, and precisely because of it, demands immediate 'reporting'.

The main difference between journalism and Facebook's News Feed – besides editorial responsibility on the part of journalism – is their approach to personalization. Whereas journalistic principles of newsworthiness are grounded in an understanding of public importance, Facebook's News Feed is grounded in personalized notions of interestingness. If, as Ekström and Westlund write, 'the democratic role and authority of news journalism depends on being able to reach out to citizens who engage in news consumption to become informed' (2019: 260), Facebook's impetus is not the informed citizen but a monetizable friendship connection. Yet, as research in digital journalism shows, clear distinctions between news journalism and algorithmically driven platforms have become harder to sustain (Bell et al., 2017; Lewis and Westlund, 2015). In recent years, we have seen how news journalism is changing, partly as a result of their increased dependency on platform companies (Ekström and Westlund, 2019). Journalism and its boundaries are being contested as people's news consumption has moved to social media spaces, suggesting that we do not just take their differences for granted but also investigate how these domains become similar or even influence each other. As we will discuss in the next chapter on Facebook's advertising infrastructure, understanding Facebook's business model means grappling with the fact that everything that happens on the News Feed is meant to support Facebook's ad-tech-surveillance complex. While much of news journalism is, of course, also financed by advertising revenue, Facebook is not just financed by advertising revenue but engineered to act as an advertising company itself. An important factor in this regard is the drive towards instant personalization.

The algorithmic logic of Facebook

A core tenet of personalization is knowing what a specific person wants or is most likely to be interested in. At Facebook, the idea of ranking or sorting the feed, as we have seen, had already been addressed numerous times with different solutions to the question of how to determine the interestingness of a story. Over the years, Facebook has experimented with different display mechanisms, alternating between real-time feeds focusing on showing stories in a chronological order and more algorithmically generated feeds emphasizing some calculated notion of relevance. It was not until the f8 event in 2010 that Facebook publicly revealed more details about the algorithm filtering and organizing the News Feed. At the event, Ruchi Sanghvi and Facebook engineer Ari Steinberg explained some of the details of what was then named the 'EdgeRank' algorithm. The side effects of Facebook's rapid user growth and engagement, the engineers told the audience, was an increase in unwanted content. So the problem that the algorithm was trying to solve, was to make the feed a more habitable place by reducing the amount of noise. The amount of content flowing through Facebook also had to be sorted and ranked into a feed that felt meaningful and interesting to the viewing user.

Edgerank was thus introduced as the algorithm that would both filter and rank the News Feed in order to provide 'the right content to the right people at the right time so they don't miss the stories that are important to them' (Kacholia and Minwen, 2013). During their talk, Sanghvi and Steinberg presented a power point slide with a two-element system representing a formulaic expression of the algorithm. The formula featured objects (content) and edges (relational inter-actions). The edges in turn, had three main components:

affinity between the viewer and the item creator, type of edge (with comments being more important than Likes), and time decay. EdgeRank was basically presented as the sum of each element multiplied together. The higher the EdgeRank, the more likely it would be to be displayed in the feed (DeVito, 2017: 6). For all its visual modesty, this formula was at best a distilled and much simplified version of what is actually going on when making sure that the most interesting stories reach the right user at the right time.

What is sometimes glossed over as *one* algorithm, should in reality be understood as an algorithmic system.[5] On Facebook, this system is comprised of a number of elements, including code and variables, but not at all reductive to them. As Bernhard Rieder writes, the conception of developers 'meticulously arranging metrics such as affinity between users, post engagement, and some function of time to produce a clear decision recipe that is guarded like a precious secret' is 'increasingly incomplete and outdated' (2017: 110). Indeed, the algorithms powering the News Feed cannot easily be captured and visualized in a formula to be displayed on a power point slide. However, when they are, the complexity becomes evident in the fine print. For example, in another much circulated visual depiction of the formulae, the fine print states how Facebook 'also looks at roughly 100,000 other highly-personalized factors when determining what's shown' on the News Feed (Constine, 2016). These 100,000 plus factors are not just computed according to some rule-based determinants, but classified and categorized according to generative models produced by machine learning algorithms.

Facebook patent applications and other publicly available documents describing its technical systems, show how the company has evolved by using machine learning to infer user interests (Deeter and Duong, 2017; Kendall et al., 2014; Naveh and Karnas, 2019; Zhou and Moreels, 2013). Machine learning algorithms are particularly useful for analysing large quantities of data, as these algorithms typically work to classify input data (or features) in order to produce and predict certain outcomes (Burrell, 2016). For a company whose bread and butter it is to create the world's largest database of social data, applying machine learning to derive workable models from those data has been central to the goal of generating actionable and profitable insight. These patents usefully show how machine learning enables decision models to be derived from the encounter between different types of data. In other words, what matters is not so much the code with the step-by-step instruction to a computer for solving a task (textbook definition of an algorithm), but the models that the machine learning techniques help to generate. User actions on Facebook, such as liking an object, do not automatically produce a clear-cut endpoint that the algorithm can use to compute a ranked result. Rather they provide input to 'an adaptive statistical model containing potentially hundreds of thousands of variables' (Rieder, 2017: 110) that the system in turn can use to make the data signify *in relation* to other data. Based on a changing set of variables (though factors such as affinity, time and content type have remained important throughout), each potential News Feed story is assigned a relevancy score that determines its position on feed. Importantly, those scores are highly personalized, As Adam Mosseri, VP of Product Management for News Feed, explained, the relevancy scores for each story are relative to the viewing user (Mosseri, 2016). In other words, just as there are thousands of stories competing to be displayed on the News Feed, there is not really *one* News Feed to speak of, but as many versions as there are Facebook users.

In essence, the News Feed algorithms work to deliver users 'the most personalized experience possible every time they visit Facebook' (Muraleedharan, 2017). The personal is pivotal and always already relational. Machine learning systems work by adapting to and changing in response to user activity. What someone sees on the News Feed is thus a mirror of sorts, a picture of the prediction of a likelihood computed by orchestrating previous events. That is, Facebook's News Feed works by inferring future worlds from the exposure of past data. However, as Wendy Chun (2021) points out, 'the term "personalized" is a misnomer', since machine learning systems are 'built on the principal of homophily'. The 'personalized' experience in the case of Facebook's News Feed, then, is not so much the result of an user's individual traits and actions. Rather, the personalized is derived from clustering the patterns recognized in the traits and actions of 'people like me'. Moreover, these systems do simply mirror reality but help to shape the world they purport to merely reflect. Quite simply, Facebook's 'inference systems are optimized to support the company's revenue goals' (Thorson et al., 2019: 3). As Thorson et al. point out, Facebook's systems are designed to 'learn which features of users' data (a) create interest classifications that produce sales for advertisers and (b) maintain user engagement on the newsfeed' (ibid). These two objectives are deeply related, as engaged users are more monetizable, and ads are created to spur more engagement (see also next chapter).

The News Feed algorithms have been pivotal to our understanding and experience of Facebook. Not only have the algorithms shaped what is made visible to individual users on the News Feed, but in making certain things visible at the expense of other things, algorithms have influenced how we keep in touch with other people. Perhaps more so than with any other platform, the algorithms organizing and programming sociality on Facebook have accustomed people to an algorithmically sorted and curated world of news and updates. Algorithms constitute an important element in support of the assertion that Facebook is Facebook. This is not limited to thinking of the algorithmic in purely technical terms. As I have argued in my previous book *If ... Then* (Bucher, 2018), what we take an algorithm to be, shapes how we come to think of its potential power and politics.

Arguably, the algorithmic also includes the many cultures and practices that have evolved around the Facebook algorithms, the kind of content that those algorithmic logics encourage and support, the kind of publishers and third parties that have taken advantage of these logics but also emerged because of them, and the imaginaries and narratives that have helped to shape how this algorithmic landscape looks and feels today. All of these things are equally part of Facebook's algorithmic logic, because they in turn help to shape the algorithms and operational logics of Facebook. Take a publisher like BuzzFeed. Rather than developing content independently of Facebook, BuzzFeed evolved in tandem with what Facebook's algorithms seemed to privilege. More than simply offering a platform upon which new businesses could emerge, businesses like BuzzFeed also impacted how Facebook's algorithms would evolve. The more algorithmically-oriented businesses became, say becoming experts of Facebook's algorithms like BuzzFeed, the more Facebook had to counter these experts with their own changes to the algorithms, ranking and curatorial logics (in this case, motivated by countering click-bait).

Interviewing dozens of news professionals for my previous book (Bucher, 2018), it quickly became evident how much of a powerful force Facebook has become in the publishing and news industry. None of the actors I interviewed (mainly senior executives, chief editors, digital managers) said their business stayed unaffected by Facebook. In fact, the opposite seemed to be the case. At the time of conducting these interviews in Scandinavian newsrooms around 2015–16, many of the participants voiced their concern with regards to making their businesses too dependent on Facebook. At that time, Facebook had just announced that its algorithms would give more prominence to video, resulting in many of the informants talking about video as an important feature to be strategically used in order to drive traffic to their respective sites. Regardless of what content and formats Facebook prioritizes in the News Feed (e.g. video, catchy headlines or the always nebulous notion of 'quality content'), the fact that so many different actors stay tuned, focused and oriented towards the inner logics of Facebook and its algorithmic workings suggests its central role in a much wider informational ecology. As the News Feed and its algorithms gained currency as something that not only organized how friends appeared (or disappeared) to each other, but also as something that became indispensable to most business, Facebook turned into a central informational organizing unit.

Building an empire, becoming a platform

Before 'world domination', Facebook, like any company, was looking for ways to grow and scale its product. Although Zuckerberg said in many early interviews that Facebook was never meant to be a company, he also suggested to his shareholders in advance of Facebook's IPO that he had developed a 'deep appreciation for how building a strong company with a strong economic engine and strong growth can be the best way to align many people to solve important problems' (Zuckerberg, 2012). Even when talking about the company's economic goals, Zuckerberg found a way to spin it back to Facebook's social mission. As Zuckerberg (2012) tellingly put it, 'we don't build services to make money; we make money to build better services'. This romantic and technocratic vision of an altruistic entrepreneurial geek is now a staple of Facebook's origin history. Essentially a story about white college dudes with connections in the right places, strategic hiring decisions, plenty of capital investments, a corporate culture infused with tons of dorm-like casualness and Californian ideology, and the mythical figure of Mark Zuckerberg himself, the early days of Facebook certainly fit right into the Silicon Valley mystique.

As technology writer David Kirkpatrick (2011) suggests in one of the first trade books on Facebook's early years, theFacebook.com was surrounded by a culture of communal cool. The employees were allegedly each other's best friends, and of course, everyone worked around the clock. Zuckerberg would allegedly come into the office at noon in his flip-flops and start typing away on his little iBook. Facebook made an explicit effort to be the coolest company in Silicon Valley (Kirkpatrick, 2011: 338). Advertising mattered, but only to the extent that it was needed to cover costs. While Facebook kept making advertising deals, mainly using banner ads on a CPM basis, the real gold mine was its growing database of users and their interests, activities and relationships. Although it would still take some time before that database truly showed its enormous power, what followed were years of growing the company. Feature by feature, Facebook was on a mission – to connect the whole world.

Early on, in 2007, Facebook established a growth team that was given the task of figuring out how to scale the platform. The growth team, or the growth circle as it was later renamed to give it a sense of uniqueness, was headed by Chamath Palihapitiya and played a major role in defining the strategies and tactics through which the company understood and optimized for growth (Levy, 2020). Faced with slowing user growth around early 2008, Palihapitiya came up with a new solution: instead of simply counting registered users, Facebook would now focus on measuring 'monthly active users' (Schultz, 2014). In a lecture at Stanford University in 2014, Alex Schultz, now VP of growth at Facebook, explained how every start-up needs a 'North Star' shining light on where the company wants to go. At Facebook, Schultz said, the North Star was monthly active users, a metric that everyone internally at Facebook was held to, and the most important number published externally as the company's benchmark.

In order to get at 'monthly active users', there first had to be what Schultz described as a 'magic moment' that got people hooked to the site. At Facebook, the magic moment was achieved when a user had at least ten friends. At ten friends, the feed would feel interesting and diverse enough for users to return, it figured. A key strategy for Facebook, as already described in the previous chapter, was to build a system around the 'real identities' of people using friendship connections as a unique selling point. Unlike the long-defunct social networking site MySpace where users could create any identity they liked (Angwin, 2009: 55), Facebook was premised on real names, real identities and real friends. The profile and the profile picture were one of the most valuable resources that Facebook deployed in order to attract new users. As Schultz explained, seeing the face of your friends helped create that magic moment, which made people want to come back to the site and keep using it.

As a consequence, Facebook put much effort into developing features to find, maintain and service friendship practices. One of the most prominent features to come out of the growth team was the People You May Know (PYMK) feature. Launched in August 2008, PYMK is a feature that selects potential friend candidates for each user. There are not many 'rules' when it comes to growing an online business, but 'network effects' or Metcalfe's law is one of them – the idea that the value of a network grows exponentially with the number of people joining. Based on the realization that new users are likely to abandon the site if they don't have ample reason (read: friends) to stay, the friend suggestion feature proved one of the most effective tools for growing a consistent user base.

Platform programmability

In Facebook's formative years, much emphasis was put on the role of third-party developers in growing its business. In doing so, Facebook has opted for two main strategies: an aggressive acquisition strategy of buying up all real competition and a platform strategy of teaming up with and granting crucial data and software resources to third-party developers. The former strategy has led to the acquisition of, among others, the virtual reality technology Oculus VR, Inc. in 2014, the messenger application WhatsApp Inc. and the popular photo-sharing application Instagram, both in 2012. This acquisition strategy did not just allow Facebook to keep possible competition in check or create new franchises to expand its business domains. Importantly, buying services and products that did something that Facebook had not yet found a way to do well, meant that it acquired the desired service and the brain-power behind. As Martinez (2018) suggests, acquiring seemingly small start-ups also served to revitalize Facebook's internal culture, making sure that the entrepreneurial spirit reminiscent of the company's early days still persisted. The latter strategy of granting data access and offering software development tools to third-party developers is really just the other side of the coin. If the acquisition strategy internalized outside resources, the third-party strategy made sure to externalize and crowdsource new solutions. By offering various technical resources, such as APIs and software development kits (SDK) to external developers and organizations to build applications, Facebook in effect created institutional dependencies among its vast network of partners (Helmond et al., 2019; Nieborg and Helmond, 2019). Both strategies significantly helped Facebook's grow, both as a platform and as a business partner.

Helmond et al. (2019) describe the expansion of Facebook's programmability as an evolution comprising four distinct stages. In stage one (2006–2010), the company was primarily concerned with expanding its social networking site, including the scaling efforts of the growth team described above as well as the launch of the Facebook Development Platform. Launched at a major press/developer event on 24 May 2007, Facebook Platform offered a number of third-party developers almost unrestricted access to Facebook data and functionality. Though 'platform' has become one of the most debated terms in internet studies during the past decade, the Facebook

Platform can be understood in the computational sense as 'an infrastructure that supports the design and use of particular applications' (Gillespie, 2010: 349).[6] Programmability, by extension, describes the process through which platforms are both changeable and mutable, and in its very mutability creates flows of data collection that seem to strengthen its position amid a wider ecosystem of developers and new products and services.

Only a year after the launch of Platform, 'Facebook created a new way for developers to access information from Facebook and for Facebook to bring software companies into its ecosystem' (Levy, 2020: 169). Facebook Connect, as it was called, allowed developers to use Facebook as an authentication service. By lowering the threshold for new users to start using an app and feed off the already existing user base of Facebook, Facebook Connect naturally incentivized third-party developers to build new services on top of the platform. Facebook essentially enacted its programmability through APIs and SDKs (Helmond, 2015; Plantin et al., 2018). 'Platformization', as Helmond (2015) calls it, is the process by which Facebook works to decentralize data production and recentralize data collection, making everything part of the wider Facebook ecosystem (see also Chapter 2). In turning Facebook into a developer environment, Helmond (2015: 1) argues, Facebook essentially transformed from being a social network site into a social media platform.

Games, in particular, have played a pivotal role in expanding Facebook's ecosystem. Premised on the assumption that people would spend more time on Facebook when playing games, game developers were particularly welcome as platform partners. This core investment strategy paid off. In 2009, Zynga had become the most popular developer on Facebook, with its hit game FarmVille claiming the title 'most popular video game in America' in 2010 (Liszkiewicz, 2010). Zynga's success was in no small part due to its symbiotic relationship with Facebook (Goggin, 2014; Poell, Nieborg and Duffy, 2021). For Facebook, its partnership with Zynga proved very lucrative too, accounting for 12% of Facebook's total profits in 2011 (Willson and Leaver, 2015). Facebook's Graph API enabled developers like Zynga to access important information about Facebook users, including their friendship connections, Likes, locations, updates, photos and more. As we will discuss in Chapter 6, the repercussions of this very open door policy for data access led to one of the biggest scandals Facebook has faced to data, its permissive data sharing with the analytics company Cambridge Analytica. In practical terms, the Graph API allowed apps and games to post 'updates on people's profiles, which would be seen by players' friends and potentially encourage them to play, too' (Solon and Farivar, 2019). One of the first things that FarmVille offered was to give 'gifts' to your Facebook friends, providing an effective nudge for new potential players (Levy, 2020: 162). Grabbing the attention of potential new users by means of their friends and seemingly harmless games ultimately created a lucrative pathway for profit. As Dave Morin, one of Facebook's key executives, put it, more apps meant more inventory for ads: 'One of the things about Facebook that's always been very straightforward is that we create experiences that are highly engaging; the business model is ads, and so the more engaging, the more ads, right?' (Levy, 2020: 170). By providing as many actions and pathways for engagement with friends as possible, games included, Facebook had designed a system that was geared towards getting people to spend as much time on the platform as possible, all the while repackaging this 'social data' and putting it back into the marketplace for monetary gain.

Stage two of Facebook's programmability (2010–14) centred on Facebook's IPO in May 2012 (Helmond et al., 2019). In one of his IPO pitches, Zuckerberg reportedly described Facebook as a 'passport' to the internet with its many integrated apps and partnerships (van Dijck, 2013a: 164).[7] This metaphor speaks directly to Facebook's empire-building efforts. As

Eric Snodgrass notes, Facebook 'sees its service as a kind of travellers' document with which one might access all domains of connectivity, breaking down a strict sense of being 'inside' or 'outside' of the Facebook platform' (2017: 182). The passport metaphor highlights the interconnectedness of Facebook's programmability, business model, and mantra of making the world more open and connected. One of the companies that fully embraced Facebook's passport metaphor from the get-go was the music streaming service Spotify. As was discussed in Chapter 2, in 2010 Facebook introduced the concept of the Open Graph along with the infamous Like button at the fourth f8 developer conference. If the social graph was the name given by Zuckerberg for mapping people's personal networks, the Open Graph would be the equivalent for mapping the activities and interests of those personal networks (Levy, 2020: 171). Spotify was one of the key partners in this highly publicized event, acting as a test case for the prospect of having apps broadcast their activities to people's personal networks via the Facebook News Feed. This strategic partnership also coincided with Spotify – a native of Sweden – looking to enter the American market. Using Facebook Connect and the Open Graph, Spotify announced that all new Spotify accounts would require a Facebook login: 'Think of it as like a virtual "passport", designed to make the experience smoother and easier, with one less username and password to remember', Spotify's representative told Evolver. fm (Baym, 2011).

Once the third-party development platform was firmly in place, Facebook turned its attention more directly to partnerships with other businesses and advertising technology companies. Just as the Graph API and SDKs made it possible for all kinds of third-party developers to build apps and businesses on top of Facebook's platform, the introduction of the Ads API in August 2011 made it possible for developers to build their own advertising technologies on top of Facebook's programmable platform (Helmond et al., 2019: 130). Up until

2011, for about two years, the Ads API had only been available in limited private beta to a few select vendors. The highly restricted API access in the interim years meant that the ad clients who did have access got a huge head start in the advertising race and marketplace of Facebook. Companies such as Marin Software, Kenshoo and Brand Networks, who received early access, are now long-term official partners and leading advertising companies. As Helmond et al. found in their work on the evolution of the Facebook partnership ecosystem, at least 42 of Facebook's marketing partners have been long-term partners, showing just how entangled Facebook is, both computationally and organizationally, 'with the global network of leading advertising and marketing technology companies' (2019: 136).

If the second stage of Facebook's programmability was all about embarking on strategic business and advertisement partnerships, the third stage (2014–18) continued the solidification and professionalization of 'Facebook's marketing development platform and its integrations in other global markets and industries' (Helmond et al., 2019: 139). Some of the major acquisitions were made in this period, including Oculus VR and WhatsApp. According to Helmond et al. (ibid.), the fourth (and so far, current) evolutionary stage (2018 to present) is marked by Facebook's efforts to 'address criticism about its market dominance and shortcomings with new programs to combat data abuse and misinformation'. As we discussed in Chapter 1, this stage involves the gradual shift in Facebook's empire-building rhetoric and rebranding efforts that seeks to render Facebook a 'privacy-focused communications platform' by integrating its 'family of apps'.

The mobile revolution

For all its focus on apps and services, by the time of its IPO, Facebook was lagging behind with its own mobile solutions (Levy, 2020; Martinez, 2016). If Facebook had put considerable efforts into its platform approach, giving third-party developers what they needed in order to create new products and services on top of the Facebook platform, they still had to find a good way to make money from their first-party mobile apps. In the face of Facebook's public offering, it became obvious that the company did not make much revenue from mobile technology. While Facebook's stock crashed, the mobile revolution was a fact, and Zuckerberg had to find a way to turn Facebook into a viable mobile company. Though Facebook had launched a mobile platform in 2007, the company had always been reluctant to integrate with existing operating systems such as Apple's iOS. Zuckerberg had been critical of developing a Facebook phone, yet persistent voices within the company thought it might be the only viable option for Facebook in facing a new mobile world. Most forcefully advocated by the growth team's Palihapitiya, Facebook did in fact launch its version of a phone in April 2013. Facebook Home, as the software was called, was designed to turn every Android device into a Facebook phone. It flopped instantly (Levy, 2020: 284). It did not take many months after the IPO, however, for Facebook to generate some revenue from mobile apps and services after all. As we will discuss in more detail in the next chapter, what proved to be Facebook's viable business model for mobile was the successful introduction of in-feed advertising and sponsored stories.

While Facebook's career in the early years was mostly focused on the desktop application, especially in the US and European context, the take-up of mobiles was substantial in the rest of the world. Despite being late to the mobile revolution, in early 2012, Zuckerberg finally 'redirected the entire company to focus on mobile' (Wagner, 2018). As Goggin (2014) writes in an article tracking Facebook's mobile strategies, much of Facebook's mobile efforts early on had to do with the internationalization of mobiles and the internet. A relatively slow bandwidth and a lack of the latest generations of wireless mobile telecommunication networks, however, meant that Facebook could not simply roll out any mobile solution but also had to get into the game of developing and contributing to the necessary infrastructure for Facebook's services to work in the first place. In order to enter the global market and get the 'next billion users' hooked to Facebook, the company had to 'make a version of Facebook that was cheaper to use' (Levy, 2020: 231), resulting in the Internet. org project launched in 2013. In practice, connecting the whole world meant entering into strategic partnerships with mobile network operators and equipment manufacturers in different parts of the world. Over the years, Facebook has collaborated with local governments and technology vendors to build and test new wireless technologies and business models. This has, for example, entailed the deployment of satellite-enabled community Wi-Fi hot spots and technologies that help expand rural connectivity in various places such as Mexico, Peru and Kenya. In Nigeria, Africa's most populous country, where over 150 million people lack access to high-speed internet, Facebook is involved in building the country's digital backbone by connecting cell towers and laying new fibre-optic cables. Similar projects have been conducted in South Africa, Uganda and many other countries (Rabinovitsj, 2019). In its effort to make the world more open and connected, especially as the world turned mobile, Facebook wasn't merely a platform but also an infrastructure.

Facebook's infrastructural mission is enacted in a number of ways, most notably through its Connectivity team. Set up to conduct research and development on new technological solutions for internet connectivity, the team works on everything from lasers to drones, satellite, terrestrial links, wireless networks and high-altitude platforms. Together with many external partners and stakeholders, Facebook Connectivity works as an umbrella platform for Facebook's global internet connectivity initiatives, including: Free Basics, Magma, the open-source software solution geared towards deploying mobile networks in hard-to-reach areas, OpenCellular, a project that seeks to expand cellular coverage to rural less densely populated areas, and Terragraph, high-speed internet solutions for dense urban areas.[8]

Facebook's first attempt at dismantling global disparities in internet access, also known as a 'first-level digital divide' (Gonzales, 2016; Hargittai, 2002) was launched in 2010 in the form of Facebook Zero. In order to combat the problem of expensive data plans and slow internet connection in large parts of the world, Facebook partnered with fifty international mobile phone operators to provide a text-only version of Facebook, without incurring data charges. These zero-rating plans, as they are called, later became the heart of Zuckerberg's more organized efforts at providing internet (aka Facebook) access for all, through the Internet.org initiative and its Free Basics app. In a white paper accompanying the launch of Internet.org, Zuckerberg described internet connectivity as a basic human right (Zuckerberg, 2013). Internet access should not just be confined to the richest, most developed countries in the world, Zuckerberg claimed. Describing internet connectivity as one of the 'greatest challenges of our generation', Zuckerberg's white paper outlined a 'rough plan' for 'connecting the world', including: (a) working to improve infrastructure solutions such as data centres and servers to make internet access more affordable and more efficient in delivering data; (b) reducing the cost and use of data, by developing data compression methodologies; and (c) providing zero-rating data plans that would benefit people, mobile operators, phone manufacturers and *the world* (ibid. [emphasis mine]). Facebook was not just framed as a humanitarian actor but a global rescuer of sorts. The internet is good for the world – even a human right – the argument went, and by serving as a proxy for the internet, Free Basics would be Facebook's greatest humanitarian project. Free Basics would be the door that allows access to a room full of 'knowledge, experience and progress' (Zuckerberg, 2013: 9). As of July

2019, Free Basics is available in 65 countries, half of which are African countries (Nothias, 2020).

'Who could possibly be against this?' Zuckerberg asked in an op-ed for the *Times of India* (Hempel, 2018). As it turned out, quite a lot of people. While Facebook maintained that Free Basics was part of its larger effort to 'connect the unconnected' (Prasad, 2018), others see it as an attempt to colonize the global south by infrastructural means (Arora, 2019; Madianou, 2019). As Madianou writes, Free Basics is colonial in attitude, it claims to 'give "free" internet to poor populations' when all it does is to provide access to Facebook's bare bones and a handful of other apps (2019: 3). To many, Facebook's Free Basics is a walled garden, a commercial trap that seeks to convert the global poor into Facebook users by purporting to provide the internet for free (Arola, 2019). While the use areas for people connected to Free Basics are rather limited – a few services and some generic Western-produced content – the potential gain for Facebook is huge. For Facebook, providing a door to the internet is ultimately a vital part of its business model. In other words, access for all in this case means access to Facebook non-users, or a business opportunity worth five billion eyeballs.

Facebook's infrastructuralism does merely reflect dubious political projects such as Free Basics but also necessitates a lot of power and energy at the material level. Important research has been conducted on the environmental impacts, energy expenditures, power use and data footprints of computational media (Brodie, 2020; Cubitt et al., 2011; Gabrys, 2013; Hogan, 2015; Thylstrup, 2019). If, as Facebook product manager Anuj Madan says in a video about Facebook's Terragraph project, '[e]qual access to data across the city is something that is becoming as fundamental as having access to water or electricity', then we must also question the increased environmental costs of the mobile revolution. As Mél Hogan writes, questions of the 'material impacts of Facebook's perpetual feed' and 'Facebook's social, political, material, and environmental impacts' have largely gone unanswered (2015: 4). In examining Facebook's data centres, Hogan argues that media researchers need to move beyond the notion of Facebook residing in the cloud to also consider the very real environmental tolls created by Facebook's data centres.[9]

To be clear, Facebook and other tech companies are not oblivious to their environmental responsibilities. In fact, discourses of sustainability and renewable energy proliferate in Facebook's own promotional materials. Zuckerberg often talks about climate change. As he wrote in a Facebook post after a visit to North Dakota in 2017 to learn about the fracking community: 'I believe stopping climate change is one of the most important challenges of our generation' (Zuckerberg, 2017c). For Zuckerberg, this means speaking up against environmental issues, condemning Trump's decision to withdraw the US out of the Paris Agreement, and to build all Facebook's data centres on 100 percent renewable energy. Yet, as Hogan (2018) argues, for all of Facebook's greening efforts, the company is still responsible for monumentalizing consumption. 'No matter how green data centers become, and no matter how innovative renewable energy is', Hogan writes, 'there is a larger media ecosystem undergirding it – a world of limited natural resources, technotrash, toxic bodies, and e-waste – driven by ideals of innovation based on the perpetual marketing of the new' (2018: 647). That is, no matter how green Facebook's cycle of production becomes, it is still a cycle of production geared to generate more and more consumption at a time when we should be doing exactly the opposite, if saving the planet is what we want.

Concluding remarks

As we are writing in 2020, at a time of perpetual crisis, some reflections on Facebook's alleged expansion seems in place. While we have mainly discussed the core features and moments of Facebook's techno-economic evolution as it pertains to the company's earlier stages of programmability, explaining how Facebook became an empire of sorts, the current evolutionary stage poignantly reveals the limits of Facebook's expansionist and imperial logics. User backlash and tech criticism has always been part of Facebook's development as a platform and global communication infrastructure. Yet, the current environment of heightened political turmoil, racial injustice, misogyny, polluted information is putting Facebook to a real test. We are no longer merely witnessing occasional missteps or glitches in the ways in which Facebook handles privacy, data access or political advertising. The missteps have become normal and as such not missteps but steps to be expected instead. These days, Mark Zuckerberg seems to spend more time apologizing and witnessing in Congress than on developing new 'cool' features. As with all infrastructure, previous decisions can be difficult or impossible to undo. If Facebook used to be more than generous with how it handled access to user data before (especially during its empire-building phase *c.* 2010–14), now hubris bites its tail.

To understand where Facebook is at today, politically and socially (as will be the topic of Chapter 6), we must understand the decisions made in the past and how those still linger in the system (the topic of this chapter). Whether we are talking about the ways in which Facebook's algorithms have been geared towards optimizing the popular and the spectacular, the annexation of the News Feed for commercial purposes, Facebook's mobile colonization of emerging economies or deceptive sustainability, the story of expansion necessarily also entails its possible downfall. Unlike the never-ending News Feed that is designed to update in real time, responding to users' scrolling patterns, the story about Facebook is not that seamless. Only time will tell what consequences Facebook's hubris has in the long run. What we do know, however, is that for the time being Facebook has *won* the internet. It won the social networking game. It *did* provide a place for people to connect. It is *the* platform of choice for most people in the world. Facebook did not just win the internet, but increasingly also owns it. Together with a handful of other companies, including Google, Facebook has become a global advertising bastion. What this means and how it plays out will be the topic of the next chapter.

CHAPTER FIVE

Monetizing You: Facebook's advertising ecosystem

> [W]hat we want to do with our ad system is have something that fits very organically into what people are already doing on our site.
>
> Mark Zuckerberg (2008)

> Nothing influences a person more than a recommendation from a trusted friend.
>
> Mark Zuckerberg (2007)[1]

In an interview with Sarah Lacy at the 2008 SXSW, Zuckerberg quite tellingly lays bare his vision on monetization that suggests a fundamental intertwining between people's communicative desires and commercial opportunities through advertising: 'We're part of a larger trend that people are communicating more with each other and we think that there is a way of advertising that is basically just people endorsing it' (AllFacebook, 2008). In this early interview, Zuckerberg does not distinguish between users' way of using the site and monetization. As he elaborates, these things are part of the same 'organic' monetization system that was driving Facebook's 'economic engine'. All Facebook wants to do, Zuckerberg explained, is to 'help people share information' and because people already 'advertise on the site and endorse things', developing a monetization system that naturally feeds off this type of behaviour is just the most obvious thing to do. Zuckerberg elaborates:

> People are sharing information and if that can be used in endorsements that people agree to then that can be a very

effective ad system. The performance of those ads means
they're trusted. Someone actually cared about or said they
wanted to use something. It fits way better and that's what
people are coming to our site to do, to learn what's going on
with their friends and communicate. (AllFacebook, 2008)

This is the crux: Facebook is an advertising company through
and through, though it took Facebook many years to find a
way to viable avenue for monetization and to openly admit
that advertising was in fact at the core of its business model.
While Zuckerberg did openly talk about advertising and
Facebook's ad strategies (or lack thereof), the emphasis
seemed to be on the inconspicuousness of the ads as part
of an organic and natural social experience. That is, ads
were not to distract from the 'real' purpose of Facebook,
which was to connect friends and family. Early on, Facebook
worked on refining its business model and ad systems. For
all the insistence on hacker culture and the cultivation of the
nerdy coder, 'Facebook was always supposed to be profitable'
(Levy, 2020: 177). As we discussed in the previous chapter on
growing the company and shaping up its platform approach,
making money from Facebook became an intrinsic part of
product development and the growth team's efforts to inter-
nationalize and expand the platform beyond its immediate
boundaries. If Facebook was mostly concerned with growing
its user base and expanding its platform during the early
years, once it had reached critical mass and status as the
world's leading global social network site, it became clear that
Facebook, unlike any other company, was sitting on a gold
mine ready to be extracted.

Facebook is not only an advertising company, but a special
kind. It is an advertising company that works not by simply
distributing ads to people, but by using people actively in the
production and distribution process. Facebook's social graph
also extends to ads. Over the years, Facebook has created a
system that fundamentally hinges on people's immaterial
labour, via their clicks, Likes, shares, comments, buys, listens,

watches, even their lurking. This system was carefully archi-
tected, engineered and designed. In the previous chapter, we
looked at how Facebook built its empire, feature by feature,
product by product, via strategic hiring, by turning itself into
a developer environment offering APIs and SDKs, creating a
universal Facebook login for connected websites and apps,
becoming a mobile company and much more. However, what
really set Facebook apart from the rest were the News Feed
and the Like button, two features that helped Facebook gather
the 'behavioural surplus' (Zuboff, 2019) needed to drive the
social advertising and surveillance complex that the company
would eventually turn into.

If we want to understand what makes Facebook Facebook,
we also need to think of Facebook as a data-driven advertising
business and ecosystem. Two questions will guide the discussions in this chapter: How did the techno-economic context
of the Web, through advertising and tracking technologies,
shape Facebook's business model and monetization strategies? What form of advertising company did Facebook
evolve into, and how can we think of Facebook's position
amid a broader ad-tech-surveillance complex?

The chapter proceeds as follows. First, it provides a brief
history of digital advertising. In order to understand how
Facebook is an ad business, we need to understand how
digital advertising evolved in the context of the commercial
Web and the technical, economic and political developments
that tied the advertising industry and the Web together
around the logic of what Shoshanna Zuboff calls surveillance capitalism. For Zuboff, 'surveillance capitalism claims
human experience as free raw material for translation
into behavioural data' (2019:8). Instead of feeding mainly
on labour as in Marx's notion of capitalism, the vampire
constituting surveillance capitalism feeds on all aspects of
human experience, including, but not confined to, labour.
As Zuboff explains, Google invented and perfected surveillance capitalism by developing a business model around

the expropriation of people's online behaviours, profiling browsing habits, Likes and clicks for commercial purposes. Facebook took on this logic wholeheartedly. If Facebook insists on being a technology company, as it often does, then we are well reminded that 'technologies are always economic means, not ends in themselves' (Zuboff, 2019: 15). For a company that earns virtually all its money from advertising revenue, understanding the digital advertising ecosystem and Facebook's place in it is imperative. The chapter then proceeds to describe the specifics of Facebook's advertising infrastructure.

Monitoring and targeting YOU: The rise of behavioural advertising

Approaches to advertising have changed dramatically throughout the history of mass media, from radio, cinema and television to the internet and social media. Advertising subsidies have been, and continue to be, one of the core ways of financing the media and tech industries. Whereas publishers make and produce content, advertisers subsidize it by paying for the right to persuade the publisher's audience to purchase the product or service (Couldry and Turow, 2014: 1712). The biggest challenge for the advertising industry has always been to understand the impulses of the marketplace and to target consumers more effectively. Yet, as Dallas Smythe (1981) has influentially argued in what is known as the 'audience commodity' thesis, the audience has never been a passive consumer but a central part of the advertising-oriented political economy of the media. For Smythe, the value of audiences extended beyond their quantity (i.e. the number of viewers), to also include their demographics and their buying habits on a general level (Elmer, 2019). The value of audiences at a general and habitual level is very much at the core of behavioural advertising as we know it today, understood as the tracking and monitoring of users' online and increasingly offline behaviours and the process of displaying digital advertisements based on this tracking.

While the extent to which people are tracked and profiled at the individual level online is unique, quantified audience insights for targeting audiences in a fragmented media landscape are not. Couldry and Turow (2014) note how the fascination with data crunching in media planning, buying and evaluation in the advertising industry had already begun in the 1980s. Others claim that the principles of automation and optimization in advertising could already be found in the 1950s (McGuigan, 2019). Traditionally, advertisers have tried to identify consumer segments along demographic lines such as age, gender, income, geography and other social economic indicators. With the rise of big data and consumer insight based on ubiquitous data-gathering and surveillance mechanisms, the advertising industry has changed accordingly. Now, the audience and consumer are no longer confined to profiling according to the same grand demographic segments as before, but can use much more fine-grained and personalized categories. That is not to say that demographics do not matter any more, or that targeting doesn't happen using demographic markers. As evidenced by stories of racially biased ads in the housing market and many other accounts, demographics matter quite a bit.

Yet, the plethora of available technologies aimed at tracking people's actions offline and online means that ads can now be targeted based on very specific individual and behavioural traits rather than merely demographic variables. To take my own Facebook 'ad preferences' as an example.[2] According to the information available in my ad settings, Facebook currently lists hundreds of my alleged interests that influence what ads I will see, including: 'Scandinavian design', Office chair', 'Cloud computing', 'Soul music', 'Alaska', and 'Surfing'. While I sort of admit to liking how Facebook seems to 'see me', the granularity emerging from the accumulated set of data is creepily precise. Although I do not surf, I might indeed want to be a person who knows how to surf. Yes, I love Scandinavian design and Alaska is my dream vacation destination. These categories need not be reflective of my actual purchases, actions or hobbies. In fact, as John Cheney-Lippold argues, 'you are rarely "you" online [...] rather, we are temporary members of different emerging categories' (2017: 4). What the detailed targeting options of Facebook advertising allow for, is not just the targeting of an already existing person but more importantly, the making up of people, as the philosopher Ian Hacking (1990) would say. In writing about the history of statistics, Ian Hacking (1990; 2007) offers the idea of 'making up people' as a way of thinking through the fabrication of categories of people in the service of managing populations, epitomized through insti-tutionalized technological means such as census statistics. As Hacking suggests, 'those kinds of people would not have existed, as a kind of people, until they had been so classified, organized and taxed' (Hacking, 2007: 288). What this means is that the 'personal' is an emerging category based on 'algorithmic identities' (Cheney-Lippold, 2017) that are temporarily assembled to reflect and promote corporate goals (Kant, 2020). What counts is how good the algorithms are at extracting meaningful patterns from whatever explicit or implicit information users have provided and how well those patterns in turn map onto individuals' dreams, desires or aspirations. As we will see in the next chapter, it was precisely the kind of psycho-demographic data reminiscent of the Facebook ad preference section that served as the basis for Cambridge Analytica's profiling work.

The turn to micro-targeting – the use of detailed demographic, behavioural and personal information to target specific attributes of people – and identity profiling in the ad industry was very much propelled by a combination of new technological methods and media-buying processes. As Joseph Turow explains in his book *Daily You*, digital advertising evolved through 'digital fingerprinting', including cookies, flash cookies, tracking pixels, Web beacons and mobile apps, and new media-buying processes based on new actors and systems that allowed for 'buying' individuals with particular characteristics, in real time (2012: 5). In particular, the 'click' and the 'cookie', Turow writes, became key mechanisms around which digital marketers and publishers planned their content strategies and digital futures. As the Web evolved into a free and open space (see Chapter 1), at least in terms of rhetoric and user expectation, publishers soon had to juggle with an environment in which people were not accustomed to paying, or willing to pay, for content. What followed were years of experimenting with new ad formats, including banner advertising, hot links, clickable ads, clickable banners and much more.

Yet, of all the technologies besides the browser itself, the cookie 'would do more to shape advertising – and social attention – on the Web than any other invention' (Turow, 2012: 48). Cookies are memory devices that track and remember a user's browsing history. Cookies are basically small pieces of data used by Web servers to track and monitor information relating to various 'states' (e.g. items added to a shopping cart, logins, clicks and visits to websites) and stored locally on the client computer by the Web browser. For advertisers, cookies proved revolutionary insofar as they allowed them to measure clicks and user behaviour beyond a single website. As Turow notes, savvy marketing entrepreneurs realized that by placing cookies across sites, they could learn what individuals did after visiting one site and thus serve more targeted ads. Moreover, 'data about what the cookie owner learned about the individual could be added to the cookie and revenues could be shared with all participating sites' (Turow, 2012: 55).

What followed from these new possibilities for tracking a user's journey across the Web was a new type of advertising company – the ad network. As Elinor Carmi explains, 'advertising networks are companies that work with multiple websites to have better insights of what and where people do things across many spaces' (2020a: 129). Ad networks emerged as an intermediary between Web publishers and marketers, offering fully outsourced advertising services. Importantly, ad networks eased the 'burdens of labour and technical expertise' and lowered the 'barriers to participation in the Web advertising market' (Crain, 2019: 334). DoubleClick, one of the most successful of these ad networks, which was acquired by Google in 2007, developed a technical system as early as 1997 that could deliver targeted ads in nearly real time under the tag line of delivering the 'right message to the right person at the right time'. Sounds familiar, right? This is just what Facebook promises when describing the purpose of its News Feed as delivering 'the right content to the right people at the right time'? (see previous chapter).

In order for the commercial Web to work, and for ad networks to flourish, Web browsing essentially had to be de-anonymized. Third-party cookies played an instrumental role by helping to identify the 'right person' to be targeted. A common distinction is made between first-party and third-party cookies (Hoofnagle et al., 2012). While only the website owner can read the information encapsuled by first-party cookies, third-party cookies are set by other websites and are thus outside of the website owner's direct control. Usually, third-party cookies are operated by companies in the advertising industry. For example, as explained on the BBC's cookie and browser setting information page, BBC web pages may contain a plethora of third-party cookies set by the owners of the website (BBC, 2020). Also, if a user shares a link to a BBC page on Facebook, Facebook may set a cookie on the user's browser. How convenient, then, that Facebook was built around a culture of sharing, where users are habitually encouraged to share links and content from around the Web – not to mention the fact that it enabled Facebook to track users across the Web, outside of its own domain.

In tandem with ad networks, search advertising grew as a dominant form of Web advertising. While different approaches and players existed at the turn of the 2000s, Google seized this market and quickly became the market leader. As Crain (2019: 336) describes, instead of inferring from consumers' shopping habits, Google used people's search terms as the basis for their profiling and targeting of potential consumers. For Zuboff, the discovery of 'behavioural surplus', as she calls Google's expropriation of people's search terms for ads, constitutes a decisive moment in the nascent development of surveillance capitalism. Originally, Google had been reluctant to build its search engine on an advertising model. However, following the burst of the dotcom bubble in the early 2000s Google changed its approach to satisfy investors, utilizing the growing stores of search signals to improve the profitability of ads (Zuboff, 2019: 75). Taking a cue from the business model of ad networks, Google created an ad program called 'AdSense' in 2003, offering Web publishers the opportunity to host Google contextual ads, turning every single website into a monetizable object. An important reason for why AdSense became such a success was the way in which it allowed every single blogger and website owner to add ads to their website, thereby exploding the opportunities and possible ad inventory. All of a sudden, advertisers could advertise on millions of blogs and websites and everyone could potentially start to earn money from their blog or website. In a matter of just a few years, AdSense captured as much as 40% of all Web advertising expenditures (Crain, 2019). In 2007, Google finally acquired DoubleClick in a bidding war with Microsoft, becoming the biggest leader in Web advertising. Until Facebook's rapid growth, Google reigned over the ad market more or less alone. Today, their combined power is commonly referred to as a 'digital ad duopoly', where the two companies as of early 2020 are reported to share approximately 60% of the global online ad market.[3]

The combination of systems aimed at consumer monitoring and the gathering of data to create fine-grained personal profiles in order to be able to target customized audiences have led to a digital advertising industry centred on micro-targeting, behavioural and programmatic advertising. As we have seen, these kinds of advertising models based on data tracking evolved in a digital landscape designed to monitor individuals' use of the internet in order to feed the gradual segmentation and classification of people into advertising-friendly profiles. Technically, as Hoofnagle et al. (2012) write, behavioural advertising was fuelled by a shift from standard cookies to more advanced tracking technologies, including ETags, Flash Cookies, HTML5 local storage and Evercookies. While cookies revolutionized online advertising by allowing advertisers, brands and Web publishers to learn more about users' browsing and consumption patterns, it was not until social network sites allowed those insights to be mapped onto personal identifiable information that the potential of behaviour advertising became more mainstream. Not only do platforms like Facebook have access to much richer data, including user-generated content, self-reported demographics, information about friends, Web browsing traces etc. But, as Andreou et al. (2018: 1) point out, Facebook also knows the 'detailed personally identifiable information of users, and they often allow advertisers to target users based on this information. In comparison, traditional advertisers often only track user browsing behaviours via opaque cookies.'

Although micro-targeting, behavioural and programmatic advertising is now commonplace at Facebook, the company's first attempts at mobilizing user data for advertising purposes was a complete disaster. Facebook first introduced behavioural targeting through its now infamous Beacon advertising program. Launched in autumn 2007, Beacon was modelled on a word-of-mouth principle, whereby users' interactions and behaviour with 'partners' who had signed up for the program were packaged into a commercial message and then distributed to their friends on Facebook, illustrated with the familiar face of the purchasing friend (Hoy and Milne, 2010: 30). According to the Beacon program, users' actions could potentially be repurposed into a commercial message on their friends' News Feeds. For example, whenever a user would post an item for sale, complete a purchase, score a high score on an online game or just view a video, these actions could potentially be formatted into a Facebook ad (Facebook, 2007c). In one highly publicized account, boyd and Harigittai (2010) recount how '[A] man purchased a diamond ring from Overstock.com only to learn that this information was shared via Facebook.' Not only did his wife learn about this via Facebook, but the message that contained a link to the site also highlighted that the ring had been purchased on sale. Needless to say, the Beacon advertising program sparked a huge public outcry. Not only was it a very transgressive way of using people's trusted relationships for commercial gain, but the default settings were opt-in. The diamond ring incident was one of many mentioned in a class action lawsuit against Facebook, which eventually led to the Beacon program being shut down in September 2009. However, as we will see, Facebook held onto the core idea of using friends as advertising billboards.

Facebook, the ad company

Facebook has repeatedly emphasized in its News Feed FYI blog series that: 'Our goal is to show the right content to the right people at the right time so they don't miss the stories that are important to them' (Kacholia, 2013; Ge, 2013; Owens and Vickrey, 2014). As already hinted at, it is no coincidence that the News Feed's tag line resembles DoubleClick's mission to deliver targeted advertising to the right people at the right time. Just like DoubleClick and Google, Facebook is an advertising company at heart. Building an effective ad system based on people's organic behaviour and transactional data reflects the kind of surveillance capitalism and 'behavioural surplus' described by Zuboff (2019). If Google laid the ground for this kind of business model, especially in the context of search, Facebook was sitting on a gold mine of a completely different kind – trusted relationships and friends. As Zuckerberg suggested in that early interview quoted at the beginning of this chapter, friendships can be a very effective ad system. He was right. Today, Facebook makes a substantial amount of its revenue from ad sales, which amounted to $55 billion (out of $55.8 in total) in 2018. In other words, Facebook is an advertising company insofar as it makes money from selling advertising space on its various sites and services. Compared to traditional ad agencies, Facebook offers easy-to-use self-service software tools for advertising placement, measurement and management. This means that the barrier has been considerably lowered for small and medium-size enterprises to buy ads directly. With Facebook's ads for every budget and easy tools, these smaller-scale enterprises indeed account for a respectable share of Facebook's overall ad revenues (Nieborg and Helmond, 2019). Yet, one of the longest-lasting confusions and controversies surrounding Facebook is whether the company is also in the business of selling user data directly to advertisers. Pressed on this question during the 2018 congressional hearings in early April that year, Mark Zuckerberg explained it to Senator Cornyn:

> What we allow is for advertisers to tell us who they want to reach, and then we do the placement. So, if an advertiser comes to us and says, 'All right, I am a ski shop and I want to sell skis to women', then we might have some sense, because people shared skiing-related content, or said they were interested in that, they shared whether they're a woman, and then we can show the ads to the right people without that data ever changing hands and going to the advertiser. (Zuckerberg quoted in Gilbert, 2018)

Rather than reiterating the data selling meme, former product manager of ads targeting at Facebook, Antonio Martinez, portrays Facebook as an advertising infrastructure that provides the ground on which ad exchanges and transactions of value can take place. As Martinez argues, 'Facebook doesn't sell your data, it buys it.' 'By providing services to advertisers that incentivize them to let Facebook ingest the data users have generated outside Facebook', the system resembles more that of a rental agreement than a one-time purchase (2018: 328). Rather than selling the data to advertisers, Facebook insists it's in the business of doing the work for and as them. In this sense, Facebook acts both as an ad network and ad company, providing not only virtually all stages of the advertising process but also the making of the ad itself. We might think of these processes in two broad terms: from the advertiser's point of view – how to place an ad on Facebook?; and the user's point of view – why am I shown this ad? The following sections will describe these in more detail.

Facebook ads from the advertiser's perspective

Facebook ads allow businesses to publish content straight onto News Feed, with no prior connection or relationship required. An advertisement is made from the advertiser's own Facebook page. Either the ad is created and published directly from the business page or it is done through the platforms Facebook Ads Manager or Facebook Business Manager.[4] There are two types of general ads within Facebook: boosted posts and actual Facebook ads. A boost is not the same as launching an ad – instead it means the user, regardless of whether this is a regular user or business, puts some money behind a post in order to boost its visibility and longevity on the platform.[5] In what follows, I will mostly describe the more typical ads created using the Facebook Ads Manager. The whole process can be summarized as follows: an advertiser first selects an audience, then chooses some optimization criteria, uploads some text and image, and finally places a bid. Often advertisers run several ads that are related, called an ad campaign.

One of the first steps in placing an ad on Facebook involves selecting an audience in order to target people with specific interests and behaviours. Facebook offers advertisers the ability to target real user IDs and specific attributes set by Facebook.[6] This not only involves user profile data but behavioural targeting as well, that is, selecting an audience based on which pages users have previously liked and interacted with, or which websites they have visited. The ad interface allows advertisers to choose from a range of demographic characteristics, including age range, gender, language and location. As we saw with the example of my own Facebook 'ad preferences' section, advertisers may also select an audience based on interests (e.g. 'liked' pages) and online behaviour (e.g. purchases, device use, interactions). These attributes can be quite specific: for example, people who are 'new parents', have an 'affinity for high-value goods', are 'likely to engage in politics (conservative)' or are in an 'open relationship' (Andreou et al., 2018: 5).

In addition to the targeting attributes that Facebook provides by virtue of users' self-reported demographic information and actions on the platform, Facebook also offers targeting attributes sourced from data brokers (until mid-2018 through its Facebook Marketing Partners). Data brokers are companies specializing in collating as much data as possible about individuals in order to resell or share that information with others. In the US, Facebook has worked with many different data brokers, including some of the biggest players in the field: Epsilon, BlueKai, DLX, Experian and Acxiom (Martinez, 2018).[7] The attributes derived from these data brokers mainly concern financial information (e.g. income level, net worth, purchase behaviours, charity and use of credit cards), which is 'presumably more difficult for Facebook to determine from its data alone' (Andreou et al., 2018: 5). Collaborating with data brokers has the benefit of adding considerable data from offline contexts to the totality of data available to advertisers using the Facebook platform. As Venkatadri et al. (2019a) found in their study of data brokers, more than 90% of Facebook accounts in the US are linked to some kind of data broker information. Besides critical financial information, data brokers provide data from diverse sources such as voter records, criminal records, surveys and other data providers such as automotive companies, grocery stores, chemists and supermarkets (Andreou, 2018; Tynan, 2013). To give a sense of the granularity of the data that data brokers trade in just consider a US Senate hearing from 2013 in which Acxiom was described as trading in information as diverse as the kinds of holidays people take, the diseases people show an interest in, how tall they are and whether they gamble. Even more fine-grained, the company Equifax was described as trading 'information as specific as whether a consumer purchased a particular soft drink or shampoo product in the last six months, uses laxatives or yeast infection products, [...] and the number of whisky drinks consumed in the past 30 days' (US Senate Committee on Commerce, Science and Transportation, 2013).

The simplest form of audience selection, whereby an advertiser only uses Facebook attributes and manually selects a target audience, is called a core audience. Traditionally, advertisers relied on Facebook's drop-down menus and pre-formatted options to select their intended audiences. For example, an advertiser might specify that they wish to show ads to 20- to 25-year-old males who live in Oslo and who like a particular TV show. To allow advertisers to target this selection on multiple occasions, Facebook creates a group for the advertiser, which is essentially the core audience.

In addition, Facebook introduced a feature called custom audience in 2012.[8] This is an audience already known to the advertiser by virtue of an existing relationship. An advertiser may target a custom audience either by uploading a list of users' personal identifiable information or by deploying Web tracking pixels on third-party sites (Ali et al., 2019a). Technically, a pixel is just an image used to set a cookie on someone's browser. However, pixels are centred on individual people rather than on IP addresses as is the case with cookies, and are thus better suited for retargeting (e.g. showing ads to people who have already visited a specific website). In other words, pixels are for people, cookies for devices. The custom audience may, for example, contain people who have already visited a specific website, or previously bought one of the company's products. The tracking of Facebook Pixel is based on the visitor's user ID from Facebook when it registers the behaviour on the website. In this way, it is able to track actions across different sessions and devices (cookies would log actions from different devices as unique users).

A big change from traditional advertising is the use of personally identifiable information in targeting ads. This includes emails, addresses, phone numbers and birth dates. Custom audiences works by letting advertisers move their existing customer records into the Facebook advertising platform. It is probably no coincidence that subscribing to email lists and signing up for a company newsletter has become such a widespread strategy. Custom audiences are essentially a linking mechanism, enabling businesses to match their customer databases to existing Facebook profiles in order to better be able to target customers who have already engaged with them in whatever capacity before (Venkatadri et al., 2019b). By allowing advertisers to cross-reference various databases, Facebook provides a platform for businesses to develop ads/content targeted at specific users. Unsurprisingly, this feature has proven widely popular with advertisers. No longer do advertisers have to opt for approximate audiences based on attributes, as Facebook can now give them the actual users they want to target.

In addition to the core and the custom audiences, Facebook allows advertisers to target a third kind of audience, what they term the *lookalike audience*. Facebook describes it as a 'way to reach new people who are likely to be interested in your business because they're similar to your best existing customers' (Facebook for Business, 2020a). This feature 'takes a list of Facebook users provided by an advertiser (called the 'source audience') and creates a new audience of users who share 'common qualities' with those in the source audience' (Sapiezynski et al., 2019: 1). As Nadler et al. suggest, audiences created in these ways might include 'women commuters in the market for a fuel-efficient car, or registered voters in Michigan's Fifth Congressional District who share traits with gun rights activists' (2018: 14). Lookalike audiences are essentially about micro-targeting, the practice of automatically segmenting people into highly specialized and specific audiences, based on people sharing one or more particular traits or qualities. As with the 'algorithmic identities' and emerging categories described by Cheney-Lippold (2017), the members of these audiences may differ in all other respects, but because they fall right into the target group of a specific commercial product at a specific point in time, they are deemed alike.[9]

After selecting an audience, advertisers can choose to optimize for different objectives, each of which tries to maximize a different *optimization event*. As for the objectives, advertisers can choose to focus on 'Reach' (showing the ad to as many as possible), 'Traffic' (optimizing for clicks), or 'App Installs' (showing the ad to people who would be likely to install the advertiser's app) (Ali et al., 2019b). 'Optimization events' may include 'awareness' (e.g. optimizing for view), 'consideration' (e.g. optimizing for clicks) and 'conversion' (e.g. optimizing for sales) (Ali et al., 2019a). For each objective, the advertiser bids on the objective itself, in addition to speci-fying a budget cap. After the advertiser has told Facebook what their budget is – how much they are willing to spend on an ad or an ad campaign, Facebook selects which ads to show users.

Like most ad platforms, Facebook uses an 'ad auction' to determine the selection and delivery of specific ads. Whereas the advertising buying process used to take weeks to complete, with real-time bidding (RTB) processes, ads can be bought and displayed in the time it takes to load the web page. As Martinez puts it: '[E]very time you go to Facebook ... you're unleashing a mad scramble of money, data, and pixels that involve undersea fibre-optic cables, the world's best database technologies, and everything that is known about you by greedy strangers' (2016: 40). The bidding and selling process works in a similar way to stock exchanges, utilizing algorithms to automatically buy and sell one ad impression at a time. Unlike the traditional buying process of segmenting audiences and targeting larger groups of people at the same time, programmatic advertising allows advertisers to buy only the impressions they need at the price they are willing to pay.[10] Programmatic advertising is an umbrella term for a media buying and selling process that is fully automated and optimized using data and networked computing. It includes tactics such as behavioural targeting, real-time bidding and retargeting (Carmi, 2020b). The idea is that anyone can run ads on Facebook, at any budget. The exact cost of a particular ad is determined through the auction. Advertisers may set budgets according to a daily or a lifetime version of the ad, allowing Facebook to spend the 'money between and within auctions according to an algorithm that is not publicly known' (Ali et al., 2019a: 4). Whether the amount is $5 or $50,000, Facebook will try to get as many results as possible for that amount (unless advertisers manually set a bid strategy).[11]

A bid essentially represents how much an advertiser is willing to pay to achieve an optimization event from a specific user. Yet, the budget itself is not enough to determine which ads are shown to whom and when, as Facebook values 'relevant ads' over higher bids (Facebook for Business, 2020c). Facebook uses a relevance score between one and ten, with ten being the highest, to infer the positive feedback and impact a specific ad would have on a target user. According to Facebook, 'the higher the relevance score, the less it will cost to be delivered' (Facebook for Business, 2015).[12] While the different elements and stakeholders in a programmatic advertising process, like it was just described, are usually distinct and not integrated as part of the same company, this is not the case with Facebook. At Facebook, everything is integrated as part of the same ad infrastructure, turning Facebook effectively into one gigantic integrated ad tech platform.

Why users are shown specific ads

As Vaidhyanathan puts it, on Facebook 'everything is an advertisement and advertisements are everything' (2018: 82). Because ads are such an intrinsic part of Facebook, users can never be sure exactly why a certain ad is shown. Or more accurately, the why is quite simple: to earn money. What is more uncertain, however, is why exactly *that* ad, with exactly that content, at exactly that time. The only thing users can be certain about is that the why, what and when of ads are not coincidental. As we have just seen, the why of an ad is most likely a combination of many parameters, such as the advertiser's budget, optimization options, underlying assumptions and values embedded in image classifications, audience-targeting options, the bidding process and much more. Just like Google, which pioneered the idea of behavioural surplus to target 'relevant' ads, Facebook is in the business of data-driven advertising where nothing is left unpredicted.

On a general level, then, the question of why a particular user is shown an ad can be answered on an equally general level: in order to maximize profit for Facebook and its partners. Yet, Facebook patents reveal many more detailed and granular explanations worth considering. As specified in a Facebook patent called 'Communicating information in a social network system about activities from another domain', users' own actions provide one of the most important input data for generating and showing ads on Facebook:

> Rather than simply deliver an advertisement that is targeted to a particular user based on the user's preferences as,

for example, declared by the user in the user's profile page, particular embodiments present advertisements that communicate information about, or take into account, actions taken by the user as well as potentially other users in the user's network (i.e. the user's friends and other relationships and connections in the social network system). (Schoen et al., 2018)

The actions performed by a user and the user's friends need not be confined to Facebook, but can, as this and other patents describe, be related to third-party websites, the sensors and tracking of mobile devices, or to other apps and databases. For example, when a user purchases something on a particular website, Schoen et al. (2018) describe how the confirmation page typically generated by websites after a purchase may include code snippets that immediately inform Facebook about the action. This information is logged, analysed and stored by Facebook, serving to target future ads and help advertisers create more personalized ad campaigns based on the accumulated purchase history of the user. As Schoen et al. write, 'such information may also be combined with information from the user's friends to develop recommendations or to tailor ads to be targeted to the user or the user's friends' (2018: 4).

If user action plays an important role in determining which ads are shown, so do friends. On Facebook, friends play an explicit transactional role. What friends do and say and their individual relations to a specific user are all valuable data to the advertising infrastructure and company that is Facebook. There are many aspects to the understanding of friendships as a business model. There is the very basic sense in which users are fundamentally tethered together, the very connected and networked form of generating the conditions for visibility and invisibility in the first place. In Chapter 3, we discussed how friendship is big business on Facebook, how friends are put to work (e.g. recruit friends to games and other apps) and how they hold economic value. The fact that user data get assembled and aggregated with other connected users' data makes for a situation in which friendships are traded for profit. In other words, what I say and do as a Facebook user may not just fall back on myself, but may also be used to target and predict the desires, actions and interests of my Facebook friends.

More specifically, friendships may function as participation and engagement proxies, helping to generate traffic and provide traction for advertisers. Just as broadcasting and television programming used to provide a common ground and conversation starter in different social contexts (Lull, 1980), so Facebook programs sociality for financial optimization by using friendships. More than simply providing an empty vessel on which people talk to each other, or rather publish carefully crafted status updates and respond to others, Facebook helps to shape communication and conversations in specific ways. Far from leaving the happening of the social to chance, Facebook informs and packages communicative actions into an engagement-inducing form. Early on, Facebook started to package people's actions into communication stories of the type 'John commented on Anne's story', presenting it on John's friends' News Feeds as a potential story of interest. The same logic of nudging people into communicative exchanges can be seen when it comes to ad creation and presentation. On the one hand, Facebook shows ads based on friends' common affiliations and interests. On the other hand, ads are also used as social nudges. For example, as stated in a Facebook patent application on targeting advertising of groups, even if friends share 'a very low affinity based on musical taste, [they] would still receive the advertisement for the CD as a group so that they could talk about it' (Yan and Senaratna, 2013: 5). This is just one of many similar examples that show how communication is strategically informed to induce engagement and further participation on the platform.

Even more explicitly, friendships play a key role in Facebook's 'sponsored stories'. Introduced in January 2011, sponsored stories are ads rendered from Facebook user's posts and posted on their friends' News Feeds. Using 'naturally' occurring communication on Facebook, such as liking a page, as the basis for these ads, Facebook's sponsored stories are essentially founded on audience labour (Fisher, 2015). Not unlike the original Beacon framework and the social ads that were originally implemented in late 2007 (and discontinued a year later), sponsored stories piggybacks on the idea of using Facebook friends as digital ad billboards. In Chapter 3, we discussed how friendships are annexed by Facebook to generate profit. More than simply monetizing user-generated content, what people do in the name of friendship is work. As Eran Fisher writes, information about something as mundane as visiting a restaurant can be 'articulated and rendered into commodified social communication through sponsored stories' (2015: 60). By turning friends' actions into brand endorsements, this new way of social advertising arguably made ads seem more personal and relevant. Because sponsored stories are based on already occurring News Feed content, this type of advertising is even more insidious than targeted advertising, considering the very blatant way in which it is promoted as organic and natural. Fisher points out how sponsored stories are successful precisely because of 'their dissociation from marketing, persuasion and propaganda' (ibid.). That is, users tend to not think of them as advertising, which has always been the ultimate goal for any advertiser.

Concluding remarks

As we have seen in this chapter, Facebook, the ad company must be understood within the broader parameters of the commercial Web turning into a surveillance complex. By tracking people using cookies, beacons and ever-more sophisticated tracking technologies, Facebook was able to build a massive distributed database made up of user's personal information, connections and communicative actions. When Zuckerberg suggested in a 2008 interview that their ad system is something that 'fits very organically into what people are already doing on our site' (AllFacebook, 2008), he set the tone for the kind of ad company Facebook would become. While Facebook at first seemed like a fun place to share what users were thinking and doing, to Facebook, these actions and their behavioural surplus, were always meant to fuel the core of their ad-tech infrastructure and business model.

Importantly, this chapter has shown how Facebook is not just an intermediary platform but also an active producer and distributor of ads. On the one hand, Facebook's ad infrastructure is based on audience labour, both in the sense of mining user-generated data and personal information, but also in terms of enlisting users as ad billboards by translating their communicative actions into sponsored stories. When it comes to advertising, then, the platform label obviously comes too short. To think of Facebook as producing and intervening in the creation, publishing and dissemination of ads would be much more accurate. Just consider the audience selection and optimization events described above. Although an advertiser sets the target audience, Facebook may intervene. According to a Facebook patent document, if the right opportunity presents itself, Facebook may choose to show the ad to other people outside of the target group (Morris et al., 2017).

Understanding how Facebook's ad infrastructure is set up and works is also helpful for understanding how injustices and bias may be built into and perpetuated by the system. As research by Ali et al. (2019a) suggests, preventing advertisers from selecting discriminatory target audiences is only half the story. Experimenting with the Facebook ad delivery process, their research suggests that advertiser budgets and ad creative may skew the ad delivery along gender and racial lines, even when neutral ad targeting settings are used. Because women generally tend to click more on ads, Facebook charges more to reach them. As they explain, 'the higher the daily budget, the smaller the fraction of men in the audience' (Ali et al., 2019a: 14). Moreover, the researchers found images to have a relatively large effect in the ad delivery process. By changing the images only and using the same neutral ad targeting setting, Ali et al. observe how the experiments yielded significant differences in ad delivery across both racial and gender lines. Ads for jobs in the lumber industry were significantly skewed towards a white (72%) male (90%) audience, ads for cashier positions in supermarkets reached an 85% female audience and ads for taxi drivers reached a 75% Black audience (Ali et al., 2019a: 4). While it may be tempting to attribute potential ad discrimination to the choice made by advertisers in selecting their target audience (e.g. White, male, highly educated), Facebook's design choices significantly affect the ad delivery and results as well.

Ultimately, this deep dive into the advertising infrastructure of Facebook shows how framing Facebook as merely a conduit and intermediary misses out on the many ways in which Facebook itself intervenes and shapes the where, how and when of the delivery process. As Ali et al. argue, targeting audiences is not the only problematic aspect of discriminatory ads. The whole process, from the ad creation through to the bidding, has the potential for creating skewed outcomes. If the regulation of platforms such as Facebook is partly dependent on them *not* being considered as publishers or materially contributing to unlawful conduct, then the question remains as to how the systemic discrimination uncovered by Ali et al.'s research or the highlighting and promotion of users' mundane communication into explicit brand promotion isn't exactly an example of such properties.

CHAPTER SIX

Personalized politics: Facebook's profiling machinery

Breaking news: Mark Zuckerberg and Facebook just
endorsed Donald Trump for re-election.
You're probably shocked, and you might be thinking,
'How could this possibly be true?'
Well, it's not.

This is how US senator Elizabeth Warren's Facebook ad
begins. On 10 October 2019, Warren, who has become
known for her hard line on US tech companies, launched a
political ad campaign on Facebook that purposefully included
false claims about Mark Zuckerberg and President Trump.
The ad went on to say that despite the headline being false,
'what Zuckerberg has done is given Donald Trump free rein
to lie on his platform [...] If Trump tries to lie in a TV ad,
most networks will refuse to air it. But Facebook just cashes
Trump's checks.' What triggered this snarky move was a
Facebook ad released by the Trump campaign a week earlier,
falsely accusing former Vice-President Joe Biden of offering
Ukrainian officials a billion dollars to drop a case against his
son Hunter Biden. Trump's ad was seen by over five million
people (Kang, 2019). Not only did Facebook allow Trump
to run the ad, but they also refused to take it down after
Biden asked the company to remove it. The reason given by
Facebook was that the ads were from a political leader and
thus in the public interest. As Facebook's ad policies state:

> Posts and ads from politicians are generally not subjected to
> fact-checking [...] If a claim is made directly by a politician
> on their page, in an ad or on their website, it is considered
> direct speech and ineligible for our third party fact checking

program – even if the substance of that claim has been
debunked elsewhere. (Facebook for Business, 2020e)

At approximately the same time as this controversy over
misinformation in political ads went down, Mark Zuckerberg
delivered a grandiose defence of free expression in a speech he
held at Georgetown University in Washington (Zuckerberg,
2019b). In it, Zuckerberg called Facebook and other social
media platforms a kind of 'fifth estate' integral to modern
society. Tech platforms, he said, have given people a voice
without having to rely on traditional gatekeepers in media
and politics. Recounting the many times in history that
free expression has been curtailed or put to question for
the greater protection of society, Zuckerberg took a clear
stance: 'I'm here today because I believe we must continue
to stand for free expression' (Zuckerberg, 2019b). 'At the
same time', he said, 'free expression has never been absolute.'
The question of whether to remove certain content or not is
about negotiating boundaries: 'Where do you draw the line?'
(Zuckerberg, 2019b).

As we will see in this chapter, lines and boundaries
are indeed fluctuating and continually negotiated. While
policies get drafted and defended, the world does not always
obey such abstract rule-making. Unruly politicians, public
concerns, accusations, manufactured truths, democratic
values, misguided actors and capital investments intervene
and live side-by-side in a world that is more than messy.
Making decisions about what content should stay and what
to take down, Facebook is by no means exempt from this
messiness. While Zuckerberg has remained firm in his
decision not to prohibit or regulate political ads on Facebook,
what constitutes legitimate political speech is not always easy
to delineate. In spring 2019, Facebook removed some of
Warren's political ads that were calling for the dismantling
of Facebook monopoly, only to reverse course later, claiming
it would restore those ads to support 'robust debate' (Lima,

2019). More recently, in March 2020, Facebook for the first time removed some of Trump's ads for misleading information related to census participation. Indeed, as Twitter CEO Jack Dorsey wrote in a Twitter thread following Twitter's announcement to ban political ads in response to the backlash faced by Facebook's permissive policy: 'While internet advertising is incredibly powerful and very effective for commercial advertisers, that power brings significant risks to politics, where it can be used to influence votes to affect the lives of millions' (Dorsey, 2019). In the most recent turn of events, Facebook announced in early September 2020, that it would roll out 'new steps to protect the US election', for example, by not accepting new political ads in the week prior to the election and removing any misinformation about voting (Facebook, 2020b).

The controversies over political ads on Facebook reveal some important questions regarding the political role of platforms. Has Facebook become too big to handle? Do we really want a CEO of a tech company in charge of setting the rules for what is considered acceptable speech online? Why should we entrust a private company to act as one of the most important global conduits for news, especially when it comes to core democratic processes and political elections? Warren's false ad campaign quite effectively illustrates the murky business of platform politics. Taking this case as a starting point for this chapter on Facebook as a political entity, it usefully makes visible a number of issues that seem central to framing the discussion, including debates over polluted information, political advertising, electoral politics, regulation, free speech, technology, democracy, platform policies, content moderation and governance of various kinds.

We must also be wary of framing Facebook politics as a story about Western democracies only. As journalist Julia Carrie Wong points out in the *Guardian*, for all the emphasis on 'free expression' and 'free speech', Zuckerberg seems to forget 'that only a small fraction (less than 10%) of Facebook's

2.45 billion users live in *this* [US] democracy, and many live in countries that are not democratic at all' (Wong, 2019 [emphasis in the original]). Moreover, while the events of 2011, colloquially referred to as the Arab Spring, may have helped boost Facebook's reputation as a global platform for social movements and democratic change, far darker stories have continued to emerge about the ways in which authoritarian regimes use Facebook to organize counter-movements and fuel atrocities. As such, we need to ask questions about Facebook's global impact and political power, especially in countries that suffer from authoritarian control and undemocratic processes. If Facebook is both a propaganda machine and a conduit for free speech, what do these apparently irreconcilable dimensions mean for an understanding of Facebook's political role?

The politics of the political

As with most aspects of Facebook, whether we are talking about friendships, sociality or community, the politics constitutive of and constituted by Facebook are fraught with deep ambivalence and a need to be understood holistically. What this means is that there is no one way in which Facebook is political or involved in politics. On a basic level, we might want to distinguish between two nominal definitions of politics. According to standard dictionary definitions, politics in a more narrow sense pertains to the 'activities associated with the governance of a country or area'. In a broader sense, politics refers to 'the principles relating to or inherent in a sphere, activity, or thing'.[1] If the former encompasses party politics, government, public and state affairs, the latter addresses the ways in which various domains (beyond electoral or state politics) are involved in power struggles, often described as the politics *of* X. The adjective 'political' may refer both to the practices of government and other state actors, and the practices of those who are engaged in influencing the actors in power. Furthermore, the political can be understood as that which pertains to the public sphere and ideas of good government (MacCabe and Yanacek, 2018). What complicates matters more is the proliferation and different uses of both 'politics' and 'political'. As Gerard de Vries notes, 'we carelessly speak of the politics of almost anything' (2007: 781–2). What used to be a concept referring to the particular decision-making capacities and activities of state-related actors is no longer confined to such a narrow understanding.

When speaking alternatively of Facebook politics, the politics of Facebook, or Facebook as political, what I mean is really a mixed bag. Firstly, there is the most common understanding, pertaining to electoral politics: how Facebook has become a central part of electoral and party politics, its role in political campaigning, and how it may potentially be used to influence voter behaviour, and the ways in which Facebook's advertising tools are extensively mobilized in elections. Secondly, there is the contentious sense: how Facebook is used to organize political protests, mobilize social movements or mediate political activism (e.g. Treré, 2018; Howard et al., 2011; Wolfsfeld et al., 2013; Valenzuela, 2013). There is also the extreme case: how Facebook is utilized as a disinformation machine, or the ways in which Facebook is used by authoritarian regimes to curtail said protests, control populations and, in some cases, lead to atrocities. Fourth, there is the regulatory sense: how Facebook is governed by the law and how the platform in turn governs use by way of its policies and standards. There is, too, the technical sense in which things have or perform politics: how data-driven mechanisms shape publics and help to orient information flows in various ways, or how the algorithmic logic of the News Feed works to make some actors and messages more visible than others based on metrics that prey on emotions and popularity. Sixth, there is the vernacular and every-dayness of politics: how Facebook is used in everyday life, and how Facebook is understood as political by the people using the platform across different sites (see Miller et al., 2016). This also corresponds to Foucault's (1982) notion of the microphysics, or micropolitics, of power, understood as a kind of power that exists at the local level of individuals' social and cultural practices. Finally, there is the ontological sense, highlighting a domain or thing's world-making capacities: how Facebook shapes realities in different ways, making some things matter more than others, and setting the conditions around which things take shape and people get oriented in various ways.

Needless to say, there are many more senses in which Facebook is political. Like Facebook itself, its politics are multidimensional and therefore difficult to grasp. The seven dimensions outlined above are not exhaustive of what might be considered Facebook politics; nor are they necessarily distinct. For example, the political economy of Facebook is not distinct from the regulatory, technical or ontological sense, but is implicated in all of them. As science and technology studies remind us, technologies both embody social relations and have profound social consequences, which makes them political (Winner, 1986). For example, Facebook's News Feed and its algorithmic ordering and ranking carry descriptions or 'scripts' (Akrich, 1992) of what is considered desired use of the system (see Chapter 4). By no means a neutral platform, then, the very design of Facebook discriminates against certain actors while privileging others (see Chapters 2 and 3). On Facebook, design and engineering intersect with the possibilities for free and equal expression, information access and news consumption.

The opening example illuminates the many intersecting versions of the political: how ad policies help to shape the conditions for public speech, electoral processes and campaign politics. More fundamentally, ad policies that allow false political ads to be distributed when their sender is a recognized politician do not just help to define what is considered a legitimate politician, but also perform an ontological politics (Mol, 1999). This is not a politics concerned with who gets to speak, but rather with the kind of reality that takes shape around and because of it (in this case, the rules laid down in the Facebook ad policies). In Facebook's terms, this means a reality in which so-called legitimate political actors enjoy the privilege of distributing false claims without being held accountable by the distributing platform. It is also a reality that operates with a specific definition of politicians as 'candidates running for office, current office holders – and, by extension, many of their cabinet appointees – along with political parties and their leaders' (Facebook Business, 2020). It is also a reality that makes no distinction between politics and consumption, a reality that is increasingly shaped by the intertwining of advertising, data-driven electoral politics and the algorithmic shaping of targeted publics. While these world-making capacities may not always be easy to grasp, the following sections telling some of the more conventional political stories about Facebook's political role should ultimately be understood as forming part of Facebook's ontological politics.

Elections and political campaigns

When we think of Facebook and politics, we often think of how Facebook is being used as a platform for political communication, in political campaigning, and as part of elections. Much has been said and written about these topics, of course, and there are multiple scholarly fields that have specialized in studying how the internet and social media are used by politicians and other political actors. One of the main questions that scholars have been grappling with is whether platforms like Facebook have the power to influence elections and their results. The 'no' camp might say that Facebook does not influence elections because there is no causal relationship to speak of. The 'yes' camp might say that Facebook indeed influences elections because even the smallest margins may have profound effects. A much-cited study published in *Nature* on Facebook's role in the 2010 US congressional elections indicated that Facebook could indeed be a factor in affecting real-world voting behaviour (Bond et al., 2012). Both camps are right, provided we do not take them at face value without interrogating their contexts. More accurate would be to say that there is no simple or one-dimensional answer to this question. It depends on what else we take into account in the claim-making process.

As with most social phenomena, the relationship between media and politics is not a one-way street. To take the 2016 US presidential election as the most obvious example, if we were simply to answer 'no' to the question of Facebook's influence, we would run the risk of stopping the conversation even before it started. Answering 'yes', however, would be to let a lot of other actors off the hook. The 2016 US presidential election resulting in Donald Trump becoming the 45th President of the United States may have come as a great shock and utter surprise, but to say that Facebook caused it to happen is a truth that needs modifying. Alongside Facebook's undeniable role in the election, we find many other ingredients that played their part, including (but not limited to) growing populist sentiments, hyper-partisan news outlets, internet trolling, media manipulation, neoliberalism, and personalized and mediatized politics (Benkler et al., 2017; Enli, 2017; Hallin, 2019; Marwick and Lewis, 2017). Rather than considering the question of Facebook's role in electoral politics in isolation, then, we need to understand the relationship as part of larger developments occurring in the media sphere.

As scholars in political communication have long argued, changes in the media shape the conditions for political communication in important ways (Blumer and Kavanaugh, 1999; Chadwick, 2013; Kreiss, 2016; Norris, 2000). Where television and mass media shaped a communication environment that was characterized by information abundance and a 24-hour news service, the internet and digital communication technologies have only intensified this logic and added to the 'hydra-headed beast [...] clamoring to be fed' (Blumer and Kavanaugh, 1999: 213). Before the rise of social media, political campaigns were all about 'message discipline and message control', as relying on paid media for political communication was 'horrendously expensive' (Johnson and Perlmutter, 2010: 555). The internet and social media changed the conditions for political communication quite dramatically. This is, of course, a long and complex story that cannot be paid justice in a few sentences, but suffice it to say at this point that new digital communication technologies such as blogs and Facebook significantly changed candidates' and parties' control over their message.[2]

Importantly, the emergence of a hybrid media system (Chadwick, 2013) in which older and newer media forms intermingle in complex relations highlights the need to be cautious about revolutionary claims. That is, new media do not make older media obsolete, but change their existing logics in important ways. For example, while the 'rise of the internet as a source of campaign information is genuinely significant', so is the fact that 'television has not declined' (Chadwick, 2013: 52). In other words, the influence of mass broadcast media on political communication is still strong, yet, as Andrew Chadwick suggests, the range of sources of information has extended to the degree that the media system of the early twenty-first century is a much more fluid and contested place (Chadwick, 2013: 21).

A significant change in political communication has to do with the availability of digital technologies, social media platforms, and data analytics. If television is generally thought to have given rise to the candidate-centred campaign, networked media seem to support a user-centred campaign. By user-centricity, I do not mean the interaction design kind where features are built to fit users' documented needs, but a kind of user-centricity that leverages and hinges on users' digital footprint. In a day and age where 'campaigning has entered a new technology-intensive era' (Kreiss, 2016: 3), electoral campaigns are no longer as dependent on the ongoing efforts of a political candidate or party locked into a permanent campaign (Blumenthal, 1982; Elmer et al., 2012) as they are on the ongoing efforts to analyse the footprint of the electorate.[3]

Facebook's central role in data-driven campaigning

In the contemporary environment of computational politics (Tufekci, 2014), campaigns are not just able to but are expected to leverage digital tools to target the right person with the right message at the right time. These tools may encompass everything from content management systems to social media platforms, email lists, databases, canvassing systems, internet fundraising, websites, phone bank and data management platform, to name but a few. According to Chadwick and Stromer-Galley (2016: 284), political campaigning has undergone an 'analytics turn', characterized by the use of 'experimental data science methods to inter-rogate large-scale aggregations of behavioral information from public voter records and digital media environments'.[4] Facebook plays a decisive role in this turn towards data analytics. As a company whose business model is built on gathering as much data about individuals as possible in order to yield better predictive models for advertising purposes, Facebook is a treasure trove for political actors seeking to trace and target the right people. However, Facebook is not just a political collaborator in terms of providing access to data and analytics, but is also a staffing aid of sorts, offering manpower and technical expertise to political campaigns on all sides of the political spectrum.

Facebook is also intimately intertwined with the political landscape insofar as digital campaigning came of age in the

Facebook era, especially with regard to the 2008 and 2012 US election campaigns. This is not just the case because the 2008 Obama campaign 'made the most sophisticated and intensive use of digital media of any major candidate for office in the US' (Bimber, 2014: 131), but, more importantly, because the media landscape had changed significantly between the 2004 and 2008 election cycles. This is not to suggest that the 2008 US presidential election hosted the first digital campaigns. Scholars often consider the 2004 Howard Dean campaign to be the first US presidential campaign to really integrate online efforts with traditional campaign functions, with a long-lasting impact on subsequent campaigns (Bimber, 2014; Kreiss, 2012). As political communication scholar Daniel Kreiss suggests, the 'Dean campaign became a prototype that spurred party actors to invest in new technologies, setting into motion the historical party dynamics that helped produce the comparative technological, digital, data, and analytics sophistication of Obama's 2012 bid' (2016: 18).

When the media practices of the electorate, activists and journalists change, campaigns change accordingly (Kreiss, 2016: 115). If Facebook seemed like a fun and a great way to mobilize potential voters in 2008, its influence on the political sphere had become even more evident in 2012, not least because of the Arab uprisings the year before. In 2012, Facebook's user base had exceeded one billion, making it the world's biggest social networking site. More users meant more data, and ultimately new possibilities for targeting individual voters in manners that had not been possible before (Pilkington and Michael, 2012). These possibilities did not just emerge because of new technical advancements, but were largely also the result of an ongoing investment in digital media, data and analytics over time. As Kreiss (2016: 123), points out, the 2012 Obama re-election had the assets of the 2008 campaign at its disposal, including massive email lists to potential donors, voter files, data on volunteers and social network data. What set the 2012 re-election bid apart from earlier elections was the extent to which the campaign used data-driven techniques for predictive modelling. Kreiss points out how the Obama campaign made extensive use of probabilistic models to identify 'whether someone was likely to support Obama or not, likely to turn out to vote, likely to be persuadable, and likely to be responsive to specific appeals' (2016: 127).

Data-driven campaigning refers to the techniques used to 'construct predictive models to make targeting campaign communications more efficient' (Nickerson and Rogers, 2014: 54; Dommett, 2019). These predictive models depend on a regime of ubiquitous testing and experimentation. Facebook has been an important platform for political online ads since at least 2010. As discussed in the previous chapter, Facebook offers the opportunity to target ads by a variety of demographic variables, such as location, gender and education, making it an important tool for reaching potential constituencies. More than simply targeting people based on the usual demographics, however, Facebook advertising offers the possibility to isolate and target very specific groups based on behavioural and personality traits.

The power of Facebook advertising is not just used strategically to target one's own voters but, perhaps more worryingly, to discredit the opposing party and candidate and to keep people from voting in the first place. According to Brad Parscale, the digital media director of the 2016 Trump campaign and responsible for the 2020 digital re-election campaign, Facebook played a decisive role in winning the election. Parscale routinely presents himself as the clever Facebook person. When interviewed, Parscale tells the story of how he used Facebook's ad tools to swing 'persuadable' voters at a critical time close to the election day.[5] Earlier in 2016, Parscale had been responsible for creating Project Alamo, a database containing 'data from the Republican National Committee, Cambridge Analytica, Facebook, donor lists, email addresses gathered at campaign rallies, and other sources' (Green and Issenberg, quoted in Brym et al., 2018: 628). When the polls started to look bleak for Trump, Parscale launched a massive digital last-stand strategy using Facebook ads to discourage Hillary Clinton supporters from voting. According to Brym et al. (2018: 629), Parscale used this database to 'identify 13.5 million persuadable voters in sixteen battleground states where the race was tight', sending these electors 'made-to-measure appeals' using Facebook. Two groups were particularly targeted by this strategy: 'alienated, older, white, small-town and rural electors' reluctant to admit their affiliations to pollsters, and 'scores of thousands of African Americans who only tepidly supported Hillary Clinton' (Brym et al., 2018: 629). Targeting these voters with custom-made messages through Facebook advertising proved effective: while the first group voted for Trump on election day, the second group decided not to vote at all.[6]

Regimes of experimentation

Driven by data, collected and aggregated through various sources, political campaigns are now in a position to target the electorate in hitherto unmatched ways. Not only are campaigns using Facebook's microtargeting tools for more precision and prediction, but they are also buying into the regimes of experimentation that come along with it. Facebook's operational logics are fundamentally premised on responding and adapting to the continuous feedback loops generated by the data points that users produce. To optimize their features and offerings, Facebook experiments with data in various ways. Whether through A/B testing of the News Feed or the kind of feature engineering required of machine learning, experiments at Facebook are not the exception but rather the default.

Some experiments naturally gain more attention due to their possible political impact. For example, in a much-cited experimental study on the possible impact of a Facebook feature on the likelihood to vote, Facebook researchers in collaboration with other academics demonstrated a small but measurable impact on voting behaviour (Bond et al., 2012). By placing different versions of an 'I Voted' button on the pages of 61 million users belonging to one of two test groups (excluding the control group), the study indicated an increase in actual voter turnout by at least 340,000. By transforming Facebook into a voter megaphone of sorts, the Facebook research team concluded 'it is possible that more of the 0.60% growth in turnout between 2006 and 2010 might have been caused by a single message on Facebook' (Bond et al., 2012: 297). This form of experimentation using a variant of A/B testing (to see which version performs better or comes closest to the target threshold) is one of the most common approaches used in developing and assessing the functionalities and effectiveness of a given user interface.

In another highly publicized case of News Feed alteration – more colloquially known as the emotional contagion experiment – data scientists and Facebook researchers experimented on more than half a million people over the age of thirteen for one week in 2012 to test whether emotional states could be transferred to others via emotional contagion (Kramer et al., 2014). The study, published in 2014, gained much public attention. Luke Stark calls it 'a seminal event in the history of digital technology's social impact', as it represented 'a moment when the tacit co-development of the psychological and computational sciences became exposed to public view' (2018: 206). Its findings suggested that Facebook posts may have the power to affect users' moods both positively and negatively, albeit with small effect sizes. Yet what seemed to get to people was the extent to which a company like Facebook could use its power to conduct experiments and engineer the public, whether at the time or in the future (Tufekci, 2014).

Despite the occasional reporting and public outcry, the data-driven test regime is far from an once-in-a-while occurrence and nor is it limited to A/B testing. At Facebook, every feature, every algorithmic weighing, every fine-tuning of the thresholds to be used on its machine learning models, every classifier and cluster, every button on the user interface is subject to ongoing experimentation. As Dommett suggests, these data-driven logics of experimentation have also 'become an important part of how we understand political campaigns' (2019: 2). Be it the possibility of combining new sources of data to generate targeted communication strategies or tracing the electorate, campaigners are expected to use these data for actionable insights.

Political advertising on Facebook

'While the data advantage is held, for the moment, by the Democratic party in the United States', Tufekci wrote in 2014, 'it will likely be available to the highest bidder in future campaigns.' The 2016 US presidential campaign made this statement painfully obvious. While both major parties in the US 2016 presidential election invested heavily in digital strategies, their tactics were different. On the face of it, Hillary Clinton did what was expected of a professional politician of her standing. She was well prepared, ran a professional and sophisticated campaign using a mix of different media, and generated more content across different social media platforms than any other candidate, along with big and focused television commercials (Graber and Dunaway, 2017; Karpf, 2016). Trump's campaign, on the other hand, seemed to be the exact opposite, which is probably why his victory came as a great shock and surprise to most analysts. Instead of investing in television ads, Trump went digital. In an interview with CBS's 60 Minutes, Parscale said the campaign had spent most of its digital advertising budget on Facebook, 'testing more than 50,000 ad variations each day in an attempt to micro-target voters' (Beckett, 2017). Much like the Clinton camp, the Trump team started out as Facebook novices (Levy, 2020). While Clinton declined Facebook's offer to help the campaign by optimizing the use of Facebook's tools, the Trump team readily accepted.

As recent work on technology-intensive campaigning has shown, Facebook's role in electoral politics exceeds its role as a platform provider and extends into human manpower and expert consultation. In one of the first studies to examine the role that technology companies play in staffing and consulting political campaigns, Kreiss and McGregor (2018: 161) document how Facebook and other tech companies 'have partisan teams, often made up of practitioners with backgrounds in Democratic and Republican politics, which work with campaigns and parties of the same political affiliation' to help them maximize usage of their digital tools. Drawing on field observations at the 2016 Democratic National Convention and interviews with digital staffers working on presidential campaigns on both sides, the researchers demonstrate how Facebook (and other companies) provide free consultants to campaigns in order to 'help them optimize, create more engagement around, and tailor and expand audiences for their ads' (Kreiss and McGregor, 2018: 167). For a short-staffed campaign like Trump's 2016 bid, this free technical help proved invaluable. For Facebook, entering into close relations with the political arena in this manner offers the opportunity for growth, advertising sales, and the creation of relationships with potential future legislators (Kreiss and McGregor, 2018: 161). This increasingly close interdependent relationship between platforms and candidates is far from unproblematic.

It matters what we are oriented towards, Sara Ahmed (2010) reminds us. What happens when public institutions and democratic processes are increasingly oriented towards the logics and business models of private companies like Facebook?[7] This is in part a question of the political realm adapting to changing media logics, as has always been the case (Chadwick, 2013)[8] – that is, how politics get shaped by the norms, values and practices of the media, and how changes in media culture help to configure what we take 'politics' to be. Facebook plays no small part in shaping the political conditions in our current media landscape. This is not just the case because of Facebook's capacity to allow people to connect and share content and thus to talk back to people and institutions of power (albeit in more or less successful ways); more fundamentally, as we have seen throughout this book, Facebook's infrastructural power and central role in the ad-tech-surveillance complex makes Facebook almost inescapable. As much as the 2016 Clinton campaign may have wanted to avoid Facebook (a noble pursuit for sure) to diminish its importance, it also failed to see how Facebook is more than a communications platform useful for broadcasting a political message or an effective microtargeting tool. This failure speaks to the mistaken notion of treating Facebook as just another social media platform, a tool to be used in instrumental ways to reach the electorate. As this book argues, treating Facebook as a social medium, a platform, or even synonymously with the internet itself, fails to grapple with a much more fundamental question, namely what it means to live in a world that is increasingly structured and shaped by the power of a handful of Silicon Valley companies. Even if some actors refuse to buy into the shaping power of platforms, the rest of the world turns in their direction. This is not to say that anyone refusing to use Facebook automatically loses, but rather that Facebook's power derives from its capacity to shape the conditions under which politics is happening in the first place.

While the political context has been relatively slow to succumb to the totalizing logics of Facebook (and Google) compared to other domains such as news and journalism, the increasing power of Facebook as an advertising tool has gradually changed this.[9] To paraphrase Kreiss and McGregor (2019), Facebook has become an arbiter of what voters get to see. As they suggest, 'Facebook and Google are increasingly the platforms that candidates are reliant upon for their strategic digital communications, and especially paid media', which makes it 'crucial to understand how these platform companies engage in the private regulation of paid political speech' (Kreiss and McGregor, 2019: 2). Unlike the regulatory constraints put on political advertising on television, political advertising on Facebook operates in the murky terrain of private self-regulation. In the case of Facebook, this mostly means no regulation, or a peculiar kind of liberal indifference.

As was stated in the beginning of this chapter, Facebook's ad policies state how political ads are generally not subject to fact-checking. In effect, politicians can speak their mind, no matter how truthful or accurate the content. While Facebook may not have *caused* the critical events of the 2016 presidential election, at the time it certainly did nothing to prevent them. For all its non-partisanship and apparent neutrality, Facebook's traditional hands-off stance on political advertising has been touted as one of the most important factors helping to sway the election in Trump's favour. As we have come to learn, truthfulness can mean many things. To speak truthfully is not necessarily the same as speaking about factually correct things. As became evident with the election of Trump, by being perceived as 'true to himself', his madness became not a liability but a sign of authenticity (Enli, 2017). Besides, who is to say what is factually correct? Certainly not Trump, and apparently not Facebook either – though Facebook is starting to show signs of acknowledging its powerful effects on public discourse with its most recent announcement 'to protect democracy' (Facebook, 2020b). Exactly two months prior to the US presidential election 2020, Mark Zuckerberg announced that Facebook would implement a series of changes to its existing policies on political advertising and content moderation. These steps include, to 'block new political and issue ads during the final week of the campaign', 'work with election officials to remove misinformation about voting' and 'remove threats related to Covid-19 to discourage voting' (Facebook, 2020b).

For all of Facebook's new self-proclaimed image as protector of the upcoming US election, it remains to be seen whether or not the temporary solutions envisioned, will actually translate into more systematic change. Just as Ruha Benjamin (2019) warns against taking quick technological fixes as signs of real cultural change, Facebook's approach to political advertising is perhaps better understood as a malleable and strategic business decision. Design and policy choices are never neutral, we are reminded, potentially impacting people in severe ways. Consistent with the experimental ethos discussed earlier, these new design and policy changes posit Facebook not just strategically as an apparent protector of democracy but more fundamentally as an explicit political actor with regards to governing political speech.

Platform governance and content moderation

Political decision-making is not beholden to those who vote at times of elections, but is part and parcel of the work that platforms do in governing the conditions of the sensible and the sayable. As we have seen, figuring out what is and what is not allowed to be published on Facebook is a thorny business. The controversies over political advertisements reveal how policing speech and content is not just a difficult task, but one that Facebook cannot solve by itself. In the regulatory sense, policing content is political insofar as it involves rule-setting and boundary-making practices. Company policies set the rules and draw the boundaries for what can and cannot be said within that space. These rules, and the practices that come with them, are not peripheral to how we come to understand platforms like Facebook: as Tarleton Gillespie (2018) argues, they are a central aspect of what makes a platform a platform. 'Platforms must moderate', he suggests, not just to protect their users from potentially disturbing and harmful content, but also for platforms to present their best face to advertisers and partners (Gillespie, 2018: 5). While all platforms have rules in place, through terms of services and community guidelines, they themselves are, of course, bound by the rules of law, states and transnational governing bodies, such as the EU or the ICANN.

In the US context, regulation of platforms needs to be understood against the backdrop of market liberalism, which puts great faith in companies' ability to self-regulate without too much interference from the state. Historically, there have also been different regulatory regimes for broadcasts and telecommunications. It is important to note the particular role played by section 230 in the US telecommunication law (originally passed as part of the Communications Decency Act of 1996) that makes a distinction between publishers 'that provide information (and therefore can be held liable for it) and distributors that merely circulate the information of others (and thus should not be held liable) – known as the "content/conduit" distinction' (Gillespie, 2018: 31). According to the safe harbour of section 230, ISPs and other network services were treated as conduits of information, free from liability for the content that users were distributing. What's more, even if a network service were to 'police what its users say or do, it does not lose its safe harbor protection by doing so' (Gillespie, 2018: 30). The regulation of Facebook elsewhere in the world is a matter of both 'conditional liability' and 'strict liability'. Most European countries, Russia, and most South American nations operate with a kind of 'conditional liability' that Gillespie compares to the US copyright rules, where platforms are only liable if they had 'actual knowledge' that the content distributed was illicit. Countries like China and many of the nations in the Middle East, however, impose 'strict liability', requiring Facebook to actively prevent the circulation of unlawful content (Gillespie, 2018: 33).

How these rules are enforced and come to play in the daily work of policing platforms, however, is much more ambiguous and difficult in practice. As Gillespie writes, the work of content moderation entails:

> not just determining what is unacceptable, but balancing offense and importance; reconciling competing value systems; mediating when people harm one another, intentionally or otherwise; honoring the contours of political discourse and cultural taste; grappling with inequities of gender, sexuality, race, and class; extending ethical obligations across national, cultural, and linguistic boundaries; and doing all that around the hottest hot-button issues of the day. (Gillespie, 2018: 10)

It is therefore not surprising that protecting users against potentially harmful speech and disturbing content has become a real headache for a global company like Facebook. News reports routinely emerge about important and legit content being removed for violating Facebook's terms of services, while problematic and disturbing content is allowed to stay. Often, these controversies centre on questions of agency and responsibility. Who or what was part (or not part) of the decision-making process? Was it an algorithm or human making the decision, and what were the possibilities for mitigating harm and correcting for potential bias?

When and how to intervene in removing or sanctioning content is something that rarely has a definite or static answer as it often is a matter of distributed actions. Moderating content on Facebook is performed by a plethora of different actors, some of whom are low-paid workers contracted by Facebook to keep their sites 'user-friendly'. Behind the screen, commercial content moderators, as Sarah T. Roberts (2019) calls these invisible contract workers, are performing the tedious task of filtering out any potentially harmful or disturbing messages or images. Equipped with a company protocol, these outsourced and freelance labourers sift through the internet's garbage in order to ensure end-users can remain blissfully ignorant. As documented by Roberts (2019) and a growing body of literature on the phenomenon of content moderation (e.g. Gerrard, 2018; Gillespie, 2018; Myers West, 2018; Ruckenstein and Turunen, 2019), not only is their work likely to be monotonous, but the decision as to whether or not an image or message will stay on the site or be removed is often made in just a matter of seconds.

How Facebook polices content and speech is important, but this alone does not determine the fate of democracy or electoral outcomes. What matters even more is the kind of reality that takes shape around and because of the fact that content is policed through a complex assemblage of content moderation, policies, community guidelines, algorithmic infrastructure and business concerns. The politics of Facebook then, is not just concerned with *who* gets to speak. What the indifference and technological solutionism of Facebook reveal, more fundamentally, is the politics embedded in producing the conditions for reality to take shape in certain ways rather than others. If the territory and topology of this political space are created through complex entities in relation, then grappling with the question of Facebook politics is necessarily also about addressing Facebook's ontological politics. As was stated in the introductory chapter, thinking of Facebook as topological means thinking about the ways in which relationships between various points/agents make certain realities and spaces come alive. In other words, it is not just a question of an indifferent stance towards political advertisements and the specificity of particular ad policies, but of what those things make more or less probable in the world. The question is what is allowed to take root, to evolve, and to take shape in a space shaped by Facebook occupying a central position in the contemporary information ecology.

The politics of the polluted information ecology

Let us return to the opening example of the Elisabeth Warren Facebook ad. The false ad campaign did not just seek to highlight the liberal hand-off stance of Facebook's ad policies: it mobilized discourses and sentiments constitutive of a much deeper and arguably more worrisome tendency in the current media landscape – the increased weaponization of information for the purpose of manipulation, propaganda and micro-targeting. Here I am following Whitney Phillips and Ryan Milner (2021) in their use of the notion of 'network pollution' to talk about a set of interrelated phenomena that have normally been described using different terms such as misinformation, disinformation and malinformation.[10] Subsuming these terms into a notion of polluted infor-mation, they suggest, 'sidesteps questions of motive', which are not just 'tricky to parse in the digital environment' but also do not always matter for the outcomes they generate (Phillips and Milner, 2021). The point I want to make is that the politics of Facebook is also concerned with the role that Facebook has played and continues to play in shaping a polluted information environment. There are many aspects to this network pollution, some of which Phillips and Milner helpfully highlight, others that are more specifically related to Facebook's position as a network hub for the spreading of polluted information. Again, the US 2016 election of Trump plays an important role in determining the perceived urgency of this matter, but we should not forget that tactics of infor-mation disorder and pollution are far from new phenomena. As Phillips and Milner point out, it was not that masses of people woke up 'one morning in 2016 suddenly repulsed by those with opposing political beliefs, any more than the sun rose one morning to record-breaking high and low tempera-tures. Polarization reflects, instead, fundamental changes in the information ecosystem' (2021). In other words, even if the election took many people by surprise, there was more to it than failed predictions, authentic representations, polarized positions, populist messages, algorithmic amplification, news feeds, media manipulation or the spreading of false news. This is not to say that these were not important elements

– on the contrary. Yet no single one of them could adequately explain the current state of affairs. Taken together, however, they are emblematic of what Phillips and Milner diagnose as a network crisis fuelled by hardening polarization and a polluted media landscape. Facebook plays no small part here.

Throughout this book we have traced some of the core technical developments and business decisions that have contributed to the kind of information environment we are witnessing today. These decisions include, but are not limited to: (a) the platform programmability of Facebook's expansion phase, during which the company offered almost unlimited and certainly uncontrolled access to core functionalities and data in exchange for developer resources and third-party applications that helped the company extend its platform to the rest of the Web; (b) the continued reinvention of the Facebook News Feed and its drive towards popular and sensational content and user engagement; (c) Facebook's vision of world domination that resulted in identity lock-ins and global development projects such as Free Basics; (d) the development of an advertising infrastructure premised on easy-to-use tools aimed at making everybody an advertiser, along with ever more fine-grained micro-targeting options. In the remainder of this chapter, I want to focus on two concrete examples of network pollution that have made their distinctive mark on our understanding of Facebook politics, capturing the interplay between complex political tendencies, business opportunism and technical affordances: the infamous Cambridge Analytica scandal and the prosecution and genocide of the Rohingya minority population in Myanmar.

Haunted data: Cambridge Analytica and the inertia of infrastructure

First of all, there should have been nothing surprising about the Cambridge Analytica so-called data scandal revealed in early 2018. In a huge exposé in the *Guardian*, journalists Carole Cadwalladr and Emma Graham-Harrison, published a classic whistleblower-story with all the 'elements of spy-novel theatrics' (Stark, 2018: 219). Christopher Wylie, a Canadian-born data nerd, told the reporters how Cambridge Analytica had 'exploited Facebook to harvest millions of people's profiles. And built models to exploit what we knew about them and target their inner demons. That was the basis the entire company was built on' (Cadwalladr and Graham-Harrison, 2018). The company had worked with both the 2016 Trump team and the winning Brexit campaign to target millions of users, based on something as inconspicuous as a Facebook personality quiz that found its way to some 270,000 Facebook users and their network of friends. There was nothing particularly unique about the app called 'thisisyourdigitallife'. In fact, it worked just as Facebook intended third-party apps to work at the time it was created by Aleksandr Kogan in 2013. While the story broke as a data breach story, Facebook's spokespersons made it clear that there had not been a breach as such, but that the extent to which Cambridge Analytica had been able to harvest user data was in fact a product of Facebook's rather liberal API policies and terms of service a few years earlier (which the company restricted in 2015). Up until 2015, Facebook had allowed developers to access information about friends of a user without having to ask for permission. If a user signed up to a third-party app in 2014 – a game personality quiz, for instance – the developer of the app would also be able to access information about the user's friends. While Facebook's unobstructed Graph API had made the data collection and creation of personality profiles possible, what it did not allow was to take these data elsewhere and use them for any commercial purpose, which is what Kogan ended up doing with Cambridge Analytica.

Cambridge Analytica, a political consultancy firm formerly known as SCL and headed by Alexander Nix and owned by

Republican hedge fund and machine learning pioneer Robert Mercer, came into contact with Kogan in early 2014. Kogan met with Wylie to discuss the possibilities for collaboration. In exchange for interesting data, Kogan would consult the company on personality-based information. To do so, Kogan sat up his own consultancy firm, Global Science Research (GSR), together with his friend Joseph Chancellor, who went on to work for the Facebook data science team (Lewis and Wong, 2018). Eventually, Cambridge Analytica went on to use its psychometric data to consult the Trump campaign. Steve Bannon, Cambridge Analytica's vice president at the time and chairman of Breitbart news, the 'platform for the alt-right', was appointed manager of the Trump campaign in August 2016 (Posner, 2016).

Here the story becomes messier. Experts disagree over the extent to which psychometric targeting played much of a role in the US 2016 election. Zuckerberg himself maintains that he had never heard of Cambridge Analytica or Kogan before the original story broke in 2015.[11] Parscale says the Cambridge Analytica scandal was blown out of proportion, and what really made the difference were Facebook audience segmentation tools (Marantz, 2020). For Bannon, it was not Facebook that helped Trump win, but 'economic nationalism' (Calia, 2018). Economic nationalism may have been a branding strategy and a euphemism for populist and right-wing desires, but growing polarization, a rise in income inequality, racism and misogyny clearly did play a role (Gaughan, 2016). Scholars of media manipulation remind us that no one single element can adequately explain the 2016 election or where we are at right now, no Cambridge Analytica, no single alt-right group, no Facebook (Marwick and Lewis, 2017). What we have instead is an assemblage of stories, actors and affects that together help to shape and amplify a landscape of polluted information.

While the Cambridge Analytica scandal may have been snake oil, its importance lies not in the question of whether it played a role in the US 2016 election, Brexit referendum or any of the other 25 countries that it has claimed to work on campaigns for: what the story helps to reveal is the multiplicity of politics at play in the making of reality. From an infrastructural point of view, the Cambridge Analytica scandal helped reveal how technical decisions coded into protocols and APIs may have significant inertia, and how infrastructures can be very difficult if not impossible to change or undo (see Chapter 2). Even if access to data were curtailed a long time ago, the data may still come back to haunt us in sometimes unanticipated ways. Rather than seeing the scandal as the outcome of big data misuse, we are better served by a kind of topological mapping of entities-in-relation: big data, small data, academic ambitions, shady political consultancy, empty promises, smart branding, polarization, populism, the alt-right, the culture of sharing, API policies, software development kits, growth strategies, the business of friendships, privacy, personality quizzes, psychometric profiling, algorithms, mainstream media, leaks, breaking stories, advertising, micro-targeting, data aggregation, predictive analytics and political campaigning. The case also goes to show the limits of tracing origins or motives. As Phillips and Milner (2021) put it, 'motives don't always matter to outcomes, and outcomes matter more than motives'. Networked pollution is not easily traceable; nor should we necessarily think that by tracing motives we can find the answers that we are looking for. We should also be wary of treating any of these stories about data scandals and large-scale psychometric studies as isolated incidents. Not one greedy academic trying to find a quick path to academic fame, or a dubious data analytics firm trying to find a quick fix to collecting Facebook data. The Facebook emotional contagion study and the psychometric data profiling by Cambridge Analytica are part of the same continuum. As Stark (2018: 221) reminds us, algorithmic psychometrics 'proliferate in the devices and dreams that Silicon Valley sell us'.

Facebook in the wild: The case of dangerous speech in Myanmar

Recall how, in the introductory chapter, Nyan characterized Facebook's role in Myanmar as all-encompassing. Nyan, who is a human rights activist and founder of a local NGO working on government transparency in Myanmar, suggests Facebook played a vital role in the ongoing atrocities against the Rohingya minority population in Myanmar.[12] Facebook's role as a trusted news source in Myanmar must be understood against the country's unique political history of authoritarian rule between 1962 and 2010, and the rapid and explosive dissemination of telecommunications from 2010 onwards (Fink, 2018). In a matter of a couple of years, an entire country went from 'no information' to getting online at the same time. As we discussed in the introduction chapter, when the first mobile phone companies started to establish themselves in Myanmar in 2014, they came with a mobile phone plan and Facebook preloaded and free to use. In 2016, Free Basics was introduced, Facebook's global endeavour to convert the global poor into Facebook users by providing access for free. Because Facebook is such an intertwined part of what it means to be connected and have access to information and news in Myanmar, Facebook means everything. As Nyan tellingly put it when I interviewed him in the autumn of 2019, to most people in Myanmar 'Facebook is something called Facebook.' For the first-time internet users of Myanmar, 'Facebook is not a social network, Facebook is not the internet, but something they would do when using their phone', he said. It is not so much that Facebook is indistinguishable from the internet, as it is commonly held, but that you don't need a preconception of the internet to make sense of this thing called Facebook.

In a country where most people had known no other reality than military dictatorship, suddenly being 'released into the wild online' (Arora, 2019: 204) was both exciting

and horrific. As Facebook quickly turned into the primary
news source for most people in Myanmar, the military and
ultranationalist Buddhist groups knew how to exploit this
to spread false news. Since 2012, Buddhist ultranationalist
groups had gained momentum, in part by using Facebook
to spread fear and hatred against the minority Muslim
population of the country (Fink, 2018). The Muslim Rohingya
population concentrated in parts of Rakhine State was
particularly severely hit and affected by the Facebook-induced
information pollution. In 2012, the president's spokesperson
called for action on Facebook, calling the Rohingya minority
'terrorists'. In another incident in 2014, Wirathu, a prominent
ultranationalist monk, reposted on his Facebook page what
later were revealed to be false reports of a 'Buddhist female
employee's rape by the proprietor of a local teashop' (Fink,
2018: 46). The post spread, resulting in the deployment of
600 officers in an attempt to control the angry crowd, and the
deaths of two people.

However, these were not minor glitches or exceptional
events. Facebook-induced protests, boycotts and violence
against Muslims have become commonplace in Myanmar (as
they have in many other countries of the world). As detailed
by reporter Paul Mozur of the *New York Times*, Facebook
has been strategically weaponized by the military to pollute
the information environment in Myanmar. At one time, as
many as 700 people worked on Myanmar military's Facebook
operation. Their strategies included setting up what appeared
to be Facebook news pages about Burmese pop stars and
other celebrities. Once these pages had reached a large
enough follower audience, they became useful vehicles for
the spreading of false news and inflammatory posts. Using
Facebook as a form of reaching the masses is a common
strategy in the dissemination of mis- and disinformation.
As Marwick and Lewis describe in their report on media
manipulation, major social media sites such as Facebook
and YouTube are used by 'members of the far-right to spread

extreme messaging to large numbers of people and to seed topics for journalists' (2017: 26). Private Facebook groups are commonly used to share memes, which are then spread more publicly through personal networks.

In Myanmar, 'troll accounts run by the military helped spread the content, shout down critics and fuel arguments between commenters to rile people up' (Mozur, 2018). Having used Facebook strategically for the purpose of psychological warfare, in 2017 the Buddhist ultranationalists, backed by the military, carried out genocidal attacks on the Rohingya population in Rakhine State. As described in several UN human rights reports on Myanmar, Facebook is not just a useful instrument for those seeking to spread hate, but it is *the* leading platform for hate speech, or 'dangerous speech' as Fink (2018) usefully calls it (Human Rights Council, 2018; 2019). The notion of dangerous speech designates 'language meant to persuade "one group of people to fear and hate – and eventually to condone violence against – another group"' (Fink, 2018: 43). The advantage of using a term like dangerous speech over similar terms such as hateful speech, is that the latter is not necessarily suggesting that speech can have dangerous effects.

If anything, the atrocities and weaponization of Facebook in Myanmar show the very ambivalent topological space created by extreme sides of the dis/connectivity spectrum. On the one hand, Facebook's explosive expansion in Myanmar enabled the kind of empowerment and access for all that Zuckerberg and others romanticized about. Remember Zuckerberg (2013) proclaiming internet connectivity a basic human right. Yet there is no guarantee that the disconnected, once given access to the internet, will actually use it as intended, or for their own liberation and education. As Payal Arora (2019) argues, there is a disconnect between celebratory empowerment discourses perpetuated by efforts to connect the next billion users and what those users actually do once they are connected. Her research shows that we should be wary of clichés about the global poor and the assumptions underlying the need for internet connectivity. Taking her own participation in internet development projects in India as a starting point, Arora recounts the disconnect between expectation and reality: 'We envisioned women to seek health information, farmers checking crop prices, and children teaching themselves English through these kiosks [computer stations/cafés of sorts]' Arora writes (2019: 2). The reality was that people wanted to use the internet for leisure purposes, not practical ones. Entertainment, finding love interests, new friends and watching porn trumped information-seeking by far. Why is it that we somehow expect the global poor to be 'more likely than the wealthy to use the Internet for practical purposes', Arora asks (2019: 3)? This is indeed a good question, and one that extends beyond leisure divides into the many faces of Facebook. If Facebook is a 'happy' place, especially for people whose daily lives are entrenched in poverty and violence (Arora, 2019: 164), its ugly face has become ever more apparent. The other extreme of the connectivity spectrum, then, is the increased use of Facebook by bad actors with malicious intent.

For all its efforts to connect the world, Facebook has shown time and again how ill equipped it is to take direct action when confronted with the detection and reporting of dangerous speech. It took Facebook several days to act on messages about the genocide in Myanmar. It is clear that the conduit metaphor is increasingly hard to sustain, yet Facebook continues to cling to the empty ideal of free expression and images of neutrality. Nick Clegg, former British deputy prime minister and now Vice-President for Global Affairs and Communications at Facebook, once likened Facebook to a car (yet another metaphor at play). In the case of a car crash, it is not the car's fault but that of the person driving, Clegg claimed in a speech on Facebook's global responsibility. For this analogy to make any sense at all, one would, of course, need to assume Facebook to be an empty vessel, a neutral platform, simply a conduit and a distribution channel. Clegg is obviously no media or STS scholar whose work would likely accentuate notions of hybrid agency. Had he been, though, Clegg would have known that there is no such thing as just a car or just a driver, but something more like what Dant (2004) calls a 'driver-car' whose agency emerges as a result of their interaction.[13] Similarly, Facebook, by operating the way it does – amplifying certain voices and discourses by design, allowing certain things to appear while obscuring others – is clearly not an empty vessel nor a car devoid of agency. Facebook is Facebook.

This is the case not just because most people in Myanmar have come to know Facebook as a thing in and of itself, decoupled from the concept of the internet or other social networking sites, but because its power and politics are most evidently described by reference to itself. That is, Facebook has power because of Facebook, because Facebook encompasses people, decision-makers, politicians, rule-making capacities, rule-enforcing capacities, users, global reach, powerful people, dictators, coders, a data trove of Likes and desires, friendship networks, advertising, capital, algorithms and news sources. As such, it speaks to Jane Bennett's (2010) notion of thing-power (see Chapter 2), in that Facebook's power is not so much located in a singular object called Facebook, but in Facebook's unmatched capacity to group things together to such an extent that only a few things still remain untouched.

Concluding remarks

Facebook politics, this chapter has argued, is a murky business. It is made up of stories that do not necessarily add up, yet seem strangely connected. We started with the example of a tactical ad campaign, one that blatantly presented false information in an attempt to bring the absurdity of Facebook's exceptional ad policies for politicians to light. We then went on to discuss how Facebook figures in contemporary political campaigning, especially in the US context. Facebook advertising and the microtargeting tools this infrastructure enables have become the primary means by which Facebook and electoral politics now intersect. If Facebook only a few years back figured in imaginaries of social movements and civic space-making, the cascading events of recent years, especially the 2016 US presidential election, have changed this story significantly.

Today we are increasingly confronted by stories of conflict and crisis. Discourses of participation and democracy have been supplanted by discussions on polarization, distrust and information pollution. Yet we must be wary of thinking in terms of totalizing disruptions or seductive narratives of linear transformations. The point here is not to think that Facebook was once good, perhaps because it helped people organize protests in the wake of the Arab uprisings, and that it has now become bad, perhaps because it can be used to manipulate opinions and spread hateful content. In general, we want to avoid such oversimplifications and binary classification schemes. This is not to concur with Clegg that Facebook is as good or bad as its users make it. Facebook is political in and through its very design, operations and modes of governance. It has all the power in the world to change directions, intervene and change modes of operation.

What is most evident from the stories told in this chapter is that there are many more. As Anna Tsing (2015) puts it in her wonderfully strange book *The Mushroom at the End of the World*, 'we have a problem with scale. A rush of stories cannot be neatly summed up' (Tsing, 2015: 39). Already exceeding the length I would have liked, this chapter (like all chapters in this book) remains deeply partial and patchy. Yet these stories point towards the importance of Facebook in shaping our contemporary information ecology, in its capacity to decide what is allowed to take root, to evolve, and to take shape within this ecology.

By looking at some of the conventional stories told about Facebook politics, including its role in Myanmar and the Cambridge Analytica scandal, one of the goals of this chapter has been to tell additional stories. This is not so much a piling up of stories, but more about revitalizing the ones we know in order to notice new things. In the case of Facebook in Myanmar, we may see how shying away from framing Facebook as a social networking site necessitates taking its socio-geographical context a little more seriously. While it has become almost commonplace to suggest that Facebook is synonymous with the internet for most users outside the Western context, what Nyan importantly hints at is that Facebook is not so much synonymous with the internet as a thing in and of itself. How this thing called Facebook is appropriated and made sense of, domesticated and incorporated into everyday life, is not uniform or static. To posit Facebook as a thing in and of itself is not to think of Facebook in essentialist terms. For an understanding of Facebook politics, this means that we must go beyond preconceived ideas of Facebook's ontological status (say, as a social media platform) to consider how Facebook differently materializes in situated practices and contexts.

Even the most recited story of recent years, the Cambridge Analytica scandal, reveals a host of forking paths. First there is the mainstream story about data misuse and massive psychometric targeting for political ends; but the so-called scandal is also a manifestation of how technology embodies and shapes politics. Changing API policies and platform programmability efforts show how technical decisions from the past may have unintended consequences in the present, even long after they were allegedly changed or reversed. The algorithmic amplification of sensational content and private messaging groups of like-minded users shows how technology companies like Facebook are not neutral conduits of information but help to shape the conditions under which information is allowed to appear and flow through various networks. The many intricate relationships at the human level concerning access, collaboration and partnerships show how Facebook consists of people and how those people may have ties to other stakeholders and organizations that may impact what decisions are made and how their technology is used. The discourses and promises of big data and psychometrics show how narrow the gaps are between the hopes and dreams of academics and corporate interests. As we have discussed, the scandal was perhaps not so much a scandal as a reminder that data can tell stories, too. Though much of the reporting after the events of 2016 focused on the failure of data to predict the election outcome, if anything, the Cambridge Analytica story revealed the extent to which data can take us by surprise, live their own lives, rest in long-forgotten databases, personality quizzes and academic feuds, and how they can be variously put to use in the hands of differently intentioned actors.

Conclusion: The many faces of Facebook

The little blue *f* logo sits among the many other apps on our mobile phones. In between mail, maps, a mobile game, Messenger, WhatsApp and Instagram, the Facebook app looks at me every time I open my phone. Just habitually checking Facebook every morning and several times throughout the day has become a familiar practice of everyday life for many. Often just for a minute or two, for no particular reason or responding to one of the many notifications, checking Facebook fills life with a certain tone and mood. The habitual, mindless scrolling, checking, liking and clicking is part of the felt presence of Facebook on our lives. It is exactly the atmospheric qualities of Facebook that reveal both its attraction and its danger. Writing this concluding chapter in the first half of 2020 inevitably brings new context to the ambivalence of Facebook.

For readers of the future, let me briefly set the scene. The year 2020 goes into the history books as the year that made 'social distancing' commonplace, 'quarantine' into a global experience and #stayathome yet another iteration of 'hashtag activism'.[1] As I am writing this in the midst of a global crisis, I will not elaborate more than necessary; after all, how does one adequately address that which is currently unfolding yet in dire need of analytical distance? At the same time, there is no way around *not* mentioning the Covid-19 pandemic, not least because it puts the object of analysis, Facebook, into new but familiar light. In the introductory chapter, the claim was made that Facebook has become less important as a communication channel for many of its first adopters and the younger generations. On a general level, this may still be true, but the experience of being confined to the home during societal lockdowns and quarantine measures certainly makes the habitual connections of Facebook more acutely felt.

In a time of heightened crisis and uncertainty during the pandemic, the typified functions of media were reassumed. National television and newspapers were again able to assemble their national publics, as everyone seemed to gather in front of the screen for more news. For a moment, Facebook's somewhat lost identity as a social network site became present again. Not many days after social distancing became a national protocol, people would flock to social media and particularly to Facebook. During the spring months of 2020, it was not at all uncommon to see people revitalize their more or less sleepy Facebook profiles, liking, sharing and commenting more than they had for years. Musicians would offer Facebook Live concerts, people were posting pictures of their virtual dinner parties, and the number of new neighbourhood help groups would most certainly have made Mark Zuckerberg proud. Did we just for a moment get a glimpse of what would have transpired if Facebook had actually succeeded in making the world more open and connected? Perhaps. Like every moment, however, this too was fleeting.

There are many faces to Facebook. If the communal help groups that tend to emerge during times of crisis epitomize Facebook's ideal face, polarized and polluted networks constitute Facebook's ugly face. Not long after people were asked to stay at home, seeking comfort in virtual connections via their home screens, Facebook's misinformation problem became painfully evident again. In between false rumours of 5G cell-phone towers fuelling the coronavirus and musings by Trump that drinking bleach might be an effective measure for containing the virus, Facebook was again confronted with one of its most resilient information polluters, the anti-vaccine community. In a study of anti-vaxxers' social networks on

Facebook, published in Nature during the early days of the pandemic government interventions, Johnson et al. (2020) show how anti-vaxxers were able to forge far more links and connections to the undecided masses than their outspoken pro-vaccination counterparts. Because of the anti-vaxxers' successful entanglement into clusters of people who are arguably still persuadable, Johnson et al. predict that anti-vaccination views will dominate within a decade. While this is not to suggest that Facebook generates such views or that these ideological battles are fought solely on Facebook, the extent to which polluted information is allowed to circulate, and even somewhat perversely designed into the business model of Facebook, is certainly constitutive of Facebook's ugly face.

Facebook's perverted business model has become even more acutely evident recently. According to a report by The Wall Street Journal, internal presentations at Facebook specifically showed evidence of Facebook's algorithms stoking divisiveness and polarization – without Facebook executives implementing any real changes (Horwitz and Seetharaman, 2020). The reports revealed how Facebook's 'integrity teams' found that 64% of all extremist group joins were due to Facebook's recommendation tools. Subsequent solutions to these problems were presented as 'antigrowth', requiring Facebook to take a stance that most likely have led to lower engagement, and ultimately less profit. Although these reports of blatant unwillingness on Facebook's part to combat algorithmic toxicity probably do not come as much of a surprise, Zuckerberg's fantasy world of free expression and platform neutrality is becoming increasingly harder to sustain.

Making the world more open and connected now seems increasingly more like making the world more closed and divided. When Zuckerberg (2017a) attempted to rebrand Facebook as an infrastructure for global community in 2017, he most certainly did not have in mind the rise of the alt-right, misogynist and racist groups, anti-vaxxers and conspiracy theorists. If Facebook sees itself as a platform that 'gives people the power to build community' and 'to bring the world closer together', it would be naive to assume (as Zuckerberg's rhetoric seems to suggest) that 'new moms and dads', 'people helping kids get into college' or 'lock-smiths' are the only ones who will use Facebook to do so (Zuckerberg, 2017b). What we are seeing today is a bit like parents in denial. Most parents want to see only the good in their kids, and vice versa. Like the pandemic world that disrupts the status quo and catapults people out of the comfort zone that normalcy provides (at least for those of us who have the luxury to lead protected and safe lives), Zuckerberg still seems to cling to a vision of days past.

As we are writing in May 2020 and many governments are beginning to ease their Covid-19 restrictions, multiple crises are unfolding on different fronts. Heading into the 2020 US presidential election, Facebook finds itself in the midst of a recurring controversy over free speech and content moderation. With the killing of George Floyd at the hands of the police in Minneapolis, Minnesota, on 25 May 2020, ongoing racial injustices and police brutality in the United States have resulted in nationwide and international street protests. Amid these protests over racism and police violence, President Trump went on Twitter threatening violent police retaliation and military intervention in Minnesota. In stark contrast to Twitter's decisions to moderate Trump, but consistent with the company line, Zuckerberg explained that Facebook would take no action, as 'accountability for those in positions of power can only happen when their speech is scrutinized out in the open' (Zuckerberg, 2020). As we discussed in the previous chapter, Zuckerberg has persistently positioned Facebook as a protector of free speech, saying he does not believe that social media companies should act as arbiters of truth and that people should be allowed to decide what to believe. Here, Zuckerberg and Trump seem to agree.

Pretending to have no politics beyond platitudes has its obvious limits, which is also what many of Facebook's own employees seem to realize. It is rare for Facebook employees to publicly criticize the company, but faced with Zuckerberg's hands-off approach to the president's inflammatory posts, several employees took to Twitter to publicly voice their concerns. 'Doing nothing is not acceptable [...]There isn't a neutral position on racism', one Facebook employee tweeted, while another noted how 'Facebook's inaction in taking down Trump's post inciting violence makes me ashamed to work here' and that 'Silence is complicity.' Yet, as Danielle Citron and Mary Anne Franks argue, to think of the law as requiring 'tech companies to act as "neutral public forums"' is one of the most prevailing myths confounding Section 230 speech reform (2020: 14). Another common misconception that undergirds discussions on Section 230, and thus Zuckerberg's insistence on free speech, is the assertion that the 'internet is primarily a medium of speech' (Citron and Franks, 2020: 11). While this may indeed have been the case when Section 230 was passed in 1996, to still think of the internet as primarily a medium for speech would be to ignore the many other activities people use the internet for that 'have very little to do with speech' (p. 12).

Facebook as a hyperobject

Discussions about Facebook suffer from a similar misconception. While it may have made sense to think of Facebook as a social network site or social media platform, say a decade ago, today the assertion that Facebook is primarily about connecting friends and family is clearly outdated and misconceived. Just as the internet is not used only for communication but also for searching, buying, selling, watching television, streaming music and looking for jobs (Citron and Franks, 2020: 11), not everything on Facebook is about friendships, community or social connectivity. Quite the contrary. Facebook is about many things, only a fraction of which would fall under the rubric of social (understood as companionship or an informal social gathering). While the many faces of Facebook include things like talking to friends and family, or liking and commenting on each other's pictures and posts, they also include harassment, polluted information and dangerous speech. People use Facebook to search, write, flirt, bully, livestream, endorse, watch, lurk. As digital infrastructure, Facebook is also a global identity provider and sometimes the only gateway to information. Facebook is a website, mobile app, platform, news site, digital marketplace, message board, event organizer, and much more besides. It is cloud computing, data warehouse and satellite technology. Facebook has turned into the Silicon Valley technology company par excellence, but it is also a leading media company, and one of the largest advertising companies in the world. It invests in virtual reality, owns one of the most resourceful research hubs for advancing artificial intelligence and has developed its own experimental solar-powered drone. End-users are not Facebook's only stakeholders. There are also the third-party developers, advertisers, businesses, governments, regulators, engineers, content moderators, designers, bots, consultancy firms, politicians, investors, competitors, news organizations, human rights activists, lawyers and academics, who all in one way or another have a vested interested in Facebook. In short: Facebook is both poison and cure, and everything in between.

This is not to say that Facebook is all of these things at once, or that we must account for all of them in conceptualizing Facebook. Facebook is not so much an assemblage of all of these things, but what Timothy Morton (2010; 2013) would call a 'hyperobject'. For Morton, hyperobjects materialize the presence of things that are bewilderingly huge, such as global warming, which makes them difficult to grasp and conceptualize as a result. Their enormity and scale, however, does not mean they are not real or cannot be encountered. Like global warming, which does not manifest in the same way or consistently, all the time, yet is just as real as a hammer, Facebook's presence in the world is felt. Hyperobjects, says Morton (2013: 1), are viscous, nonlocal in their manifestation and often operate at timescales inaccessible to humans. Like global warming, Facebook is sticky in the sense that it adheres to so many things in life. It orients the way in which we think about connectivity and friendships, how news gets produced and circulated, how politicians have come to think of their electorate, how small businesses try to reach customers, how advertising and surveillance work in tandem.

Facebook is quite literally sticky. Our digital traces stick to Facebook just as much as Facebook sticks to us. When our Facebook identity constitutes a key to other websites, is used as a token of trust and verification mechanism, when the data our friends provide is as important as our own traces, when we miss out on important life opportunities or vital information, when Facebook may offer the only source of comfort or support, simply leaving or disconnecting from Facebook is not necessarily an attainable option. As entities of such vast temporal and spatial dimensions, hyperobjects like global warming or Facebook 'seem to force something on us, something that affects some core ideas of what it means to exist' (Morton, 2013: 15). With the presence of Facebook in the world, we have been confronted with and urged to reflect on a great number of things. For example, Facebook's algorithms have stirred debates over polarization and misinformation (and also disinformation and false news), Free Basics has opened up conversation about techno-colonialism and net neutrality, news organizations have been confronted with their business models and journalistic values, Facebook's recurring privacy missteps and data breaches have pushed discussion about personal information and consumer protection to the forefront of internet regulation, API changes have highlighted the differential power relations between platforms and third parties, and micro-targeting and Facebook's advertising infrastructure have opened up questions of political transparency and accountability. While these examples are mostly negative in the sense that they involve some form of public controversy, Facebook's affective power is not at all confined to privacy scandals or amplification of dangerous speech. By inserting itself into every facet of life, Facebook confronts us with the seemingly mundane and ordinary. In the introductory chapter, I brought up the example of Jace, who could feel the influence of Facebook every time his dad had him stop what he was doing and pose for photos that were destined to be shared online. But we may also just think of the ways in which Facebook has inserted itself into something as habitual as wishing someone happy birthday or even generated an emotional language of Likes and other reactions. It is in this sense that hyperobjects like Facebook are very productive.

Becoming new

Over fifteen years ago, Mark Zuckerberg founded TheFacebook.com, a small college network that turned into a global information and communications empire. While history reminds us to be wary of claims of novelty, especially when it comes to the pronouncement of new shiny things, sometimes claims of newness are warranted. Part of making the argument that Facebook is Facebook is to insist on its (relative) unprecedentedness. Embedded in this statement is the assertion that Facebook cannot easily be compared or described by reference to something else. However, I argue that Facebook wasn't new from the beginning, but that it became 'new' much later on. That is to say, Facebook's newness cannot be traced to 2004 when Zuckerberg launched TheFacebook.com, nor to the early days of the company. Facebook's newness must rather be understood as something that emerged after the fact, and somewhat paradoxically, in a time when it had become habitually commonplace.

Reflecting on the term 'new media', Wendy Chun observes how the 'new' remains a surprisingly uninterrogated term (2006: 3). To call something new, she writes, 'is to categorize it, to describe and prescribe it, while at the same time to insist that "X" is wonderful, singular, without opposite or precedent' (ibid.). The question is: what does it take to qualify for such exclusive labels? When is something without opposite? Similarly to how Chun argues that the 'Internet was not new in 1995, the year it arguably became "new"' (2006: 3), but rather it emerged as new in a concerted effort by the mass media, we might think of Facebook's newness not as coinciding with the time of its invention but rather as something it became much later in the course of Facebook's lifetime. More specifically, Facebook's moment of newness became apparent when existing words, categories and concepts ceased being able to describe and explain it adequately. Becoming new in the case of Facebook can thus be understood as coinciding with its conceptual emergence. Yet, because concepts cannot be traced to a single source or origin (Berenskoetter, 2017: 169), providing an accurate starting point to Facebook's life as a concept will only ever be partial.

To be new, Chun (2006) suggests, is not simply to be singular. Dictionary definitions, she says, also emphasize repetition, positing things that can be made anew, fresh and additional. In this book, we have seen many examples of such remakings. Just as the internet seemed to renew old theories and dreams, Facebook leaned on existing techno-libertarian ideologies in shaping a company culture around the cult of entrepreneurship, start-up discourse and hacker ethic. Dreams of openness, communalism and the power of networks are part of Facebook's founding myth, as are existing conceptions of friendship, news and social behaviours. Hardly any of these things can be described as unique or unprecedented. At the same time, Facebook does not just renew existing theories and ideas, it also helps to reconfigure our understandings of the terms it merely seeks to represent.

Facebook did not just represent friendship, for example, it fundamentally changed how we think of friendships today – even shaping a new concept of the Facebook 'friend'.

Indeed, as Carolyn Marvin (1988) suggests, 'new technologies' is an historically relative term. It is relative in the sense that hardly any technology can be said to be without precedent, if we take this to mean without being modelled on previous examples, patterns or instances. Historians of science and technology remind us to be wary of claims that speak of radical innovations and transformations. History also tells us that there is nothing inevitable about the success of technological or scientific inventions. Whether we are talking about the invention of the telegraph, the electric light or the internet, these technologies, or rather sociotechnical systems, did not emerge in a vacuum but came into being as part of various social, economic and political arrangements (Bazerman, 2002). This is no different with Facebook.

If the relativity of the term 'new technologies' stems in part from resisting ideas of uniqueness and singularity, then what are the relations and propositions considered to be part of 'making Facebook new'? Put differently, if the claim that Facebook is new is relative, then to whom or what are we comparing Facebook? There are different ways of answering this, as we have seen. First, Facebook itself seems to do a good job in comparing itself to everything from the electric light, furniture, cars, public institutions, governmental bodies and communication channels through to communal gathering spaces. Moreover, we might also think of Facebook's newness in terms of 'not previously used or owned'. Facebook might be new to those who have never used Facebook before, whether these are individual users or entire countries. As we have seen in the case of Myanmar, for example, Facebook was introduced to the general public by way of a pre-installed data plan on new mobile phones rather than via internet browsers. As my informant tellingly proclaimed, in Myanmar, Facebook is everything. It cannot be compared to the internet or to social media because, in order for that comparison to hold, people would have to have a conception of what the internet or social media is. That is not to say that people in Myanmar do not know these things, or that knowing these things is important. That is to say, instead, that we cannot simply assume that these things are related or part of the propositions needed for making sense of Facebook.

There are many ways in which Facebook and newness relate. We might also think of Facebook's newness in the dictionary sense of 'additional, supplementary and extra'. Here we might think of Facebook as new in contexts where it offers the only or one of the only supplemental information channels available. Although reluctant to speak too positively about Facebook, an Ethiopian human rights and internet activist told me how she and her friends while growing up depended almost entirely on Facebook as an alternative to state-controlled media outlets for information. While the core argument is made that Facebook's newness has emerged only lately, what this newness entails is constantly up for grabs. As we have discussed as part of this concluding chapter, Facebook was arguably rejuvenated during the Covid-19 pandemic. For many users confined to their homes in different states of quarantine, Facebook offered a way to stay connected with the 'outside world'. After all, dictionary definitions suggest that the 'new' can also be understood as something that is 'already existing but seen, experienced or acquired' in new ways.

More-than-social media

If the political is ultimately about the inclusion of some moment rather than others and the suppression of alternatives, adding the political to Facebook – either as a prefix or suffix – seems rather superfluous at this point. There is nothing *un*political about Facebook. Whether we are talking about indifferent ad policies or polluted information, the many stories told in this book reveal the extent to which

Facebook has become 'more-than-social media'. Here I am drawing on Sarah Whatmore's (2006) notion of 'more-than-human' worlds. For Whatmore, the 'more-than-human' offers a way of decentering the human in cultural geography by attending to all kinds of things that help to co-fabricate the world, including animals and technological devices. Just to what exactly the 'more' in the 'more-than-human' refers, however, is often not specified. I find the notion of the 'more-than-human' to be useful for thinking through the assertion that Facebook has become more-than-social media for a number of reasons. It helps to decenter social media in an understanding of Facebook, without specifying what the more-than entails. The openness of the more-than seems useful for thinking through the variability and multiplicity of concepts, especially as it manifests in different minds, experiences and practices. The idea of 'more-than-human' is not about additions or blurring of boundaries. Instead, the 'more-than-human', or in this case the 'more-than-social media', 'operates as a strategy that asks "how those categories rub on, and against, each other, generating friction and leakage"' (Luciano and Chen, quoted in Springgay and Truman, 2017: 9). In this way it asks the analyst to attend to frictions between our understanding of Facebook and social media, asking how they might be different and related, how an understanding of social media grounds or rubs against an understanding of Facebook, and what it would entail to think of them separately.

Whether we think of Facebook as a hyperobject or concept (or neither), Facebook has become so familiar and habitual that it also exists in the minds, opinions, imaginaries, expectations and experiences of different people. It is important to acknowledge that hyperobjects, the way that Timothy Morton defines them, and philosophical concepts are not the same. To use them interchangeably can be problematic, which is not my intention. To Morton, hyperobjects are very specific things that simultaneously evade direct experience yet are considered to 'be as real as this sentence' (2013: 48).[2] To Deleuze and Guattari (1994), concepts do not represent something in the actual world; instead they are invented and created. Philosophers create concepts to reorient thought. Albeit in somewhat different terms, Deleuze and Guattari's (1994) emphasis on the generative nature of concepts is reminiscent of Morton's notion of the hyperobject as forcing thought on us.[3] When people expect Facebook to behave and work in a certain way, it is arguably not *because* they judge Facebook by the standards of something generic called a social media platform, digital infrastructure or a website. Facebook is judged by the standards of Facebook, no matter how diverse, imaginary or even unattainable those standards may be. The point is that by becoming something 'more-than' Facebook seems to have exceeded existing linguistic markers.

When politicians expect Facebook to work without the clouded subjectivities of human editors, and human editors, for their part, expect Facebook's algorithms to work like they do, this is because they have come to attach certain meanings to something they call Facebook (including its many proxies such as the algorithm, platform, content moderators, APIs etc.). The fact that many conceptions and opinions exist as to what Facebook is and how it ought to behave only speaks to the notion of Facebook becoming conceptual. We can see the 'more-than-social media' of Facebook in conversations over politics, news, misinformation, advertising, algorithms and much more. As such, we might say that 'Facebook talks'. For historian of science Lorraine Daston, 'things talk' by virtue of enabling and constraining meaning, a capacity which in part is derived from 'certain properties of the things themselves' (2004: 15). This means that things are not just objects of political deliberation, but they also shape and intervene in politics by virtue of being forceful.

Being many things at once is bound to disappoint. To paraphrase a Facebook employee in an informal meeting, when I visited the headquarters for an invited seminar: No matter what we do, or what we design, someone will complain. There is always someone who feels overstepped or bypassed. Listening to a bunch of social scientists critiquing Facebook's faulty algorithms, the employee, a product manager, was clearly frustrated by the level of abstract theoretical discussion and the complaints of the academics in the room. 'Fair compared to what exactly', she asked us, 'whom do you want to satisfy?' These are fair points, indeed. The question is not about designing for some universally recognized notion of fairness or truth. Demanding that the algorithms work in a certain way necessitates that they will not work optimally for someone else. But the question is for what we want Facebook's algorithms to be optimized, and to grapple with the question of for whom the algorithms work.

Possibilities for the future

Why is it that we have come to expect so much of Facebook, despite the relentless scandals and privacy breaches? Just like a parent, a person we have not chosen freely but whose presence continues to be part of most people's lives, Facebook exerts both control and freedom. Some love their parents, others despise them. Some wish for different parents, others couldn't be happier. Some don't care what their parents think of them, others do everything they can to be recognized and get attention from them. Even in the most loving relations, most people have a complicated relationship with their parents. No relationship is a constant and will change over time. Most parents set out rules for their children, sometimes quite randomly, at other times well founded and reasonable. Parents are not always fair, well meaning, or kind, though we expect them to be. Ideal parents raise, care for, and educate their children. They offer templates and guidelines for going about the world. We hope for our parents to act as role models, offering moral and social support. We expect much of parents, but more often than not parents expect even more from their children. Ideas of good parenting proliferate, as do ideas about ideal childhood. To most children, their parents are everything. Many of these things ring true of our relationship to Facebook as well.

Metaphorically speaking (as if we haven't already exhausted metaphors in this book), the role of Facebook resembles that of a parent, or at least, our abstract ideas and ideals of what a parent is supposed to be. Like the many missteps of parenting, Zuckerberg's apology tour and users' relative loyalty hint at the forgiveness most children show (for better or worse) when their parents do wrong. Parental media normally conjures up images of parental monitoring of children and adolescent media use. Yet many parents also lack the language or knowledge of how to respond to whatever information their monitoring yields. Facebook, a monitoring device for sure, also lacks the language or capacity to take responsibility for its actions. More than simply another word for the ad-tech-surveillance complex, thinking of Facebook in parental terms is also about acknowledging the 'complicated relationships' involved. Using such a charged metaphor, however, is not without its problems. Do we really want to think of Facebook as a parent?

While nobody wants a parent like Facebook (monitoring, controlling and extracting everything one does), the parental metaphor points to the ambiguities of power relations. Involuntary at the core, yet often voluntary at heart. Simultaneously caring and controlling, rule-enforcing and resistant, wilful and indifferent. While the parent–child relationship is often thought of as deeply asymmetric and skewed, this is only half the story. Just as children in many cases have to raise their parents as well, Facebook users are also parenting Facebook. We might think of this in at least two distinct ways: first in the technical sense, through the logic of training in machine learning, whereby user's actions and traces train computer models for generating new predictions; second, in a more hopeful and speculative way, in that playing with the idea of parenting Facebook may open up possibilities for the future.

To say that Facebook is Facebook, as I have claimed in this book, is to resist any easy labels. If, as Morton (2013) says, hyperobjects are entities that cause us to reflect on our place in the world, mobilizing a seemingly tautological conception of Facebook forces us to interrogate its meaning, rather than take it for granted. I could also have said something along the lines of 'there is nothing like Facebook' and that would have been more or less accurate, but it would not have been the same as claiming Facebook is Facebook. There are at least two sides to this. First, it would not have captured the notion that Facebook has turned into a concept of its own. Just like people invoke concepts such as love and hate, but in very different ways, Facebook does not mean the same thing and is not simply a word that can be looked up in the dictionary. To say that Facebook has turned conceptual is to highlight its multiplicity. Facebook does not exist in a singular form. Rather we are dealing with multiple conceptions that take on different forms. Borrowing from Berenskoetter, we might say that conceptions of Facebook 'evolve throughout history', 'take on different empirical forms yet still maintains an abstract unity', and 'artificially reified yet at closer inspection reveals nothing but fragments' (2017: 170). Secondly, the seemingly tautological definition makes us pause in ways that just claiming its uniqueness would not. Everyone and everything is arguably unique, but not everyone's uniqueness becomes a global political and economic force. While the statement Facebook is Facebook at first glance may seem obvious, it is precisely in the seemingly obvious that we are confronted with the fact that no precise meaning exists so that we must 'stay with the trouble' of interrogating how the concept of Facebook is made to cohere in the present moment and what we would like it to mean in the future.[4] Just as concepts can travel from discipline to discipline and take on new meanings (Bal, 2002), framing Facebook as a concept points to its generative force. Importantly, as Deleuze and Guattari (1994) have asserted, the purpose of a concept is not to confine meaning but to create intensive orientations.

The purpose, then, is not to come up with a precise definition of what Facebook is, but to think about the repercussions and implications of what its different conceptions do and the kinds of realities that are shaped by them. What do different labels do for an understanding of Facebook? What are the possible consequences of using certain metaphors rather than others? What stories are more or less likely to emerge in the different ways that Facebook gets framed? From a topological perspective there is indeed hope. Because Facebook is neither a given nor a unified actor, how we enter into and reside in a relation with Facebook is also not a given. To posit Facebook as new in the sense of its becoming, rather than to assume its newness from the start, also means that what is new about Facebook can be renewed as well. What will become of Facebook nobody knows. All we know is that new stories will inevitably emerge, as will new scandals, new controversies, new beginnings and new ends. Everybody has a Facebook story, as we said in the very beginning of the book. As this book has shown, we also enter into stories. Like children who are born into their parents' stories, their histories and legacies, as students, critics and users of Facebook, we are often introduced to the same stories about Facebook. What I hope to have achieved is not to have closed the story about Facebook but rather to have incited the curiosity for more stories.

Notes

Introduction: Facebook is Facebook

1 Market capitalization measures the total value of a company based on the stock price multiplied by the shares outstanding.
2 Foote, Shaw and Mako (2018) found that scholarship using the term 'social media' increased fivefold between 2010 and 2015. Many of the articles examined were mainly about Facebook.
3 The same could possibly also be said about Google serving as a shorthand for search.
4 This definition is itself an accumulation by merging Deleuze and Guattari's statement that a concept is composed of multiplicities and can be 'considered as the point of coincidence, condensation, or accumulation of its own components' (1994: 20), and the Wittgensteinian notion of 'family resemblance' that holds that concepts are connected by a series of overlapping similarities, where no one feature is common to all of the conceptions.
5 We might think of the consistency of concepts in terms of a Venn diagram or, as Deleuze and Guattari say: 'There is an area ab that belongs to both a and b, where a and b 'become' indiscernible. These zones, thresholds or becomings, define the internal consistency of the concept' (1994: 20).

1 Metaphors at work: Framing Facebook

1 For more on the Foucauldian understanding of discourse, see Foucault, 1970.
2 For more on the history of the internet see for example: Abbate, 2000; Castells, 2002; Driscoll and Paloque-Berges, 2017; Turner, 2006.
3 For more on the countercultural origins of the Web and its

virtual communities, see Rheingold, 1993; Baym 2010; Turner, 2006.
4 For histories of free and open-source movements, including their distinction, see Berry, 2008; Lerner and Tirole, 2002; Raymond, 1999; Stallman, 2002; Streeter, 2011.
5 David Harvey defines neoliberalism as 'a theory of political economic practices that proposes that human well-being can best be advanced by liberating individual entrepreneurial freedoms and skills within an institutional framework characterized by strong private property rights, free markets and free trade' (Harvey, 2007: 2). Neoliberalism is also an ideology that translates these principles into daily life whereby people are encouraged to regulate themselves. Moreover, as Wendy Brown has argued, neoliberalism is grounded in inequality. If everything we do as individuals is measured in terms of human capital, 'equality ceases to be our presumed natural relation with one another' (Brown, 2015: 179).
6 For more on Web 2.0 as a discursive movement see Jarrett, 2008; van Dijck and Nieborg, 2009; Zimmer, 2008.
7 See FB tech talk 'behind the code' in which Facebook engineers discuss the boot camp and the company culture.
8 https://www.quora.com/How-would-you-describe-the-Facebook-culture

2 Of electricity and chairs: Facebook as infrastructure

1 https://www.youtube.com/watch?v=SSz0DPptYNA

3 Grounded in reality: How Facebook programs sociality

1 http://miserablebliss.ca/blog/2007/07/30/what-facebook-means-to-me/
2 https://imagineannie.wordpress.com/category/food/page/22/
3 The campaign site has now been deleted, but its purpose is described in numerous news reports, for example: https://www.salon.com/2015/03/30/say_my_name_facebooks_unfair_real_names_policy_continues_to_harm_vulnerable_users
4 https://www.youtube.com/watch?v=Gy0bq9FAJRs

5 https://www.pri.org/stories/2019-02-04/we-asked-listeners-why-they-cant-quit-facebook-heres-what-you-said

6 danah boyd (2006) points out that Dunbar's number has a tendency to be misunderstood. Robin Dunbar did not claim that there is a friendship cap at 150, but that there is a cognitive limit to the number of relations that one can maintain at any given time.

7 Granovetter's thesis about the strength of weak ties has been particularly influential in research on social networks, as it describes the benefits of having access to people beyond one's close circle (e.g. employment opportunities). See Granovetter, 1973.

8 https://www.pri.org/stories/2019-02-04/we-asked-listeners-why-they-cant-quit-facebook-heres-what-you-said

9 The utility and instrumental view on friendship is by no means unique to online social network sites. In the *Nicomachean Ethics*, Aristotle (2004) famously conceived of friendship in three main ways, based on utility, pleasure and virtue. Whereas friendships based on utility are defined by people keeping each other's company in the hope of deriving some benefit from it, friendships based on pleasure exist solely for an individual's own interest. According to Aristotle's view, it is only the last form of friendship, based on virtue, that can be called real friendship. Virtue friendships are neither instrumental nor fluctuating and fun, but are based on wishing the other well for their own sake. These friendships are permanent and formed out of people's mutual appreciation of each other.

10 For more on friendships and homophily in networks, see: Chun, 2016, 2018; McPherson et al., 2001.

11 Mark Zuckerberg's favoured term for this is the 'social graph'.

12 http://wee3kids.blogspot.com/2014/03/facebooktime-suck-or-lifeline.html

13 This is closely related to Ruth Schwartz Cowan's (1983) argument in her seminal book *More Work for Mother*. The introduction of household technology, Cowan argues, did not mean less work for women but more. Technologies like the washing machine did not relieve the housewife of her work, but implied more time for raising children, managing the household and keeping up with rising cleanliness standards that developed alongside the tech.

14 See Brandom, 2018; Wagner, K., 2018: https://www.vox.com/2018/4/20/17254312/

facebook-shadow-profiles-data-collection-non-users-mark-zuckerberg

15 Social games in this context designates games played within social network sites. See Goggin, 2014; Hou, 2011.

4 ENGINEERING A PLATFORM: FACEBOOK'S TECHNO-ECONOMIC EVOLUTION

1 There are some very good accounts of Facebook that do provide a more complete history of the technological and business developments that the company has undergone over the years. For the most recent overview, see Levy, 2020. For an account of the first four to five years of the company, see Kirkpatrick, 2011. For an inside account written by one of Facebook's earliest employees that takes apart the bro-centric culture of the start-up world, see Losse, 2012. For a recent academic critique of Facebook's existential threat to democracy, see Vaidhyanathan, 2018.

2 Steven Levy's (2020) recent book on the history of Facebook provides a great account of the many mundane discussions, decisions and negotiations that went into making Facebook Facebook. Levy is a prolific American journalist who has spent his career writing about the computer industry and technology platforms. Having followed Zuckerberg since 2006, spoken to him nine times and seen how he's adapted or not adapted, Levy is well positioned to provide a readable insider account of the company.

3 For the history of the News Feed, see, for example, Chapter 4 in Bucher, 2018; Brügger, 2015; DeVito, 2017; Powers, 2017; Facebook also ran its own blog series of updates and news concerning its News Feed feature called 'News feed FYI'. The blog was regularly updated between 2013 and 2019. At the time of writing (early 2020), Facebook has revamped all news concerning its many products under the heading 'Technologies' and subheadings of 'Facebook app', 'Messenger', 'Instagram' and so on.

4 Here I am paraphrasing a tweet by Nick Seaver: https://twitter.com/npseaver/status/1163977679101734912

5 For a full-length discussion on the problematic notion of a single algorithm, see my Chapters 2 and 3 in Bucher, T., 2018.

6 As Tarleton Gillespie's (2010) seminal paper on the topic lays

out, the term 'platform' can be understood in at least four senses: computational, architectural, figurative and political. Later, in his book on content moderation, Gillespie (2018) adds a fifth dimension, which to him is central to the understanding of platforms, namely that all platforms are moderated. Other important contributions to the understanding of platforms include: Helmond's (2015) computational and Web-historical approach to 'platformization of the Web'; Srnicek (2017) on platform capitalism; van Dijck, Poell and de Waal (2018) on the *Platform Society*; and Parker and Van Alstyne's (2016) business-oriented *Platform Revolution*.

7 There is also a fascinating story about the last-minute revisions made to Facebook's IPO prospectus, told in Elmer, G. (2019).

8 See *Facebook Engineering* (https://engineering.fb.com) and *Facebook Connectivity* (https://connectivity.fb.com) for more information on the specific projects.

9 Facebook built its first data centre in Prineville, Oregon, in 2010, at the cost of 210 million dollars. As of January 2019, Facebook has built a total of fifteen data centres (with many new announced) in sites such as Papillion, Nebraska; Henrico, Virginia; Luleå, Sweden; Los Lunas, New Mexico; Newton County, Georgia; and Singapore among other places. See: https://engineering.fb.com/data-center-engineering/data-centers-2018/

5 MONETIZING YOU: FACEBOOK'S ADVERTISING ECOSYSTEM

1 This quote is derived from a *New York Times* article on Facebook's sponsored stories advertising programme (Story, 2007).

2 This example is inspired by Tanja Kant's (2020: 9) description of her own Facebook ad preferences.

3 https://www.emarketer.com/content/facebook-google-duopoly-won-t-crack-this-year

4 Facebook Ads Manager is a tool for managing and creating ad campaigns. The tool also comes in handy when you want to compare and measure your campaigns. Facebook Business Manager is a more general tool for business members to access, overview and control all the company's public Facebook pages. You can also customize the access levels between the members of the company page – for example between the roles of ad

account analysts (can only see ads), ad account advertisers (can edit and manage ads) and ad account admins (can manage all aspects of campaigns).

5 A boosted post is essentially paid content, and it will appear as 'sponsored' content to the user. This is the simplest way to advertise on Facebook. Boosted posts differ from Facebook ads because they are not created in Ads Manager and don't have the same customization features.

6 Ali et al. (2019) claim that Facebook offers over 1,000 well-defined attributes and hundreds of thousands of free-form attributes.

7 Some of these relationships were terminated in the wake of the Cambridge Analytica scandal in 2018. Following the scandal, Facebook implemented several changes. The function 'Partner Categories' was removed, in effect terminating partnerships with data brokers such as Acxiom and Datalogix. Advertisers who use the custom audience function also need to ask people for permission to reuse their personal information in this way. Facebook also established a public, searchable archive for political advertising. In addition, Facebook now forbids any advertiser actor to target an ad to less than 1,000 people. In certain countries, Facebook also offers a verification function for advertisers that offer election-related content (Datatilsynet, 2019).

8 Different platforms offer similar custom audience selection options. Twitter has 'Tailored Audiences', Google has 'Customer Match'. There is also Pinterest's 'Audiences' and LinkedIn's 'Audience Match'; see Venkatadri et al., 2019b.

9 In March 2018, civil-rights groups sued Facebook over violations of the Fair Housing Act (FHA). These groups came together accusing Facebook's ad technology of unlawfully discriminating against minorities, women and the elderly, especially as it pertained to ads for housing, jobs and credit. In an historic settlement one year later, Facebook agreed to build a designated portal for advertising in these specific ad categories to 'not allow targeting users by age, gender, zipcode, or other categories covered by anti-discrimination laws' (Dreyfuss, 2019b). As a result, Facebook created Special Ad Audiences, which works like Lookalike Audiences, except its algorithm does not consider users' demographic profile information (Sapiezynski et al., 2019).

10 The programmatic process is usually comprised of a user, a

publisher, a supply-side platform (SSP), a demand-side platform (DSP), an ad network and an ad exchange. The SSP is an advertising technology (AdTech) platform used by publishers to manage, sell and optimize their ad inventory (ad space). The DSP is an AdTech platform that allows advertisers and marketers to buy inventory on an impression-by-impression basis and to manage multiple ad exchange and data exchange accounts through one interface. DSPs do not purchase media directly from publishers, but rather communicate with SSPs through an ad exchange. The way it works, and assuming the publisher has its website rigged to display ads by making its ad inventory (ad space) available to an SSP, is that as soon as a user visits the website, the publisher sends an ad request to multiple ad exchanges via its ad server and/or the SSP. The DSPs then bid on the ad request (impression), and based on the highest and most relevant bid, the SSP picks a winner. Subsequently, the winning ad is instantly sent to the publisher and displayed to the user.

11 Bid strategies are Facebook's overall approach to spending budget and getting results. The strategy chosen by the advertiser tells Facebook how to bid for them in an auction; see: https://www.facebook.com/business/help/16195917347421 16?id=2196356200683573

12 While relevance itself is a highly relative term, in the Facebook ad delivery process it is being conceptualized as a mixture of engagement and quality; see Facebook's Advertising Policies, Facebook for Business, 2020d: https://www.facebook.com/business/help/423781975167984

6 Personalized politics: Facebook's profiling machinery

1 https://www.lexico.com/en/definition/politics
2 For a great overview and in-depth analysis of how the internet, social media and data analytics have changed politics and political communication, see, for example, Anstead and Chadwick, 2008; Chadwick, 2013; Howard, 2006; Kreiss, 2012, 2016; Stromer-Galley, 2019.
3 The concept of the permanent campaign was first coined in the 1970s to describe the blurring lines between time spent on the campaign trail and in the governing office (Blumenthal,

1982). The concept has since been frequently used to describe how digital media and the 'always-on' logic of social media seem to demand an ongoing effort by politicians to engage in campaigning and communicate with citizens (see Elmer et al., 2012; Larsson, 2016).

4 As described by scholars working at the intersection of information technology and political communication, the mobilization of data analytics and microtargeting methods was a prevalent feature of technology-intensive political campaigning during the 2010s, particularly in the US context (Karpf, 2016). Though much of the literature on technology-intensive campaigning and analytics comes out of the US, the importance of digital technologies and data analytics is evident in many other national contexts as well. See Anstead, 2017; Dommett and Temple, 2018; Jungherr, 2016; Kreiss and Howard, 2010.

5 At the time of writing this book, Brad Parscale is the digital campaign manager of Trump's re-election campaign. Given how often he named Facebook, and especially Facebook's advertising tools, as decisive features for winning the 2016 election, interviews with him often focus on the role of Facebook. See for example, Smith, 2020; Marantz, A., 2020.

6 As Brym et al. (2018: 629) exemplify: 'Campaign organizers believed that if, say, enough Haitian Americans in Miami could be reminded of the failures of the Clinton Foundation following the 2010 earthquake in Port-au-Prince; and if enough doubts could be put in the minds of a critical mass of African-American voters in cities such as Milwaukee about the sincerity of Clinton's support for racial equality, then such people would stay home on election day.'

7 For a book that tackles the question of public values in a platform society dominated by private tech companies, see van Dijck, Poell and de Waal, 2018.

8 The concept of 'media logic' was first introduced by Altheide and Snow in 1979, as a way to identify how the logics of media (e.g. formats, templates, genres, tropes, etc.) came to impact other areas of society. This concept has been widely influential as it speaks to the various degrees of dependencies dependency between media and politics.

9 Evident also from the increasing amount of political communications research on digital advertising. See, for example, Benoit et al., 2017; Fowler, 2018; Kreiss and McGregor, 2019; Williams and Gulati, 2018).

10 See for example, Søe (2018) for a good discussion on the
different meanings and approaches to these terms. Despite
inconsistencies in how these terms are used in practice,
they are often meant to signal slight differences in intent or
motive. Whereas misinformation is generally understood as a
type of 'factually false' information, disinformation does not
require the information to be 'factual' or 'false'. Unlike the
term misinformation, disinformation 'focuses on deceptive
intent of the source' (Li, 2020: 125). As Søe writes, common
dictionary definitions and journalistic accounts conceptualize
'misinformation as unintended false, inaccurate, or misleading
information' while disinformation is understood as 'false,
inaccurate, or misleading information intended to deceive and/
or mislead' (2018: 321).

11 Before Wylie, there was another whistle-blower. Kosinski told
his friend Harry Davies at the *Guardian* about the Kogan-SCL
connection in late 2014, and a year later Davies' story was
published in the *Guardian*, reporting on misused Facebook data
utilized in the Ted Cruz political campaign (Davies, 2015).

12 Similar sentiments have been regularly reported in the press and
in UN human rights reports. In an NYT feature on Facebook's
role in inciting hate speech in Myanmar, Thet Swe Win, founder
of Synergy, a group that focuses on fostering social harmony
in Myanmar, said 'The military has gotten a lot of benefit from
Facebook'. 'I wouldn't say Facebook is directly involved in the
ethnic cleansing', he said, 'but there is a responsibility they
had to take proper actions to avoid becoming an instigator of
genocide' (Mozur, 2018). Nyan also did not want to go as far
as claiming Facebook is to blame for the genocide ('it's more
complicated than that'), but that it certainly did not help to stop
it either (by deleting or governing the dissemination of hate
speech and propaganda).

13 The driver-car is much akin to Bruno Latour's famous example
of the merging agencies of humans and non-humans in his
notion of the 'citizen-gun' or 'gun-citizen'. Asking whether
guns kill people or people with guns kill people, Latour (1999)
suggests the dichotomy is misleading to begin with. Neither
entity remains the same when entering into a relationship; that
is, the citizen is transformed by the possession of a gun, and the
gun when in the hands of a human agent ready to use it changes
its meaning and agential capacities.

CONCLUSION: THE MANY FACES OF FACEBOOK

1 By common parlance and global experience, I want to stress
   how the Covid-19 pandemic has introduced a state of exception
   on a general level – for most people, in most nations around
   the world, while acknowledging that for some people, mostly
   non-whites, poor, displaced, imprisoned, chronically ill and
   otherwise marginalized, being isolated and living in a constant
   state of uncertainty and chaos is sadly not the exception but
   the norm. There will undoubtedly be much written about these
   events in the years to come, but we are already seeing some
   critical social analysis emerging. See, for example, critiques of
   'The Household' concept in the *Feminist Review* blog: https://
   femrev.wordpress.com/2020/05/26/confronting-the-household
2 Whereas Morton subscribes to a philosophical thought known as
   object-oriented ontology, the idea that objects exist independently
   of human perception (specifically aimed at breaking the spell of
   correlationism), the notion of concept is derived from the Latin
   conceptus, which refers to an idea conceived in the mind (thus
   not at all independent of human thought). Whereas Morton's
   emphasis on the nonlocality of hyperobjects refers to a specific
   understanding of quantum theory, we might also think of
   concepts as nonlocal in the sense that Deleuze and Guattari
   think of them as multiplicities.
3 These are meant only to acknowledge that we are dealing with
   terms that have their intellectual histories, legacies and different
   purposes and implications. Using the notion of both hyperobject
   and concept to make sense of Facebook does not mean to
   suggest that Facebook maps easily onto Morton's description of
   a hyperobject or that it is exactly like the concepts described by
   Deleuze and Guattari.
4 The idea of staying with the trouble is borrowed from Donna
   Haraway, whose book with the same title urges scientists to
   dismiss any faith in technofixes by continuing to 'stir up potent
   response to devastating events' (2016: 1).

References

Abbate, J. (2000). *Inventing the Internet.* Cambridge, MA: MIT Press.

Abidin, C. (2018). *Internet Celebrity: Understanding Fame Online.* Bingley: Emerald Publishing Limited.

Adorno, T. (2013). *The Jargon of Authenticity.* New York: Routledge.

Ahmed, S. (2006). *Queer Phenomenology: Orientations, Objects, Others.* Duke University Press.

Ahmed, S. (2010). Orientations matter. In D. Coole and S. Frost (eds) *New Materialisms: Ontology, Agency and Politics.* Durham, NC: Duke University Press, pp. 234–57.

Ahmed, S. (2017). *Living a Feminist Life.* Durham, NC: Duke University Press.

Akrich, M. (1992). The description of technical objects. In W. E. Bijker and J. Law (eds) *Shaping Technology/Building Society, Studies in Socio Technical Change.* Cambridge, MA: MIT Press, pp. 205–24.

Akrich, M., M. Callon, B. Latour and A. Monaghan (2002). The key to success in innovation. Part II: The art of choosing good spokespersons. *International Journal of Innovation Management,* 6(02): 207–25.

Ali, M., P. Sapiezynski, M. Bogen, A. Korolova, A. Mislove and A. Rieke (2019a). Discrimination through optimization: How Facebook's ad delivery can lead to skewed outcomes. arXiv preprint arXiv:1904.02095. https://arxiv.org/pdf/1904.02095.pdf

Ali, M., P. Sapiezynski, A. Korolova, A. Mislove and A. Rieke (2019b). Ad delivery algorithms: The hidden arbiters of political messaging. arXiv preprint:1912.04255. https://arxiv.org/pdf/1912.04255.pdf

AllFacebook (2008). Mark Zuckerberg/Sarah Lacy SXSW Interview. *Zuckerberg Transcripts,* 16. https://epublications.marquette.edu/zuckerberg_files_transcripts/16/

Anderson, B. (2009). Affective atmospheres. *Emotion, Space and Society,* 2(2): 7–81.

Anderson, M. and J. Jiang, (2018). Teens, social media and technology. *Pew Research Center,* 31. https://www.pewresearch.org/internet/2018/05/31/teens-social-media-technology-2018/

Andrejevic, M. (2010). Social network exploitation. In Z. Papacharissi (ed.) *A Networked Self.* New York: Routledge, pp. 90–110.

Andreou, A., G. Venkatadri, O. Goga, K. Gummadi, P. Loiseau and A. Mislove (2018). Investigating ad transparency mechanisms in social media: A case study of Facebook's explanations. http://www.ccs.neu.edu/home/amislove/publications/Explanations-NDSS.pdf

Angwin, J. (2009). *Stealing MySpace: The Battle to Control the Most Popular Website in America.* Random House.

Anstead, N. (2017). Data-driven campaigning in the 2015 United Kingdom general election. *The International Journal of Press/Politics,* 22(3): 294–313.

Anstead, N. and A. Chadwick (2008). Parties, election campaigning, and the Internet: Toward a comparative institutional approach. In A. Chadwick and P. Howards (eds) *Routledge Handbook of Internet Politics.* London: Routledge, pp. 72–87.

Appadurai, A. (1996). *Modernity at Large: Cultural Dimensions of Globalization.* Minneapolis: University of Minnesota Press.

Aristotle (2004). *The Nicomachean Ethics,* trans. J. A. K. Thomson and H. Tredennick. Penguin Classics.

Arora, P. (2019). *The Next Billion Users: Digital Life Beyond the West.* Cambridge, MA: Harvard University Press.

Arora, P. and L. Scheiber (2017). Slumdog romance: Facebook love and digital privacy at the margins. *Media, Culture and Society,* 39(3): 408–22.

Atlantic Live (2013). Facebook nation: Mr. Zuckerberg goes to Washington. *Zuckerberg Videos,* 243. https://epublications.marquette.edu/zuckerberg_files_videos/243

Bailey, M. M. (2011). Gender/racial realness: Theorizing the gender system in ballroom culture. *Feminist Studies,* 37(2): 365–86.

Bakardjieva, M. (2014). Social media and the McDonaldization of friendship. *Communications,* 39(4): 369–87.

Bal, M. (2002). *Travelling Concepts in the Humanities: A Rough Guide.* Toronto: University of Toronto Press.

Banet-Weiser, S. (2012). *AuthenticTM: The Politics of Ambivalence in a Brand Culture.* New York: New York University Press.

Barbrook, R. and A. Cameron (1996). The Californian ideology. *Science as Culture,* 6(1): 44–72.

Barker, H. and Y. Taylor (2007). *Faking It: The Quest for Authenticity in Popular Music.* New York: W.W. Norton and Company.

Bastone, N. (2019). Former Facebook employees reportedly say the corporate culture is like a cult where you have to be happy all the time. *Business Insider.* https://www.businessinsider.in/former-facebook-employees-reportedly-say-the-corporate-culture-is-like-a-cult-where-you-have-to-be-happy-all-the-time/articleshow/67445965.cms

Baym, N. K. (2010). *Personal Connections in the Digital Age*. Cambridge, UK: Polity.

Baym, N. K. (2011). The Swedish model: Balancing markets and gifts in the music industry. *Popular Communication*, 9(1): 22–38.

Bazerman, C. (2002). *The Languages of Edison's Light*. Cambridge, MA: MIT Press.

BBC (2020). What do I need to know about cookies? *Cookie and Browser Settings*. https://www.bbc.co.uk/usingthebbc/cookies/what-do-i-need-to-know-about-cookies/

Beckett, L. (2017). Trump digital director says Facebook helped win the White House. *Guardian*. https://www.theguardian.com/technology/2017/oct/08/trump-digital-director-brad-parscale-facebook-advertising

Bell, E. J., T. Owen, P. D. Brown, C. Hauka and N. Rashidian (2017). The platform press: How Silicon Valley reengineered journalism. *Tow Reports*. https://www.cjr.org/tow_center_reports/platform-press-how-silicon-valley-reengineered-journalism.php

Benjamin, R. (2019). *Race after Technology: Abolitionist Tools for the New Jim Code*. Cambridge, UK: Polity.

Benjamin, W. (2008). *The Work of Art in the Age of Mechanical Reproduction*. Penguin UK.

Benkler, Y., R. Faris, H. Roberts and E. Zuckerman (2017). Study: Breitbart-led right-wing media ecosystem altered broader media agenda. *Columbia Journalism Review*, 3.

Bennett, J. (2010). *Vibrant Matter: A Political Ecology of Things*. Durham, NC: Duke University Press.

Benoit, W. L., K. M. Coe, J. L. Conners, W. O. Dailey, C. de Anda, E. A. Hinck, R. S. Hinck, S. S. Hinck, A. Koehn and J. A. Kuypers (2017). *Political Campaign Communication: Theory, Method, and Practice*. London: Rowman and Littlefield.

Berenskoetter, F. (2017). Approaches to concept analysis. *Millennium*, 45(2): 151–73.

Berlant, L. G. (2011). *Cruel Optimism*. Durham, NC: Duke University Press.

Berry, D. M. (2008). *Copy, Rip, Burn: The Politics of Copyleft and Open Source*. London: Pluto Press.

Bhatia, V. K. (2010). Interdiscursivity in professional communication. *Discourse and Communication*, 4(1): 32–50.

Bille, M., Bjerregaard, P. and Sørensen, T. F. (2015). Staging atmospheres: Materiality, culture, and the texture of the in-between. *Emotion, Space and Society*, 15: 31–8.

Bimber, B. (2014). Digital media in the Obama campaigns of 2008 and 2012: Adaptation to the personalized political communication environment. *Journal of Information Technology and Politics*, 11(2): 130–50.

Bivens, R. (2017). The gender binary will not be deprogrammed: Ten years of coding gender on Facebook. *New Media and Society*, 19(6): 880–98.

Bivens, R. and O. L. Haimson (2016). Baking gender into social media design: How platforms shape categories for users and advertisers. *Social Media and Society*, 2(4): 2056305116672486.

Blatterer, H. (2019). Siegfried Kracauer's differentiating approach to friendship. *Journal of Historical Sociology*, 32(2): 173–88.

Blumenthal, S. (1982). *The Permanent Campaign*. New York: Simon and Schuster.

Blumler, J. G. and D. Kavanagh (1999). The third age of political communication: Influences and features. *Political Communication*, 16(3): 209–30.

Boczkowski, P. and L. A. Lievrouw (2008). Bridging STS and communication studies: research on media and information technologies. In U. Felt, R. Fouché, C. A. Miller and L. Smith-Doerr (eds) *New Handbook of Science and Technologies Studies*. Cambridge, MA: MIT Press.

Böhme, G. (1993). Atmosphere as the fundamental concept of a new aesthetics. *Thesis Eleven*, 36(1): 113–26.

Boltanski, L. and E. Chiapello (2005). The new spirit of capitalism. *International Journal of Politics, Culture, and Society*, 18(3–4): 161–88.

Bond, R. M., C. J. Fariss, J. J. Jones, A. D. Kramer, C. Marlow, J. E. Settle and J. H. Fowler (2012). A 61-million-person experiment in social influence and political mobilization. *Nature*, 489(7415): 295–8.

Bosworth, A. (2011). How does Facebook Engineering's 'Bootcamp' program work? *Quora*. https://www.quora.com/How-does-Facebook-Engineerings-Bootcamp-program-work

Bosworth, A. (2014). What's the history of the 'Awesome Button' (that eventually became the Like button) on Facebook? *Quora*. https://www.quora.com/Whats-the-history-of-the-Awesome-Button-that-eventually-became-the-Like-button-on-Facebook

Bosworth, A. and C. Cox. (2013). Providing a newsfeed based on user affinity for entities and monitored actions in a social network environment. *Facebook*, US 8,402,094 B2.

Bourdieu, P. (2018). The forms of capital. In M. Granovetter and R. Swedberg (eds) *The Sociology of Economic Life*. New York: Routledge.

Bowker, G. (1994). *Science on the Run: Information Management and Industrial Geophysics at Schlumberger, 1920–1940*. Cambridge, MA: MIT Press.

boyd, d. (2006). Friends, friendsters, and myspace top 8: Writing community into being on social network sites. *First Monday*, 11. http://www.firstmonday.org/issues/issue11_12/boyd/index.html

boyd, d. (2012). The politics of real names. *Communications of the ACM*, 55(8): 29–31.

boyd, d. and N. Ellison (2007). Social network sites: Definition, history, and scholarship. *Journal of Computer-Mediated Communication*, 13(1): 210–23.

boyd, d. and E. Hargittai (2010). Facebook privacy settings: Who cares? *First Monday*, 15(8). https://firstmonday.org/article/view/3086/2589

Brandom, R. (2018). Shadow profiles are the biggest flaw in Facebook's privacy defense. *The Verge*. https://www.theverge.com/2018/4/11/17225482/facebook-shadow-profiles-zuckerberg-congress-data-privacy

Brodie, P. (2020). Climate extraction and supply chains of data. *Media, Culture and Society*: 0163443720904601.

Brown, B. (2001). Thing theory. *Critical Inquiry*, 28(1): 1–22.

Brown, W. (2015). *Undoing the Demos: Neoliberalism's Stealth Revolution*. Cambridge, MA: MIT Press.

Brügger, N. (2015). A brief history of Facebook as a media text: The development of an empty structure. *First Monday*, 20(5). https://firstmonday.org/ojs/index.php/fm/article/view/5423/4466

Brym, R., A. Slavina, M. Todosijevic and D. Cowan (2018). Social movement horizontality in the internet age? A critique of Castells in light of the Trump victory. *Canadian Review of Sociology/Revue canadienne de sociologie*, 55(4): 624–34.

Bucher, T. (2013). The friendship assemblage: Investigating programmed sociality on Facebook. *Television and New Media*, 14(6): 479–93.

Bucher, T. (2018). *If … Then: Algorithmic Power and Politics*. New York: Oxford University Press.

Buchheit, P. (2009). Applied philosophy, a.k.a. 'hacking'. Paul Buchheit blog. http://paulbuchheit.blogspot.com/2009_10_01_archive.html

Burrell, J. (2016). How the machine 'thinks': Understanding opacity in machine learning algorithms. *Big Data and Society*, 3(1): 2053951715622512.

Cadwalladr, C. and E. Graham-Harrison (2018). Revealed: 50 million

Facebook profiles harvested for Cambridge Analytica in major data breach. *Guardian*. https://www.theguardian.com/news/2018/mar/17/cambridge-analytica-facebook-influence-us-election

Calia, M. (2018). Steve Bannon at FT conference: I didn't know about Facebook data mining at Cambridge Analytica. *CNBC*. https://www.cnbc.com/2018/03/22/steve-bannon-at-ft-conference-i-didnt-know-about-facebook-data-mining.html

Carmi, E. (2020a). *Media Distortions: Understanding the Power Behind Spam, Noise and Other Deviant Media*. New York: Peter Lang.

Carmi, E. (2020b). Rhythmedia: A study of Facebook immune system. *Theory, Culture and Society*, 0263276420917466.

Castells, M. (2002). *The Internet Galaxy: Reflections on the Internet, Business, and Society*. Oxford: Oxford University Press.

Castillo, M. (2018). Zuckerberg tells Congress Facebook is not a media company: 'I consider us to be a technology company'. *CNBC*. https://www.cnbc.com/2018/04/11/mark-zuckerberg-facebook-is-a-technology-company-not-media-company.html

Chadwick, A. (2013). *The Hybrid Media System: Politics and Power*. New York: Oxford University Press.

Chadwick, A. and J. Stromer-Galley (2016). Digital media, power, and democracy in parties and election campaigns: Party decline or party renewal? *International Journal of Press/Politics*, 21(3): 283–93.

Cheney-Lippold, J. (2017). *We Are Data: Algorithms and the Making of Our Digital Selves*. New York: New York University Press.

Chinoy, S. (2018). What 7 creepy patents reveal about Facebook. *New York Times*. https://www.nytimes.com/interactive/2018/06/21/opinion/sunday/facebook-patents-privacy.html

Cho, A. (2018). Default publicness: Queer youth of color, social media, and being outed by the machine. *New Media and Society*, 20(9): 3183–200.

Chun, W. H. K. (2006). Introduction: Did somebody say new media? In W. H. K. Chun and T. Keenan (eds) *New Media, Old Media: A History and Theory Reader*. New York: Routledge.

Chun, W. H. K. (2016). *Updating to Remain the Same: Habitual New Media*. Cambridge, MA: MIT Press.

Chun, W. H. K. (2018). Queerying homophily. In C. Apprich, W. H. K. Chun and F. Cramer (eds) *Pattern Discrimination*. Lüneburg: Meson Press, pp. 59–97.

Chun, W. H. K. (2021). *Discriminating Data*. Cambridge, MA: MIT Press.

Citron, D. K. and M. A. Franks (2020). The internet as a speech machine and other myths confounding Section 230 speech reform.

Boston University School of Law, Public Law Research Paper (20–8).

Clough, P. T. (2008). The affective turn: Political economy, biomedia and bodies. *Theory, Culture and Society*, 25(1): 1–22.

CNBC (2004). Mark Zuckerberg Interview on CNBC from 2004. *Zuckerberg Transcripts*, 72. https://epublications.marquette.edu/zuckerberg_files_transcripts/72

CNN Money/Fortune (2013). Mark Zuckerberg: Why we don't want to build a phone. *Zuckerberg Transcripts*, 98. https://epublications.marquette.edu/zuckerberg_files_transcripts/98

Cockburn, C. (1988). *Machinery of Dominance: Women, Men, and Technical Know-How*. Boston: Northeastern University Press.

Coleman, G. (2014). *Hacker, Hoaxer, Whistleblower, Spy: The Many Faces of Anonymous*. London: Verso Books.

Constine, J. (2016). How Facebook news feed works. Techcrunch. https://techcrunch.com/2016/09/06/ultimate-guide-to-the-news-feed/

Costa, E. (2016). *Social Media in Southeast Turkey*. London: UCL Press, p. 206.

Couldry, N. and J. Turow (2014). Advertising, big data and the clearance of the public realm: Marketers' new approaches to the content subsidy. *International Journal of Communication*, 8: 1710–26.

Cowan, R. S. (1983). *More Work for Mother*. New York: Basic Books.

Crain, M. (2019). A critical political economy of web advertising history. In N. Brügger and I. Milligan (eds) *The SAGE Handbook of Web History*. London: SAGE, p. 331.

Cranz, G. (1998). *The Chair: Rethinking Culture, Body, and Design*. New York: W.W. Norton and Company.

Cubitt, S., R. Hassan and I. Volkmer (2011). Does cloud computing have a silver lining? *Media, Culture and Society*, 33(1): 149–58.

Cunliffe, A. L. (2010). Retelling tales of the field: In search of organizational ethnography 20 years on. *Organizational Research Methods*, 13(2): 224–39.

Dant, T. (2004). The driver-car. *Theory, Culture and Society*, 21(4–5): 61–79.

Daston, L. (2004). *Things that Talk: Object Lessons from Art and Science*. New York: Zone Books.

Datatilsynet (2019). Digital targeting of political messages in Norway. https://www.datatilsynet.no/en/regulations-and-tools/reports-on-specific-subjects/digital-targeting-of-political-messages-in-norway/

Davies, H. (2015). Ted Cruz using firm that harvested data on millions of unwitting Facebook users. *Guardian.* https://www.theguardian. com/us-news/2015/dec/11/senator-ted-cruz-president-campaign-facebook-user-data

Davies, S. R. (2018). Interrogating innovation: Silence, citizenship, and the figure of the hacker. *Cultural Politics,* 14(3): 354–71.

de Vries, G. (2007). What is political in sub-politics? How Aristotle might help STS. *Social Studies of Science,* 37(5): 781–809.

Decuypere, M. and Simons, M. (2016). Relational thinking in education: Topology, sociomaterial studies, and figures. *Pedagogy, Culture and Society,* 24(3): 371–86.

Deeter, K. and M. Duong (2017). Inferring topics from social networking system communications using social context. *Facebook, Inc.* US Patent No. 9,773,283.

Deleuze, G. and F. Guattari (1994). *What is Philosophy?* New York: Columbia University Press.

DeNardis, L. (2014). *The Global War for Internet Governance.* New Haven: Yale University Press.

DeRuiter, R. J. (2016). *The Evolution of Facebook's News Feed.* Master: University of Amsterdam.

DeVito, M. A. (2017). From editors to algorithms: A values-based approach to understanding story selection in the Facebook news feed. *Digital Journalism,* 5(6): 753–73.

Dibbell, J. (1994). A rape in cyberspace or how an evil clown, a Haitian trickster spirit, two wizards, and a cast of dozens turned a database into a society. *Annual Survey of American Literature,* 47: 1.

Dreyfuss, E. (2019a). Teens don't use Facebook, but they can't escape it either. *Wired.* https://www.wired.com/story/teens-cant-escape-facebook/

Dreyfuss, E. (2019b) Facebook changes its ad tech to stop discrimination. *Wired.* https://www.wired.com/story/facebook-advertising-discrimination-settlement/

Dommett, K. (2019). Data-driven political campaigns in practice: Understanding and regulating diverse data-driven campaigns. *Internet Policy Review,* 8(4).

Dommett, K. and L. Temple (2018). Digital campaigning: The rise of Facebook and satellite campaigns. *Parliamentary Affairs,* 71(suppl. 1): 189–202.

Donath, J. S. (2002). Identity and deception in the virtual community. In P. Kollock and M. Smith (eds) *Communities in Cyberspace.* London: Routledge, pp. 37–68.

Dorsey, J. (2019). Twitter. https://twitter.com/jack/status/1189634368 081260549?lang=en

Driscoll, K. (2016). Social media's dial-up roots. *IEEE Spectrum*, 53(11): 54–60.

Driscoll, K. and C. Paloque-Berges (2017). Searching for missing 'net histories'. *Internet Histories*, 1(1–2): 47–59.

Duffy, B. E. and E. Hund (2019). Gendered visibility on social media: Navigating Instagram's authenticity bind. *International Journal of Communication*, 13: 20.

Duguay, S. (2017). Dressing up Tinderella: Interrogating authenticity claims on the mobile dating app Tinder. *Information, Communication and Society*, 20(3): 351–67.

Edwards, P. N. (1997). *The Closed World: Computers and the Politics of Discourse in Cold War America*. Cambridge, MA: MIT Press.

E-G8 Forum (2011). E-G8 Forum Mark Zuckerberg talks with Maurice Lévy. *Zuckerberg Transcripts*, 79. https://epublications.marquette.edu/zuckerberg_files_transcripts/79

Egan, E. (2016). Improving enforcement and promoting diversity: Updates to ethnic affinity marketing. *Facebook Newsroom*. https://about.fb.com/news/2016/11/updates-to-ethnic-affinity-marketing/

Ekström, M. and O. Westlund (2019). The dislocation of news journalism: A conceptual framework for the study of epistemologies of digital journalism. *Media and Communication*, 7(1): 259–70.

Ellison, N. B., C. Steinfield and C. Lampe (2007). The benefits of Facebook 'friends': Social capital and college students' use of online social network sites. *Journal of Computer-Mediated Communication*, 12(4): 1143–68.

Elmer, G. (2019). Prospecting Facebook: The limits of the economy of attention. *Media, Culture and Society*, 41(3): 332–46.

Elmer, G., G. Langlois and F. McKelvey (2012). *The Permanent Campaign: New Media, New Politics*. New York: Peter Lang.

Enli, G. (2015). *Mediated Authenticity: How the Media Constructs Reality*. New York: Peter Lang.

Enli, G. (2017). Twitter as arena for the authentic outsider: Exploring the social media campaigns of Trump and Clinton in the 2016 US presidential election. *European Journal of Communication*, 32(1): 50–61.

Espeland, W. N. and Sauder, M. (2007). Rankings and reactivity: How public measures recreate social worlds. *American Journal of Sociology*, 113(1): 1–40.

Esposito, E. and Stark, D. (2019). What's observed in a rating? Rankings as orientation in the face of uncertainty. *Theory, Culture and Society*, 36(4): 3–26.

Eveleth, R. (2019). Why are there so many weird tech patents? *Slate*. https://slate.com/technology/2019/08/amazon-sony-facebook-strange-patents.html

f8 (2008). f8 Post-Keynote Press Event. *Zuckerberg Transcripts*, 17. https://dc.uwm.edu/zuckerberg_files_transcripts/17

Facebook (2007a). Facebook unveils platform for developers of social applications. *Facebook Newsroom*. https://about.fb.com/news/2007/05/facebook-unveils-platform-for-developers-of-social-applications

Facebook (2007b). Facebook unveils Facebook ads. *Facebook Newsroom*. https://about.fb.com/news/2007/11/facebook-unveils-facebook-ads

Facebook (2007c). Leading websites offer Facebook beacon for social distribution. *Facebook Newsroom*. https://about.fb.com/news/2007/11/leading-websites-offer-facebook-beacon-for-social-distribution

Facebook (2008). Facebook expands its social platform across the web through general availability of Facebook connect. *Facebook Newsroom*. https://about.fb.com/news/2008/12/facebook-expands-its-social-platform-across-the-web-through-general-availability-of-facebook-connect

Facebook (2014). Facebook Q4 and full year 2013 earnings call. *Zuckerberg Transcripts*, 235. https://dc.uwm.edu/zuckerberg_files_transcripts/235

Facebook (2018). Facebook here together (UK). YouTube. https://www.youtube.com/watch?v=Q4zd7X98eOs

Facebook (2020a). Facebook reports first quarter 2020 results. *Facebook for Investors*. https://investor.fb.com/investor-news/press-release-details/2020/Facebook-Reports-First-Quarter-2020-Results/default.aspx

Facebook (2020b). New steps to protect the US elections. *Facebook Newsroom*. https://about.fb.com/news/2020/09/additional-steps-to-protect-the-us-elections

Facebook Careers (2020). Facebook life. https://www.facebook.com/careers/facebook-life/

Facebook for Business (2015). Showing relevance scores for ads on Facebook. https://www.facebook.com/business/news/relevance-score

Facebook for Business (2020a). How to create custom or lookalike audiences in Ads manager. https://www.facebook.com/business/learn/lessons/using-ads-manager-to-create-custom-lookalike-audiences

Facebook for Business (2020b). Help: Choosing a special ad category. https://www.facebook.com/business/help/298000447747885

Facebook for Business (2020c). About ad relevance diagnostics. https://www.facebook.com/business/help/4031104804931 60?id=56190637758703

Facebook for Business (2020d). Ad quality: What you should know. *Facebook Advertising Policies.* https://www.facebook.com/business/help/423781975167984

Facebook for Business (2020e). Fact-checking on Facebook: What publishers should know. *Business Help Center.* https://www.facebook.com/help/publisher/182222309230722?ref=MisinformationPolicy Page

Fiegerman, S. (2016). Dear Facebook, you're a media company now. Start acting like one. *Mashable.* https://mashable.com/2016/05/15/facebook-media-company/

Fink, C. (2018). Dangerous speech, anti-Muslim violence, and Facebook in Myanmar. *Journal of International Affairs*, 71(1.5): 43–52.

First Round (n.d.). 80% of your culture is your founder. https://firstround.com/review/80-of-Your-Culture-is-Your-Founder

Fisher, E. (2015). 'You media': Audiencing as marketing in social media. *Media, Culture and Society*, 37(1): 50–67.

Flanagan, M., D. Howe and H. Nissenbaum (2008). Embodying values in technology: Theory and practice. *Information Technology and Moral Philosophy*: 322–53.

Flory, J. F. (2018). A look inside Facebook's open source program. Opensource.com. https://opensource.com/article/18/1/inside-facebooks-open-source-program

Foote, J., Shaw, A. and Hill, B. M. (2018). A computational analysis of social media scholarship. In J. Burgess, A. Marwick and T. Poell (eds) *The SAGE Handbook of Social Media*. London: SAGE, pp. 111–34.

Fortunati, L. (1995). *The Arcane of Reproduction: Housework, Prostitution, Labor and Capital.* Autonomedia.

Foucault, M. (1970). *The Order of Things.* New York: Vintage.

Foucault, M. (1982). The subject and power. *Critical Inquiry*, 8(4): 777–95.

Fowler, E. F. (2018). *Political Advertising in the United States.* New York: Routledge.

Friedman, B. and H. Nissenbaum (1996). Bias in computer systems. *ACM Transactions on Information Systems* (TOIS), 14(3): 330–47.

Gabrys, J. (2013). *Digital Rubbish: A Natural History of Electronics.* Ann Arbor, MI: University of Michigan Press.

Gaughan, A. J. (2016). Explaining Donald Trump's shock election win.

Scientific American. https://www.scientificamerican.com/article/ explaining-donald-trump-s-shock-election-win

Ge, H. (2013). News feed FYI: More relevant ads in news feed. *Facebook Newsroom.* https://newsroom.fb.com/news/2013/09/ news-feed-fyi-more-relevant-ads-in-news-feed

Gerlitz, C. and A. Helmond (2013). The like economy: Social buttons and the data-intensive web. *New Media and Society,* 15(8): 1348–65.

Gerrard, Y. (2018). Beyond the hashtag: Circumventing content moderation on social media. *New Media and Society,* 20(12): 4492–511.

Gilbert, B. (2018). How Facebook makes money from your data, in Mark Zuckerberg's words (FB). *Markets Insider.* https://markets. businessinsider.com/news/stocks/how-facebook-makes-money-according-to-mark-zuckerberg-2018-4-1021179411

Gillespie, T. (2006). Engineering a principle 'end-to-end' in the design of the internet. *Social Studies of Science,* 36(3): 427–57.

Gillespie, T. (2010). The politics of 'platforms'. *New Media and Society,* 12(3): 347–64.

Gillespie, T. (2018). *Custodians of the Internet: Platforms, Content Moderation, and the Hidden Decisions that Shape Social Media.* New Haven: Yale University Press.

Goggin, G. (2014). Facebook's mobile career. *New Media and Society,* 16(7): 1068–86.

Goffman, E. (1959). *The Presentation of Self in Everyday Life.* New York: Anchor.

Gonzales, A. (2016). The contemporary US digital divide: From initial access to technology maintenance. *Information, Communication and Society,* 19(2): 234–48.

Gottfried, J. and E. Shearer (2016). News use across social medial platforms 2016, Pew Research Center.

Graber, D. A. and J. Dunaway (2017). *Mass Media and American Politics.* Los Angeles: CQ Press.

Graham, M. (2013). What does Facebook's performance review process look like? *Quora.* https://www.quora.com/What-does-Facebooks-performance-review-process-look-like

Granovetter, M. S. (1973). The strength of weak ties. *American Journal of Sociology,* 78(6): 1360–80.

Grazian, D. (2005). *Blue Chicago: The Search for Authenticity in Urban Blues Clubs.* Chicago: University of Chicago Press.

Gregg, M. (2015). Hack for good: Speculative labour, app development and the burden of austerity. *The Fibreculture Journal,* 25. http:// twentyfive.fibreculturejournal.org/fcj-186-hack-for-good-speculative-labour-app-development-and-the-burden-of-austerity/

Grossmann, L. (2014). Inside Facebook's plan to wire the world. *Zuckerberg Transcripts*, 163. https://epublications.marquette.edu/zuckerberg_files_transcripts/163

Gubin, M., W. Kao, D. Vickrey and A. Maykov (2014). Adaptive ranking of news feed in social networking systems. *Facebook, Inc.* US Patent No. 8, 768,863.

Gubrium, J. F. and J. A. Holstein (2016). The everyday work and auspices of authenticity. In P. Vannini and J. P. Williams (eds) *Authenticity in Culture, Self, and Society*. New York: Routledge, pp. 137–54.

Guyard, C. and A. Kaun (2018). Workfulness: Governing the disobedient brain. *Journal of Cultural Economy*, 11(6): 535–48.

Guynn, J. (2014). Facebook apologizes to drag queens over real name policy. *USA Today*. https://eu.usatoday.com/story/tech/2014/10/01/facebook-drag-queens/16552927/

Hacking, I. (1990). *The Taming of Chance*. Cambridge, UK, Cambridge University Press.

Hacking, I. (2007). Kinds of people: Moving targets. *Proceedings of the British Academy*. Oxford, UK: Oxford University Press.

Haimson, O. L. and A. L. Hoffmann (2016). Constructing and enforcing 'authentic' identity online: Facebook, real names, and non-normative identities. *First Monday*, 21(6). https://firstmonday.org/article/view/6791/5521

Hallin, D. C. (2019). Mediatisation, neoliberalism and populisms: The case of Trump. *Contemporary Social Science* 14(1): 14–25.

Hamilton, B. (2010). Bootcamp: Growing culture at Facebook. *Facebook Engineering*. https://www.facebook.com/notes/facebook-engineering/bootcamp-growing-culture-at-facebook/249415563919

Hamraie, A. (2017). *Building Access: Universal Design and the Politics of Disability*. Minneapolis: University of Minnesota Press.

Haraway, D. J. (2016). *Staying with the Trouble: Making Kin in the Chthulucene*. Durham, NC: Duke University Press.

Hardy, Q. (2014). The monuments of tech. *New York Times*. http://www.nytimes.com/2014/03/02/technology/the-monuments-of-tech.html

Hargittai, E. (2002). Second-level digital divide: Differences in people's online skills. *First Monday*, 7(4).

Harvard University (2005). CS50 guest lecture by Mark Zuckerberg. *Zuckerberg Transcripts*, 141. https://epublications.marquette.edu/zuckerberg_files_transcripts/141

Harvey, D. (2007). *A Brief History of Neoliberalism*. New York: Oxford University Press.

Hecht, L. (2019). A reason to not hate Facebook: Open source contributions. *The New Stack*. https://thenewstack.io/a-reason-to-not-hate-facebook-open-source-contributions

Helmond, A. (2015). The platformization of the web: Making web data platform ready. *Social Media and Society* 1(2): 2056305115603080.

Helmond, A., D. B. Nieborg and F. N. van der Vlist (2019). Facebook's evolution: development of a platform-as-infrastructure. *Internet Histories* 3(2): 123–46.

Hempel, J. (2018). What Happened to Facebook's Grand Plan to Wire the World? *Wired*. https://www.wired.com/story/what-happened-to-facebooks-grand-plan-to-wire-the-world/

Herod, A. (1999). Reflections on interviewing foreign elites: Praxis, positionality, validity, and the cult of the insider. *Geoforum*, 30(4): 313–27.

Herring, S. (1996). Posting in a different voice: Gender and ethics in computer-mediated communication. *Philosophical Perspectives on Computer-Mediated Communication*, 115: 45.

Herring, S. C. (2000). Gender differences in CMC: Findings and implications. *Computer Professionals for Social Responsibility Journal*, 18(1).

Hirsch, E. and R. Silverstone (2003). *Consuming Technologies: Media and Information in Domestic Spaces*. London: Routledge.

Hochschild, A. R. (1979). Emotion work, feeling rules, and social structure. *American Journal of Sociology* 85(3): 551–75.

Hoffmann, A. L., N. Proferes and M. Zimmer (2018). 'Making the world more open and connected': Mark Zuckerberg and the discursive construction of Facebook and its users. *New Media and Society*, 20(1): 199–218.

Hogan, M. (2015). Facebook data storage centers as the archive's underbelly. *Television and New Media*, 16(1): 3–18.

Hogan, M. (2018). Big data ecologies. *Ephemera*, 18(3): 631.

Hou, J. (2011). Uses and gratifications of social games: Blending social networking and game play. *First Monday*, 16(7).

Hoofnagle, C. J., A. Soltani, N. Good and D. J. Wambach (2012). Behavioral advertising: The offer you can't refuse. *Harvard Law and Policy Review*, 6: 273.

Horwitz, J. and D. Seetharaman (2020). Facebook executives shut down efforts to make the site less divisive. *Wall Street Journal*. https://www.wsj.com/articles/facebook-knows-it-encourages-division-top-executives-nixed-solutions-11590507499

Howard, P. N. (2006). *New Media Campaigns and the Managed Citizen*. Cambridge, UK: Cambridge University Press.

Howard, P. N., A. Duffy, D. Freelon, M. M. Hussain, W. Mari and M. Maziad (2011). Opening closed regimes: What was the role of social media during the Arab Spring?. Available at SSRN 2595096.

Hoy, M. G. and G. Milne (2010). Gender differences in privacy-related measures for young adult Facebook users. *Journal of Interactive Advertising*, 10(2): 28–45.

Hughes, T. P. (1983). *Networks of Power: Electrification in Western Society, 1880–1930*. Baltimore, JHU Press.

Human Rights Council (2018). Report of the independent international fact-finding mission on Myanmar. A/HRC/39/64

Human Rights Council (2019). Report of the Independent International Fact-finding Mission on Myanmar. A/HRC/42/50

Irani, L. (2015). Hackathons and the making of entrepreneurial citizenship. *Science, Technology, and Human Values*, 40(5): 799–824.

Jarrett, K. (2008). Interactivity is evil: A critical investigation of Web 2.0. *First Monday*, 13(3).

Jarrett, K. (2015). *Feminism, Labour and Digital Media: The Digital Housewife*. London: Routledge.

John, N. A. (2016). *The Age of Sharing*. Cambridge, UK: Polity.

Johns, A. (2014). How the growth team helped Facebook reach 500 million users. *Forbes*. https://www.forbes.com/sites/quora/2014/09/15/how-the-growth-team-helped-facebook-reach-500-million-users/

Johnson, T. J. and D. D. Perlmutter (2010). Introduction: The Facebook election. *Mass Communication and Society*, 13(5): 554–9.

Johnson, N. F., N. Velásquez, N. J. Restrepo, R. Leahy, N. Gabriel, S. El Oud, M. Zheng, P. Manrique, S. Wuchty and Y. Lupu (2020). The online competition between pro- and anti-vaccination views. *Nature*: 1–4.

Jungherr, A. (2016). Four functions of digital tools in election campaigns: The German case. *The International Journal of Press/Politics*, 21(3): 358–77.

Kacholia, V. (2013). News feed FYI: Showing more high-quality content. *Facebook: News Feed FYI*. https://newsroom.fb.com/news/2013/08/news-feed-fyi-showing-more-high-quality-content/

Kacholia, V. and J. Minwen (2013). Helping you find more news to talk about. *Facebook Newsroom*. https://about.fb.com/news/2013/12/news-feed-fyi-helping-you-find-more-news-to-talk-about/

Kang, C. (2019). Facebook's hands-off approach to political speech gets impeachment test. *New York Times*. https://www.nytimes.com/2019/10/08/technology/facebook-trump-biden-ad.html

Kant, T. (2020). *Making it Personal: Algorithmic Personalization, Identity, and Everyday Life*. New York: Oxford University Press.

Karpf, D. (2016). *Analytic Activism: Digital Listening and the New Political Strategy*. New York: Oxford University Press.

Karppi, T. and Nieborg, D. B. (2020). Facebook confessions: Corporate abdication and Silicon Valley dystopianism. *New Media and Society*, 1461444820933549.

Kendall, T. A., M. R. Cohler, M. E. Zuckerberg, Y.-F. Juan, R. K. X. Jin, J. M. Rosenstein, A. G. Bosworth, Y. Wong, A. D'Angelo and C. M. Palihapitiya (2014). Social advertisements and other informational messages on a social networking website, and advertising model for same, *Facebook*, 8,799,068.

Kirkpatrick, D. (2011). *The Facebook Effect: The Inside Story of the Company that is Connecting the World*. New York: Simon and Schuster.

Koselleck, R. (2011). Introduction and Prefaces to the Geschichtliche Grundbegriffe, trans. M. Richter, *Contributions to the History of Concepts*, 6(1): 1–37.

Kramer, A. D., J. E. Guillory and J. T. Hancock (2014). Experimental evidence of massive-scale emotional contagion through social networks. *Proceedings of the National Academy of Sciences*, 111(24): 8788–90.

Kreiss, D. (2012). *Taking our Country Back: The Crafting of Networked Politics from Howard Dean to Barack Obama*. New York: Oxford University Press.

Kreiss, D. (2016). *Prototype Politics: Technology-intensive Campaigning and the Data of Democracy*. New York: Oxford University Press.

Kreiss, D. and P. N. Howard (2010). New challenges to political privacy: Lessons from the first US Presidential race in the Web 2.0 era. *International Journal of Communication*, 4: 19.

Kreiss, D. and S. C. Mcgregor (2018). Technology firms shape political communication: The work of Microsoft, Facebook, Twitter, and Google with campaigns during the 2016 US presidential cycle. *Political Communication*, 35(2): 155–77.

Kreiss, D. and S. C. McGregor (2019). The 'arbiters of what our voters see': Facebook and Google's struggle with policy, process, and enforcement around political advertising. *Political Communication*, 36(4): 499–522.

Lai, S. S. (2021). Human Capabilities in a Datafied Society: Empirical approaches to studying the interplay between digital communication and internet infrastructures. PhD thesis, University of Copenhagen: https://comm.ku.dk/calendar/2021/human-capabilities/Lai_dissertation_sikker.pdf

Larkin, B. (2013). The politics and poetics of infrastructure. *Annual Review of Anthropology*, 42: 327–43.

Larsson, A. O. (2016). Online, all the time? A quantitative assessment of the permanent campaign on Facebook. *New Media and Society*, 18(2): 274–92.

Latour, B. (1999). *Pandora's Hope: Essays on the Reality of Science Studies*. Cambridge, Harvard University Press.

Latour, B. (2005). *Reassembling the Social: An Introduction to Actor-Network-Theory*. Oxford, UK: Oxford University Press.

Law, J. (2002). *Aircraft Stories: Decentering the Object in Technoscience*. Durham, NC: Duke University Press.

Law, J. (2004). *After Method: Mess in Social Science Research*. London: Routledge.

Lehman-Wilzig, S. N. and M. Seletzky (2010). Hard news, soft news, 'general' news: The necessity and utility of an intermediate classification. *Journalism*, 11(1): 37–56.

Lerner, J. and J. Tirole (2002). Some simple economics of open source. *Journal of Industrial Economics*, 50(2): 197–234.

Levy, S. (2010). *Hackers*. Sebastopol, CA: O'Reilly Media.

Levy, S. (2020). *Facebook. The Inside Story*. Blue Rider Press.

Lewis, P. (2017). Our minds can be hijacked': The tech insiders who fear a smartphone dystopia. *Guardian*. https://www.theguardian.com/technology/2017/oct/05/smartphone-addiction-silicon-valley-dystopia

Lewis, S. C. and O. Westlund (2015). Big data and journalism: Epistemology, expertise, economics, and ethics. *Digital Journalism*, 3(3): 447–66.

Lewis, P. and J. C. Wong (2018). Facebook employs psychologist whose firm sold data to Cambridge Analytica. *Guardian*. https://www.theguardian.com/news/2018/mar/18/facebook-cambridge-analytica-joseph-chancellor-gsr

Lima, C. (2019). Facebook backtracks after removing Warren ads calling for Facebook breakup. *Politico*. https://www.politico.com/story/2019/03/11/facebook-removes-elizabeth-warren-ads-1216757

Lingel, J. and A. Golub (2015). In face on Facebook: Brooklyn's drag community and sociotechnical practices of online communication. *Journal of Computer-Mediated Communication* 20(5): 536–53.

Liszkiewicz, A. (2010). Cultivated play: Farmville. http://mediacommons.futureofthebook.org/content/cultivated-play-farmville

Livni, E. (2017). The US Supreme Court just ruled that using social media is a constitutional right. *Quartz*: https://qz.com/1009546/the-us-supreme-court-just-decided-access-to-facebook-twitter-or-snapchat-is-fundamental-to-free-speech/

Losse, K. (2012). *The Boy Kings: A Journey into the Heart of the Social Network*. New York: Simon and Schuster.

Lull, J. (1980). The social uses of television. *Human Communication Research*, 6(3): 197–209.

Lury, C., Parisi, L. and Terranova, T. (2012). Introduction: The becoming topological of culture. *Theory, Culture and Society*, 29(4–5): 3–35.

Luyt, B. (2008). The one laptop per child project and the negotiation of technological meaning. *First Monday*, 13(6).

MacCabe, C. and H. Yanacek (2018). *Keywords for Today: A 21st Century Vocabulary*. New York: Oxford University Press.

MacCannell, D. (1973). Staged authenticity: Arrangements of social space in tourist settings. *American Journal of Sociology*, 79(3): 589–603.

McCormack, D. P. (2015). Devices for doing atmospheric things. In P. Vannini (ed.) *Non-Representational Methodologies. Re-Envisioning Research*. New York, Routledge.

McCracken, H. (2015). How Facebook keeps scaling its culture. *Fastcompany*.   https://www.fastcompany.com/3053776/how-facebook-keeps-scaling-its-culture

McGuigan, L. (2019). Automating the audience commodity: The unacknowledged ancestry of programmatic advertising. *New Media and Society*: 1461444819846449.

Mackenzie, A. (2019). From API to AI: Platforms and their opacities. *Information, Communication and Society*, 22(13): 1989–2006.

McPherson, M., L. Smith-Lovin and J. M. Cook (2001). Birds of a feather: Homophily in social networks. *Annual Review of Sociology*, 27(1): 415–44.

McRobbie, A. (2016). *Be Creative: Making a Living in the New Culture Industries*. Cambridge, UK: Polity.

Madianou, M. (2019). Technocolonialism: Digital innovation and data practices in the humanitarian response to refugee crises. *Social Media and Society*, 5(3): 2056305119863146.

Marantz, A. (2020). The man behind Trump's Facebook juggernaut. *The New Yorker*. https://www.newyorker.com/magazine/2020/03/09/the-man-behind-trumps-facebook-juggernaut

Marres, N. (2012). On some uses and abuses of topology in the social analysis of technology (or the problem with smart meters). *Theory, Culture and Society*, 29(4–5): 288–310.

Martínez, A. G. (2016). *Chaos Monkeys: Inside the Silicon Valley Money Machine*. Random House.

Marvin, C. (1988). *When Old Technologies Were New: Thinking About*

Electric Communication in the Late Nineteenth Century. New York: Oxford University Press.

Marwick, A. and R. Lewis (2017). Media Manipulation and Disinformation Online. New York: Data and Society Research Institute.

Marwick, A. E. (2013). *Status Update: Celebrity, Publicity, and Branding in the Social Media Age*. New Haven: Yale University Press.

Massumi, B. (1995). The autonomy of affect. *Cultural Critique*, 31: 83–109.

Matamoros-Fernández, A. (2017). Platformed racism: The mediation and circulation of an Australian race-based controversy on Twitter, Facebook and YouTube. *Information, Communication and Society*, 20(6): 930–46.

Mattern, S. (2017). Sharing is tables: Furniture for digital labor. *E-flux*. https://www.e-flux.com/architecture/positions/151184/sharing-is-tables-furniture-for-digital-labor

Miller, D. (2011). *Tales from Facebook*. Cambridge, UK: Polity.

Miller, D., E. Costa, N. Haynes, T. McDonald, R. Nicolescu, J. Sinanan, J. Spyer, S. Venkatraman and X. Wang (2016). How the World Changed Social Media. London: UCL Press.

Miller, D. and S. Venkatraman (2018). Facebook interactions: An ethnographic perspective. *Social Media and Society*, 4(3): 2056305118784776.

Milne, E. (2012). *Letters, Postcards, Email: Technologies of Presence*. London: Routledge.

Mol, A. (1999). Ontological politics. A word and some questions. *The Sociological Review*, 47(S1): 74–89.

Mol, A. (2002). *The Body Multiple: Ontology in Medical Practice*. Durham, NC: Duke University Press.

Money/Fortune, C. (2013). Mark Zuckerberg: Why we don't want to build a phone. *Zuckerberg Transcripts*, 98. https://dc.uwm.edu/zuckerberg_files_transcripts/98

Morin, D. (2008). Announcing Facebook connect. *Facebook for Developers*. https://developers.facebook.com/blog/post/2008/05/09/announcing-facebook-connect/

Morley, D. and R. Silverstone (1990). Domestic communication – technologies and meanings. *Media, Culture and Society*, 12(1): 31–55.

Morris, C. J., M. C. Eulenstein, T. Chakraborty, J. E. Geller and N. Mihajlovic (2017). Advertisement relevance score using social signals. *Facebook, US Patent Application*, 14/983,449.

Morton, T. (2010). *The Ecological Thought*. Cambridge, MA: Harvard University Press.

Morton, T. (2013). *Hyperobjects: Philosophy and Ecology after the End of the World*. Minneapolis: University of Minnesota Press.

Mosseri, A. (2016). From f8: How News Feed Works. *Facebook Newsroom*. https://about.fb.com/news/2016/04/news-feed-fyi-from-f8-how-news-feed-works/

Mozur, P. (2018). A genocide incited on Facebook, with posts from Myanmar's military. *New York Times*. https://www.nytimes.com/2018/10/15/technology/myanmar-facebook-genocide.html

Mueller, M. L. (2010). *Networks and States: The Global Politics of Internet Governance*. Cambridge, MA: MIT Press.

Muraleedharan, S. (2017). Introducing snooze to give you more control of your news feed. *Facebook*. https://about.fb.com/news/2017/12/news-feed-fyi-snooze/

Myers West, S. (2018). Censored, suspended, shadowbanned: User interpretations of content moderation on social media platforms. *New Media and Society*, 20(11): 4366–83.

Nadler, A., M. Crain and J. Donovan (2018). Weaponizing the digital influence machine. Data and Society Research Institute. https://datasociety.net/wp-content/uploads/2018/10/DS_Digital_Influence_Machine.pdf

Napoli, P. and R. Caplan (2017). Why media companies insist they're not media companies, why they're wrong, and why it matters. *First Monday*, 22(5). https://firstmonday.org/ojs/index.php/fm/article/view/7051/6124

Naveh, B. R. and G. Karnas (2019). Method and apparatus for identifying common interest between social network users. *Facebook*. 10,277,692. 30 April 2019.

Nickerson, D. W. and T. Rogers (2014). Political campaigns and big data. *Journal of Economic Perspectives*, 28(2): 51–74.

Nieborg, D. B. (2015). Crushing candy: The free-to-play game in its connective commodity form. *Social Media and Society*, 1(2): 2056305115621932.

Nieborg, D. B. and A. Helmond (2019). The political economy of Facebook's platformization in the mobile ecosystem: Facebook Messenger as a platform instance. *Media, Culture and Society*, 41(2): 196–218.

Norris, P. (2000). *A Virtuous Circle: Political Communications in Postindustrial Societies*. Cambridge, UK: Cambridge University Press.

Nothias, T. (2020). Access granted: Facebook's free basics in Africa. *Media, Culture and Society*, 42(3): 329–48.

O'Reilly, T. (2005). What is Web 2.0? Design patterns and business models for the next generation of software. https://www.oreilly.com/pub/a/web2/archive/what-is-web-20.html

Osofsky, J. (2015). Community support FYI: Improving the names process on Facebook. *Facebook*. https://about.fb.com/news/2015/12/community-support-fyi-improving-the-names-process-on-facebook

Owens, E. and D. Vickrey (2014). News feed FYI: Showing more timely stories from friends and pages. *Facebook News Feed FYI*. https://newsroom.fb.com/news/2014/09/news-feed-fyi-showing-more-timely-stories-from-friends-and-pages/

Parker, S. (2010). From soft eyes to street lives: The Wire and jargons of authenticity. *City*, 14(5): 545–57.

Parker, G. G., M. W. Van Alstyne and S. P. Choudary (2016). *Platform Revolution: How Networked Markets are Transforming the Economy – and How to Make Them Work for You*. New York: W.W. Norton and Company.

Pearlman, L. (2009). 'I like this.' *Facebook*. https://www.facebook.com/notes/facebook-app/i-like-this/53024537130/

Phillips, W. and R. Milner (2021). *You Are Here*. Cambridge, MA: MIT Press.

Pilkington, E. and A. Michel (2012). Obama, Facebook and the power of friendship: The 2012 data election. https://www.theguardian.com/world/2012/feb/17/obama-digital-data-machine-facebook-election

Plantin, J.-C., C. Lagoze, P. N. Edwards and C. Sandvig (2018). Infrastructure studies meet platform studies in the age of Google and Facebook. *New Media and Society*, 20(1): 293–310.

Plantin, J. C. and Punathambekar, A. (2019). Digital media infrastructures: Pipes, platforms, and politics. *Media, Culture and Society*, 41(2): 163–74.

Poell, T., D. Nieborg and B. E. Duffy (2021). *Platforms and Cultural Production*. Cambridge, UK: Polity.

Pooley, J. (2010). The consuming self from flappers to Facebook. In M. Aronczyk, D. Powers and P. Lang (eds) *Blowing up the Brand: Critical Perspectives on Promotional Culture*. New York: Peter Lang, pp. 71–90.

Powers, E. (2017). My news feed is filtered? Awareness of news personalization among college students. *Digital Journalism*: 1–21.

Posner, S. (2016). How Donald Trump's new campaign chief created an online haven for white nationalists. *MotherJones*. https://www.motherjones.com/politics/2016/08/stephen-bannon-donald-trump-alt-right-breitbart-news/

Postigo, H. (2016). The socio-technical architecture of digital labor: Converting play into YouTube money. *New Media and Society*, 18(2): 332–49.

Prasad, R. (2018). Ascendant India, digital India: How net neutrality advocates defeated Facebook's free basics. *Media, Culture and Society*, 40(3): 415–31.

Putnam, R. D. (2000). *Bowling Alone: The Collapse and Revival of American Community*. New York: Simon and Schuster.

Rabinovitsj, D. (2019) Enabling better global connectivity through new partnerships and technologies. *Facebook Engineering*. https://engineering.fb.com/connectivity/mobile-world-congress-2019/

Rangaswamy, N. and P. Arora (2016). The mobile internet in the wild and every day: Digital leisure in the slums of urban India. *International Journal of Cultural Studies*, 19(6): 611–26.

Rankin, J. L. (2018). *A People's History of Computing in the United States*. Cambridge, MA: Harvard University Press.

Raymond, E. (1999). The cathedral and the bazaar. *Knowledge, Technology and Policy*, 12(3): 23–49.

Reinemann, C., J. Stanyer, S. Scherr and G. Legnante (2012). Hard and soft news: A review of concepts, operationalizations and key findings. *Journalism*, 13(2): 221–39.

Rheingold, H. (1993). *The Virtual Community: Finding Connection in a Computerized World*. Chicago, IL: Addison-Wesley Longman Publishing Co., Inc.

Ribes, D. and C. P. Lee. (2010). Sociotechnical studies of cyberinfrastructure and e-research: Current themes and future trajectories. *Computer Supported Cooperative Work (CSCW)*, 19(3–4): 231–44.

Rieder, B. (2017). Scrutinizing an algorithmic technique: The Bayes classifier as interested reading of reality. *Information, Communication and Society*, 20(1): 100–17.

Rider, K. and D. Murakami Wood. (2019). Condemned to connection? Network communitarianism in Mark Zuckerberg's 'Facebook Manifesto'. *New Media and Society*, 21(3): 639–54.

Roberts, S. T. (2019). *Behind the Screen: Content Moderation in the Shadows of Social Media*. New Haven: Yale University Press.

Ruckenstein, M. and L. L. M. Turunen (2019). Re-humanizing the platform: Content moderators and the logic of care. *New Media and Society*: 1461444819875990.

Salisbury, M. and J. D. Pooley (2017). The #nofilter self: The contest for authenticity among social networking sites, 2002–2016. *Social Sciences*, 6(1): 10.

Sanghvi, R. (2006). Facebook gets a facelift. *Facebook*. https://www.facebook.com/notes/facebook/facebook-gets-a-facelift/2207967130/

Sanghvi, R. (2016). Facebook post. *Facebook*. https://www.facebook. com/ruchi/posts/10101160244871819

Sapiezynski, P., A. Gosh, L. Kaplan, A. Mislove and A. Rieke (2019). Algorithms that 'don't see color': Comparing biases in lookalike and special ad audiences. arXiv preprint arXiv:1912.07579. https://arxiv. org/abs/1912.07579

Sawhney, H. (1996). Information superhighway: Metaphors as midwives. *Media, Culture and Society*, 18(2): 291–314.

Schmidt, T. (2006). Inside the backlash against Facebook. *Time*. http://content.time.com/time/nation/article/0,8599,1532225,00. html

Schoen, K. M., G. L. Dingle and T. Kendall (2018). communicating information in a social network system about activities from another domain. *Facebook*. US Patent No. 10,110,413.

Scholz, T. (2012). *Digital Labor: The Internet as Playground and Factory*. London: Routledge.

Schroers, J. (2019). I have a Facebook account, therefore I am – authentication with social networks. *International Review of Law, Computers and Technology*, 33(2): 211–23.

Schultz, A. (2014). Lecture 6 growth. https://www.youtube.com/ watch?v=n_yHZ_vKjno

Schultz, A. P., Piepgrass, B., Weng, C. C., Ferrante, D., Verma, D., Martinazzi, P., Alison, T., and Mao, Z. (2014). Methods and systems for determining use and content of pymk based on value model. Washington, DC: US Patent and Trademark Office. US Patent No. 20140114774 A1.

Sengupta (2013). Facebook shows off new home page design, including bigger pictures. *New York Times*. https://www.nytimes. com/2013/03/08/technology/facebook-shows-off-redesign. html?pagewanted=all&_r=0

Shilton, K., J. A. Koepfler and K. R. Fleischmann (2013). Charting sociotechnical dimensions of values for design research. *The Information Society*, 29(5): 259–71.

Smith, D. (2020). Meet the social media master who could win Trump a second term. https://www.theguardian.com/us-news/2020/jan/30/ brad-parscale-trump-social-media-rasputin-campaign-manager

Smythe, D. (1981) On the audience commodity and its work. In M. G. Durham and D. M. Kellner (eds) *Media and Cultural Studies: Key Works*. Malden, MA: Blackwell, pp. 230–56.

Snodgrass, E. (2017). Executions: Power and expression in networked and computational media, PhD dissertation. Malmö University.

Solon, O. and C. Farivar (2019). Mark Zuckerberg leveraged Facebook user data to fight rivals and help friends, leaked documents show. *NBC News*. https://www.nbcnews.com/tech/social-media/mark-zuckerberg-leveraged-facebook-user-data-fight-rivals-help-friends-n994706

Springgay, S. and S. E. Truman (2017). *Walking Methodologies in a More-Than-Human World: WalkingLab*. London: Routledge.

Song, F. W. (2010). Theorizing Web 2.0: A cultural perspective. *Information, Communication and Society*, 13(2): 249–75.

Srnicek, N. (2017). *Platform Capitalism*. Cambridge: Polity.

Stallman, R. (2002). Free software, free society: Selected essays of Richard M. Stallman. https://www.gnu.org/philosophy/fsfs/rms-essays.pdf

Star, S. L. (1999). The ethnography of infrastructure. *American Behavioral Scientist*, 43(3): 377–91.

Star, S. L. and G. C. Bowker (2006). How to infrastructure. In L. Lievrouw and S. Livingstone (eds) *Handbook of New Media: Social Shaping and Social Consequences of ICTs*. London: SAGE, pp. 230–45.

Star, S. L. and K. Ruhleder (1996). Steps toward an ecology of infrastructure: Design and access for large information spaces. *Information Systems Research*, 7(1): 111–34.

Stark, L. (2018). Algorithmic psychometrics and the scalable subject. *Social Studies of Science*, 48(2): 204–31.

Stewart, K. (2007). *Ordinary Affects*. Durham, NC: Duke University Press.

Story, L. (2007). Facebook is marketing your brand preferences (with your permission). *New York Times*. https://www.nytimes.com/2007/11/07/technology/07iht-07adco.8230630.html

Streeter, T. (2011). *The Net Effect: Romanticism, Capitalism, and the Internet*. New York: New York University Press.

Strings, S. and L. T. Bui (2014). 'She is not acting, she is.' The conflict between gender and racial realness on RuPaul's Drag Race. *Feminist Media Studies*, 14(5): 822–36.

Stromer-Galley, J. (2019). *Presidential Campaigning in the Internet Age*. New York: Oxford University Press.

Suchman, L. (2007). *Human-machine Reconfigurations: Plans and Situated Actions*. Cambridge, UK: Cambridge University Press.

Sujon, Z., L. Viney and E. Toker-Turnalar (2018). Domesticating Facebook: The shift from compulsive connection to personal service platform. *Social Media and Society*, 4(4): 2056305118803895.

Søe, S. O. (2018). Algorithmic detection of misinformation and disinformation: Gricean perspectives. *Journal of Documentation*. https://

www.emerald.com/insight/content/doi/10.1108/JD-05-2017-0075/full/html

Taylor, C. (1992). *The Ethics of Authenticity*. Cambridge, MA: Harvard University Press.

Terranova, T. (2000). Free labor: Producing culture for the digital economy. *Social Text*, 18(2): 33–58.

Thorson, K., K. Cotter, M. Medeiros and C. Pak (2019). Algorithmic inference, political interest, and exposure to news and politics on Facebook. *Information, Communication and Society*, 21: 1–18.

Thylstrup, N. B. (2019). Data out of place: Toxic traces and the politics of recycling. *Big Data and Society*, 6(2): 2053951719875479.

Treré, E. (2018). *Hybrid Media Activism: Ecologies, Imaginaries, Algorithms*. London: Routledge.

Trilling, L. (2009). *Sincerity and Authenticity*. Cambridge, MA: Harvard University Press.

Tsing, A. L. (2015). *The Mushroom at the End of the World: On the Possibility of Life in Capitalist Ruins*. Princeton, NJ: Princeton University Press.

Tuchman, G. (1978). *Making News: A Study in the Construction of Reality*. New York: Free Press.

Tufekci, Z. (2014). Engineering the public: Big data, surveillance and computational politics. *First Monday*, 19(7). https://firstmonday.org/article/view/4901/4097

Tufekci, Z. (2018). Facebook's surveillance machine. *New York Times*. https://www.nytimes.com/2018/03/19/opinion/facebook-cambridge-analytica.html

Turkle, S. (2011). *Life on the Screen*. New York: Simon and Schuster.

Turner, F. (2006). *From Counterculture to Cyberculture: Stewart Brand, the Whole Earth Network, and the Rise of Digital Utopianism*. Chicago, IL: University of Chicago Press.

Turow, J. (2012). *The Daily You: How the New Advertising Industry is Defining Your Identity and Your Worth*. New Haven: Yale University Press.

Tussey, D. (2014). Facebook: The New Town Square. *Southwestern Law Review*, 44: 385.

Tynan, D. (2013). Acxiom exposed: A peek inside one of the world's largest data brokers. *IT World*. https://www.itworld.com/article/2710610/acxiom-exposed--a-peek-inside-one-of-the-world-s-largest-data-brokers.html

US Senate Committee on Commerce, Science and Transportation (2013). A review of the data broker industry: collection, use, and sale of consumer data for marketing purposes.

Uski, S. and A. Lampinen (2016). Social norms and self-presentation on social network sites: Profile work in action. *New Media and Society*, 18(3): 447–64.

Vaidhyanathan, S. (2018). *Antisocial Media: How Facebook Disconnects Us and Undermines Democracy*. New York: Oxford University Press.

Valenzuela, S. (2013). Unpacking the use of social media for protest behavior: The roles of information, opinion expression, and activism. *American Behavioral Scientist*, 57(7): 920–42.

Valenzuela, S., N. Park and K. F. Kee (2009). Is there social capital in a social network site?: Facebook use and college students' life satisfaction, trust, and participation. *Journal of Computer-Mediated Communication*, 14(4): 875–901.

van der Nagel, E. (2017). From usernames to profiles: The development of pseudonymity in Internet communication. *Internet Histories*, 1(4): 312–31.

van Dijck, J. (2013a). *The Culture of Connectivity: A Critical History of Social Media*. Oxford, UK: Oxford University Press.

van Dijck, J. (2013b). 'You have one identity': Performing the self on Facebook and LinkedIn. *Media, Culture and Society*, 35(2): 199–215.

van Dijck, J. and D. Nieborg (2009). Wikinomics and its discontents: A critical analysis of Web 2.0 business manifestos. *New Media and Society*, 11(5): 855–74.

van Dijck, J., T. Poell and M. de Waal (2018). *The Platform Society: Public Values in a Connective World*. Oxford: Oxford University Press.

Veldstra, C. (2018). Bad feeling at work: Emotional labour, precarity, and the affective economy. *Cultural Studies*, 25: 1–24.

Venkatadri, G., P. Sapiezynski, E. M. Redmiles, A. Mislove, O. Goga, M. Mazurek and K. P. Gummadi (2019a). Auditing offline data brokers via Facebook's advertising platform. The World Wide Web Conference.

Venkatadri, G., E. Lucherini, P. Sapiezynski and A. Mislove (2019b). Investigating sources of PII used in Facebook's targeted advertising. *Proceedings on Privacy Enhancing Technologies*, 1: 227–44.

Vitak, J. and N. B. Ellison (2013). 'There's a network out there you might as well tap': Exploring the benefits of and barriers to exchanging informational and support-based resources on Facebook. *New Media and Society*, 15(2): 243–59.

Wagner, K. (2018). This is how Facebook collects data on you even if you don't have an account. *VOX*. https://www.vox.com/2018/4/20/17254312/facebook-shadow-profiles-data-collection-non-users-mark-zuckerberg

Whatmore, S. (2006). Materialist returns: Practising cultural geography in and for a more-than-human world. *Cultural Geographies*, 13(4): 600–9.

Wang, N. (1999). Rethinking authenticity in tourism experience. *Annals of Tourism Research*, 26(2): 349–70.

Williams, C. B. and G. J. J. Gulati (2018). Digital advertising expenditures in the 2016 presidential election. *Social Science Computer Review*, 36(4): 406–21.

Willson, M. and T. Leaver (2015). Zynga's FarmVille, social games, and the ethics of big data mining. *Communication Research and Practice*, 1(2): 147–58.

Winner, L. (1986). *The Whale and the Reactor: A Search for Limits in an Age of High Technology*. Chicago, IL: University of Chicago Press.

Wolfsfeld, G., E. Segev and T. Sheafer (2013). Social media and the Arab Spring: Politics comes first. *The International Journal of Press/ Politics*, 18(2): 115–37.

Wong, J. C. (2019). The debate over Facebook's political ads ignores 90% of its global users. https://www.theguardian.com/ technology/2019/nov/01/facebook-free-speech-democracy-claims

Wyatt, S. (2004). Danger! Metaphors at work in economics, geophysiology, and the Internet. *Science, Technology, and Human Values*, 29(2): 242–61.

Yan, R. and N. Senaratna (2013). Targeting advertisements to groups of social networking system users. *Facebook*. US Patent Application No. 13/411,456.

Zhou, D. and P. Moreels (2013). Inferring user profile attributes from social information. *Facebook, Inc.*, 8,495,143.

Zimmer, M. (2008). The externalities of search 2.0: The emerging privacy threats when the drive for the perfect search engine meets Web 2.0. *First Monday*, 13(3). https://firstmonday.org/article/view/2136/1944

Zittrain, J. (2008). *The Future of the Internet – And How to Stop It*. New Haven: Yale University Press.

Zuboff, S. (2019). *The Age of Surveillance Capitalism: The Fight for a Human Future at the New Frontier of Power*. New York: Profile Books.

Zuckerberg, M. (2006). Calm down. Breathe. We hear you. https:// www.facebook.com/notes/facebook/calm-down-breathe-we-hear-you/2208197130/

Zuckerberg, M. (2009). 200 million strong. *Zuckerberg Transcripts*, 21. https://epublications.marquette.edu/zuckerberg_files_transcripts/21

Zuckerberg, M. (2010). Designing media: Mark Zuckerberg interview. *Zuckerberg Transcripts*, 73. https://epublications.marquette.edu/ zuckerberg_files_transcripts/73

Zuckerberg, M. (2011a). Startup school 2011 interview. *Zuckerberg Transcripts*, 76. https://epublications.marquette.edu/zuckerberg_files_transcripts/76

Zuckerberg, M. (2011b). Our commitment to the Facebook community. *Zuckerberg Transcripts*, 46. https://epublications.marquette.edu/zuckerberg_files_transcripts/46

Zuckerberg, M. (2012a). The things that connect us. *Zuckerberg Transcripts*, 246. https://epublications.marquette.edu/zuckerberg_files_transcripts/246

Zuckerberg, M. (2012b). 'Zuckerberg letter to shareholders in advance of IPO'. *Zuckerberg Transcripts*, 48. https://epublications.marquette.edu/zuckerberg_files_transcripts/48

Zuckerberg, M. (2012c). World perspective. *Zuckerberg Transcripts*, 313. https://epublications.marquette.edu/zuckerberg_files_transcripts/313

Zuckerberg, M. (2013). Mark Zuckerberg: Is connectivity a human right? *Zuckerberg Transcripts*, 100. https://epublications.marquette.edu/zuckerberg_files_transcripts/100

Zuckerberg, M. (2017a). Building global community. *Zuckerberg Transcripts*, 989. https://epublications.marquette.edu/zuckerberg_files_transcripts/989

Zuckerberg, M. (2017b). Live from the Facebook communities summit in Chicago. *Zuckerberg Videos*, 138. https://epublications.marquette.edu/zuckerberg_files_videos/138.

Zuckerberg, M. (2017c). Facebook post. https://www.facebook.com/zuck/posts/10103877842160021

Zuckerberg, M. (2019a). A privacy-focused vision for social networking. *Zuckerberg Transcripts*, 1006. https://epublications.marquette.edu/zuckerberg_files_transcripts/1006

Zuckerberg, M. (2019b). Standing for voice and free expression. *Zuckerberg Transcripts*, 1022. https://epublications.marquette.edu/zuckerberg_files_transcripts/1022

Zuckerberg, M. (2020). MZ post about aftermath of George Floyd's death. *Zuckerberg Transcripts*, 1222. https://epublications.marquette.edu/zuckerberg_files_transcripts/1222

Zuckerberg, M., R. Sanghvi, A. Bosworth, C. Cox, A. Sittig, C. Hughes, K. Geminder and D. Corson (2010). Dynamically providing a news feed about a user of a social network. *Facebook*. US Patent No. 7,669,123. 23 February 2010.

Zuckerman, E. (2014). Cute cats to the rescue? Participatory media and political expression. https://dspace.mit.edu/handle/1721.1/78899

Index